Data Analysis & Decision Making

with Microsoft® Excel

THIRD EDITION

S. Christian Albright

Kelley School of Business, Indiana University

Wayne L. Winston

Kelley School of Business, Indiana University

Christopher Zappe

Bucknell University

Prepared by

Kelly B. Nichols-Voss

SOUTH-WESTERN
CENGAGE Learning

Australia • Brazil • Japan • Korea • Mexico • Singapore • Spain • United Kingdom • United States

SOUTH-WESTERN
CENGAGE Learning

Student Solutions Manual to accompany Data Analysis & Decision Making with Microsoft Excel, Third Edition
S. Christian Albright, Wayne L. Winston, Christopher Zappe
Prepared by Kelly B. Nichols-Voss

VP/Editorial Director:
Jack W. Calhoun

VP/Editor-in-Chief:
Alex von Rosenberg

Acquisitions Editor:
Charles E. McCormick, Jr.

Sponsoring Editor:
Julie Klooster

Marketing Manager:
Larry Qualls

Production Project Manager:
Heather Mann

Manager of Technology, Editorial:
Vicky True

Technology Project Editor:
Kelly Reid

Web Coordinator:
Scott Cook

Manufacturing Coordinator:
Diane Lohman

Printer:
The P.A. Hutchison Company
Mayfield, PA

Art Director:
Stacy Shirley

For more information about our products,
contact us at:

Cengage Learning
Customer & Sales Support

1-800-354-9706

South-Western
5191 Natorp Boulevard
Mason, OH 45040
USA

Student Solution Manual
for Albright, Winston and Zappe's **Data Analysis & Decision Making**

Table of Contents

CHAPTER 2

Problem 2_1

Part a: Nominal: Gender

Discrete Numerical: Age, Beta Experience and Education

Continuous Numerical: Annual Salary

Part b: The age distribution (See Age Histogram.) is slightly positively skewed.

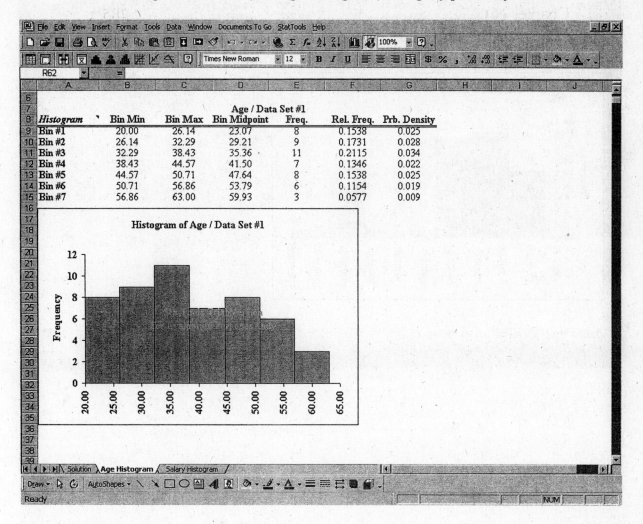

Part c: The annual salary distribution (See Salary Histogram.) is positively skewed.

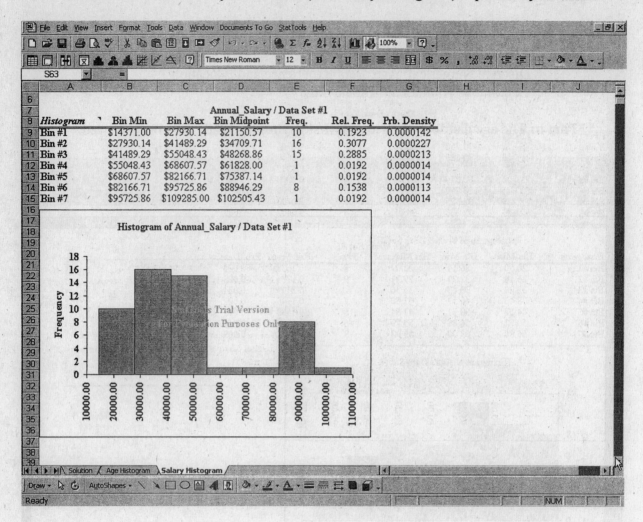

Histogram	Bin Min	Bin Max	Bin Midpoint	Freq.	Rel. Freq.	Prb. Density
			Annual_Salary / Data Set #1			
Bin #1	$14371.00	$27930.14	$21150.57	10	0.1923	0.0000142
Bin #2	$27930.14	$41489.29	$34709.71	16	0.3077	0.0000227
Bin #3	$41489.29	$55048.43	$48268.86	15	0.2885	0.0000213
Bin #4	$55048.43	$68607.57	$61828.00	1	0.0192	0.0000014
Bin #5	$68607.57	$82166.71	$75387.14	1	0.0192	0.0000014
Bin #6	$82166.71	$95725.86	$88946.29	8	0.1538	0.0000113
Bin #7	$95725.86	$109285.00	$102505.43	1	0.0192	0.0000014

Problem 2_5

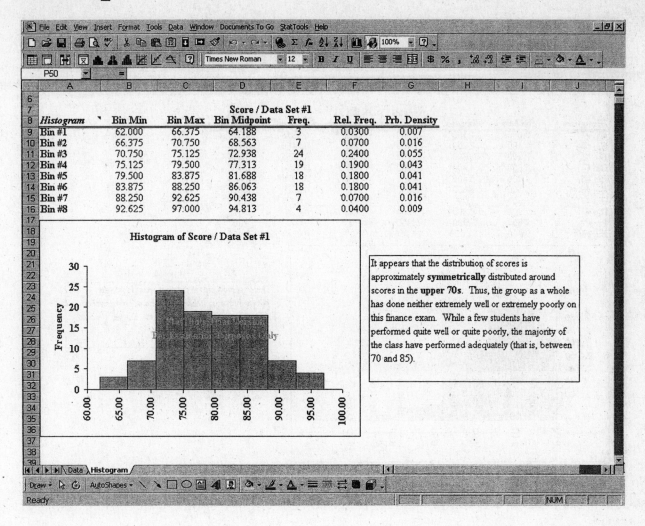

Histogram	Bin Min	Bin Max	Bin Midpoint	Freq.	Rel. Freq.	Prb. Density
			Score / Data Set #1			
Bin #1	62.000	66.375	64.188	3	0.0300	0.007
Bin #2	66.375	70.750	68.563	7	0.0700	0.016
Bin #3	70.750	75.125	72.938	24	0.2400	0.055
Bin #4	75.125	79.500	77.313	19	0.1900	0.043
Bin #5	79.500	83.875	81.688	18	0.1800	0.041
Bin #6	83.875	88.250	86.063	18	0.1800	0.041
Bin #7	88.250	92.625	90.438	7	0.0700	0.016
Bin #8	92.625	97.000	94.813	4	0.0400	0.009

It appears that the distribution of scores is approximately **symmetrically** distributed around scores in the **upper 70s**. Thus, the group as a whole has done neither extremely well or extremely poorly on this finance exam. While a few students have performed quite well or quite poorly, the majority of the class have performed adequately (that is, between 70 and 85).

Problem 2_9

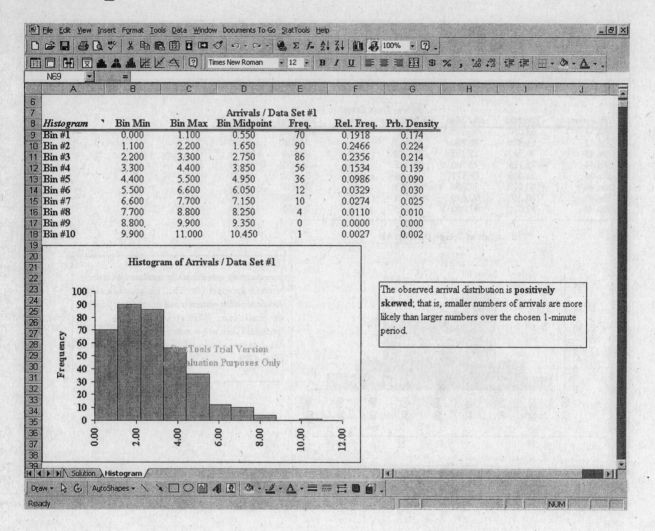

Problem 2_11

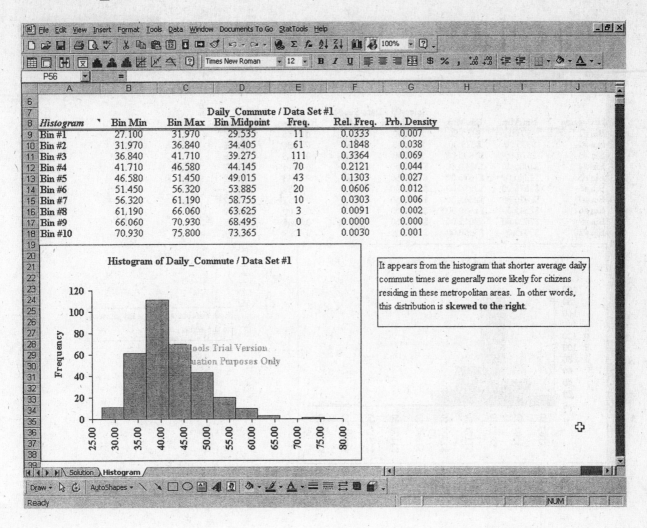

Problem 2_13

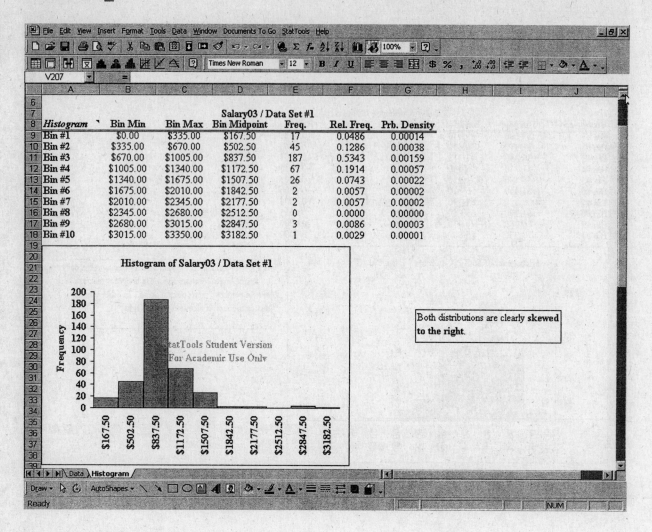

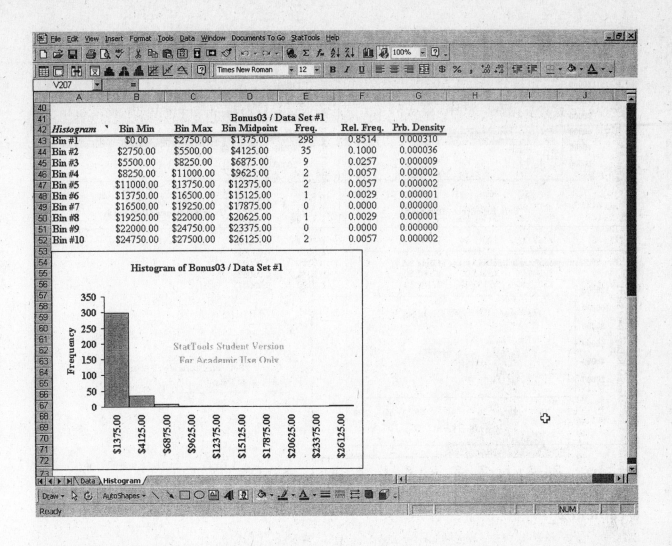

Problem 2_15

Age has the strongest linear relationship with annual salary here.

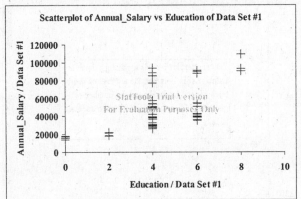

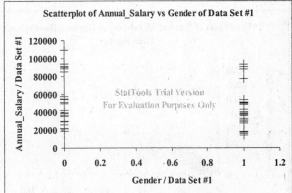

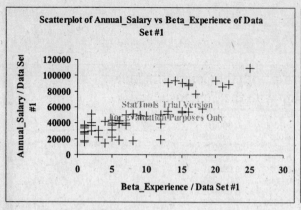

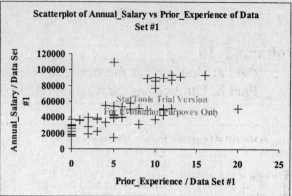

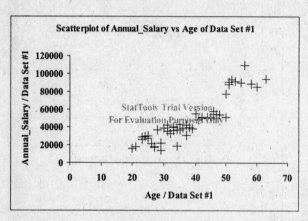

Note: The scatterplot for salary and age most closely resembles a straight line.

Problem 2_17

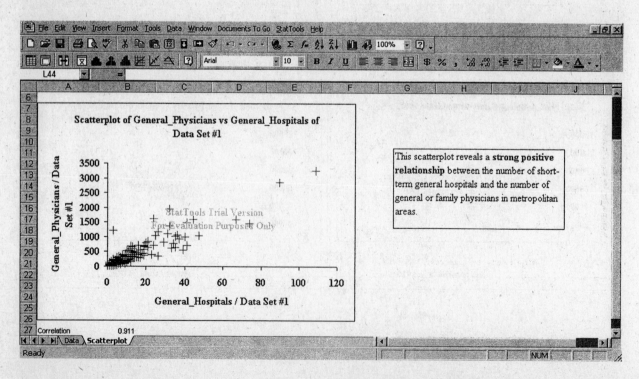

Problem 2_19

Part a: Housing has the strongest relationship with the Composite Index.

Part b: Utilities has the weakest relationship with the Composite Index.

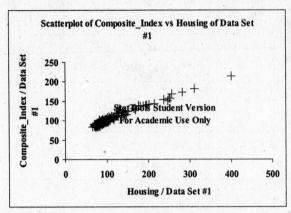

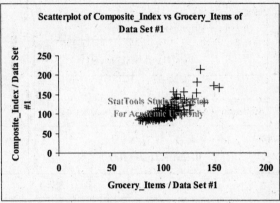

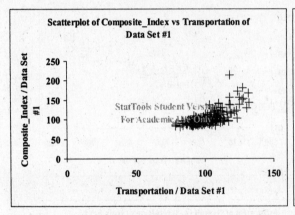

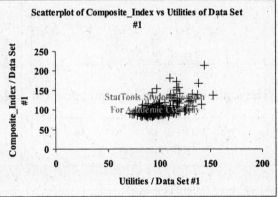

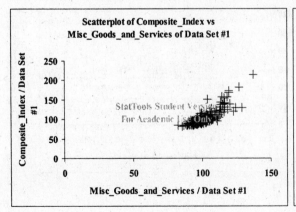

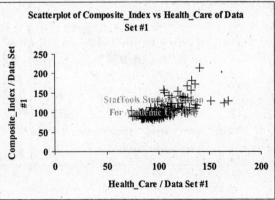

Problem 2_21

Part a: **Rank by peers, rank by recruiters, mean score on the GMAT, mean starting salary for recent graduates,** and **total program enrollment** are most strongly related to the overall score in the U.S. News & World Report ranking.

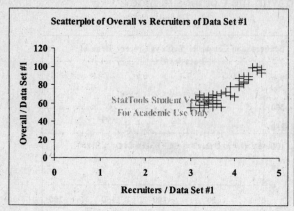

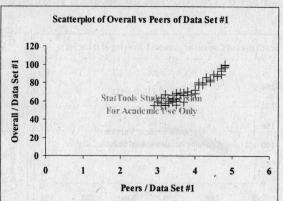

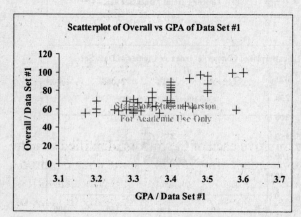

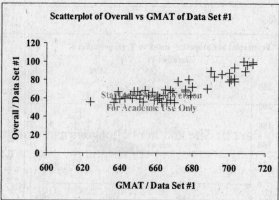

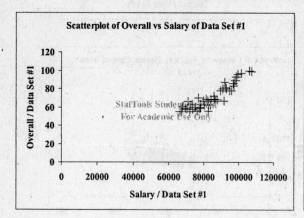

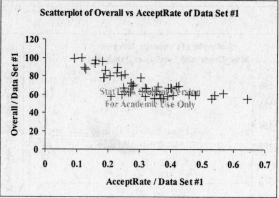

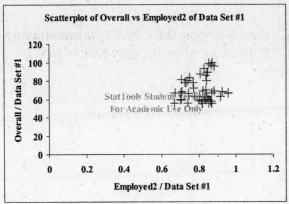

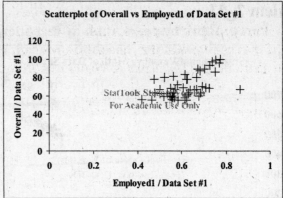

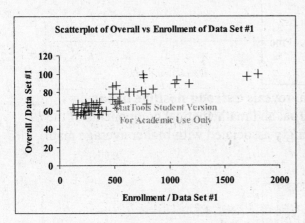

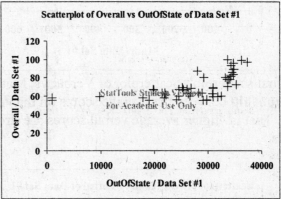

Part b: She and her colleagues can work to improve each of the factors identified in part a by revising admission policies and the program's placement efforts. Also, some consideration should be given to promoting the program more effectively among the deans and admissions officers of other top graduate business programs. Finally, she might consider growing the size of the program by recruiting more students with strong GMAT scores.

Problem 2_23

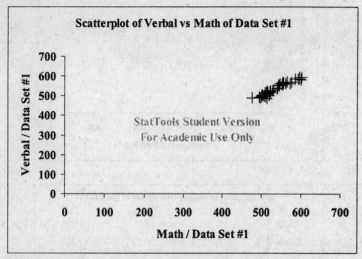

The first scatterplot, Scatterplot of Verbal vs. Math, reveals a **strong positive linear relationship** between the average scores on the verbal and mathematical components of the SAT. That is, higher average verbal scores are strongly associated with higher average math scores.

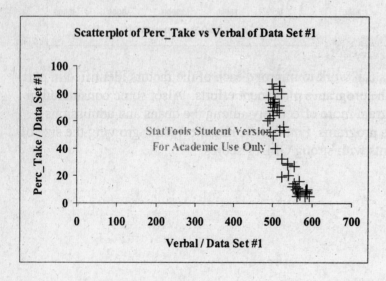

The second scatterplot, Scatterplot Perc_Take vs. Verbal, reveals a **strong negative relationship** between the average scores on the verbal component on the SAT and the proportion of high school graduates taking the SAT. In other words, average verbal scores tend to fall as the proportion of students taking the SAT increases.

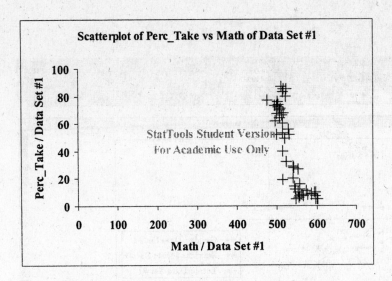

Scatterplot of Perc_Take vs Math of Data Set #1

The third scatterplot, Scatterplot Perc_Take vs. Math, reveals a **strong negative relationship** between the average scores on the math component on the SAT and the proportion of high school graduates taking the SAT. In other words, average math scores tend to fall as the proportion of students taking the SAT increases.

Problem 2_29

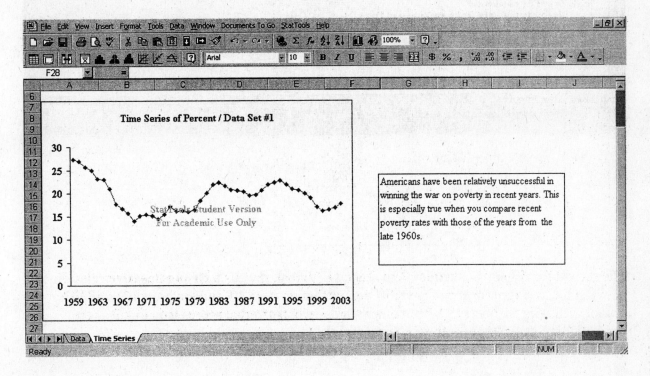

Time Series of Percent / Data Set #1

Americans have been relatively unsuccessful in winning the war on poverty in recent years. This is especially true when you compare recent poverty rates with those of the years from the late 1960s.

Problem 2_31

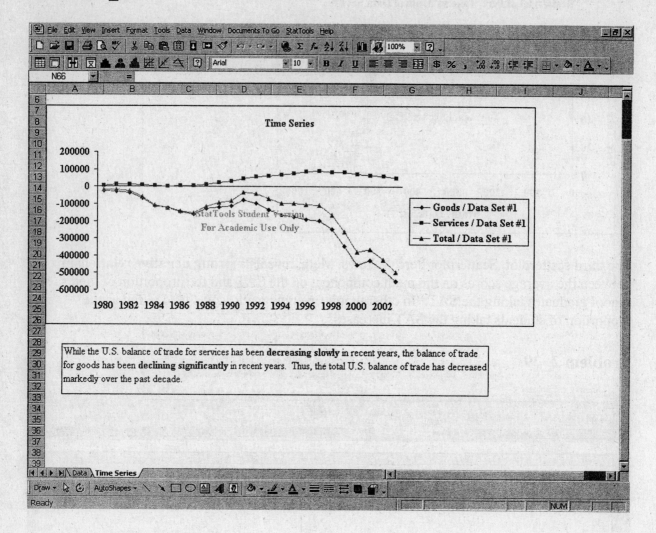

While the U.S. balance of trade for services has been **decreasing slowly** in recent years, the balance of trade for goods has been **declining significantly** in recent years. Thus, the total U.S. balance of trade has decreased markedly over the past decade.

Problem 2_37

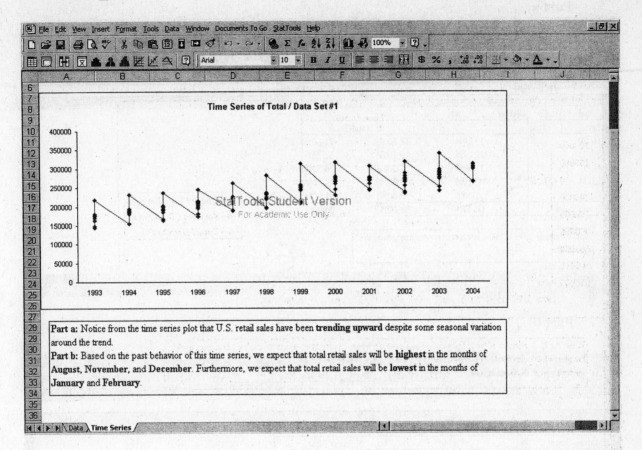

File Edit View Insert Format Tools Data Window Documents To Go StatTools Help

Arial   10   B I U

Time Series of Total / Data Set #1

StatTools Student Version
For Academic Use Only

| | 1993 | 1994 | 1995 | 1996 | 1997 | 1998 | 1999 | 2000 | 2001 | 2002 | 2003 | 2004 |

Part a: Notice from the time series plot that U.S. retail sales have been **trending upward** despite some seasonal variation around the trend.

Part b: Based on the past behavior of this time series, we expect that total retail sales will be **highest** in the months of **August, November,** and **December.** Furthermore, we expect that total retail sales will be **lowest** in the months of **January** and **February.**

Data \ **Time Series**

Problem 2_43

Part a:

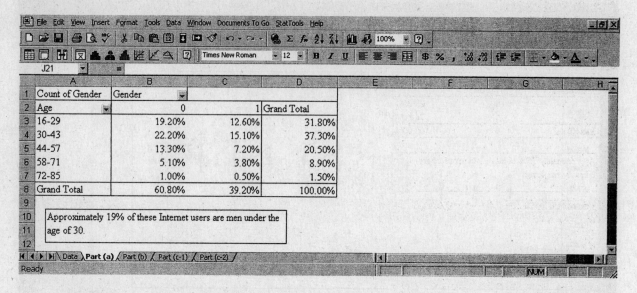

Count of Gender	Gender		
Age	0	1	Grand Total
16-29	19.20%	12.60%	31.80%
30-43	22.20%	15.10%	37.30%
44-57	13.30%	7.20%	20.50%
58-71	5.10%	3.80%	8.90%
72-85	1.00%	0.50%	1.50%
Grand Total	60.80%	39.20%	100.00%

Approximately 19% of these Internet users are men under the age of 30.

Part b:

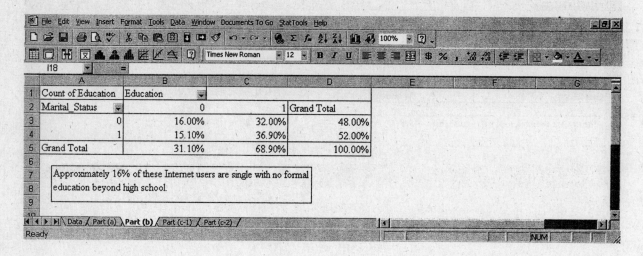

Count of Education	Education		
Marital_Status	0	1	Grand Total
0	16.00%	32.00%	48.00%
1	15.10%	36.90%	52.00%
Grand Total	31.10%	68.90%	100.00%

Approximately 16% of these Internet users are single with no formal education beyond high school.

Part c-1:

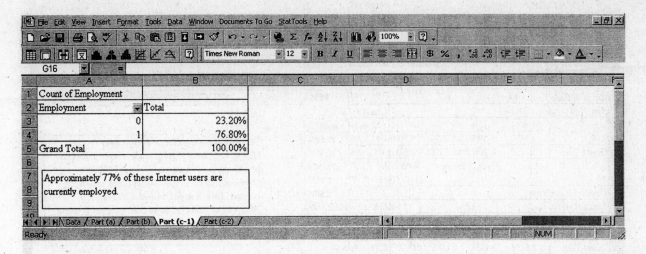

	A	B
1	Count of Employment	
2	Employment ▼	Total
3	0	23.20%
4	1	76.80%
5	Grand Total	100.00%
7	Approximately 77% of these Internet users are	
8	currently employed.	

Part c-2:

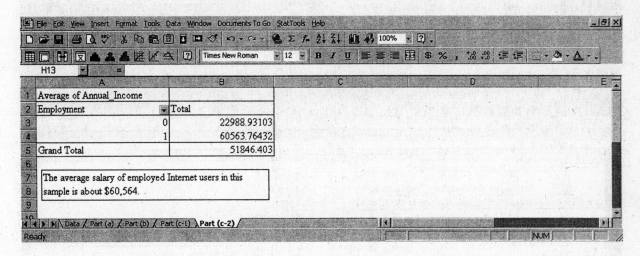

	A	B
1	Average of Annual_Income	
2	Employment ▼	Total
3	0	22988.93103
4	1	60563.76432
5	Grand Total	51846.403
7	The average salary of employed Internet users in this	
8	sample is about $60,564.	

Problem 2_45

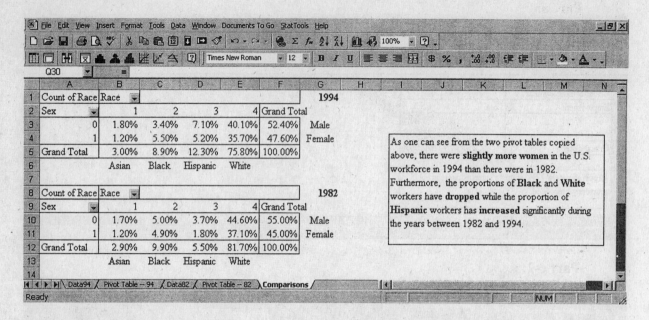

As one can see from the two pivot tables copied above, there were **slightly more women** in the U.S. workforce in 1994 than there were in 1982. Furthermore, the proportions of **Black** and **White** workers have **dropped** while the proportion of **Hispanic** workers has **increased** significantly during the years between 1982 and 1994.

Problem 2_47

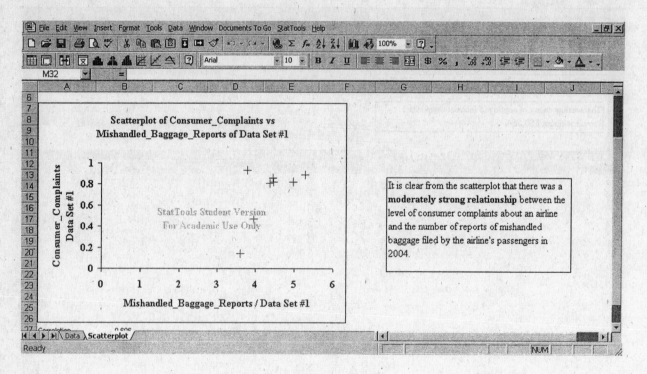

It is clear from the scatterplot that there was a **moderately strong relationship** between the level of consumer complaints about an airline and the number of reports of mishandled baggage filed by the airline's passengers in 2004.

Problem 2_55

Part a:

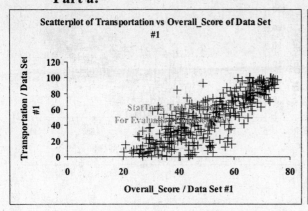

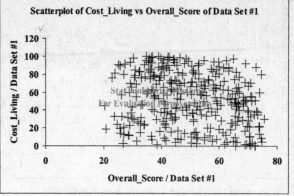

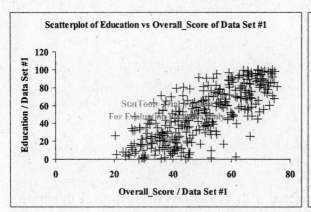

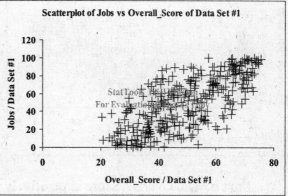

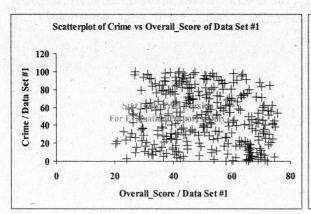

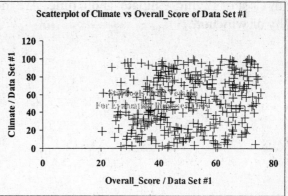

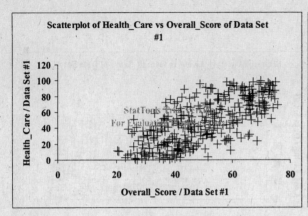

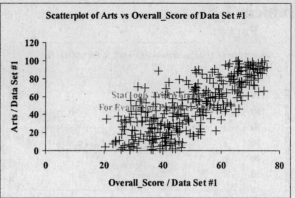

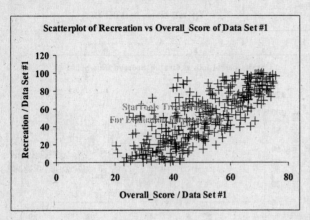

Part b: The Overall_Score is **positively** related with **Transportation, Jobs, Education, Arts, Health_Care**, and **Recreation**. Surprisingly, the Overall_Score is essentially not related with Cost of Living, Climate, and Crime. Are these results consistent with your expectations? Why or why not?

Problem 2_57

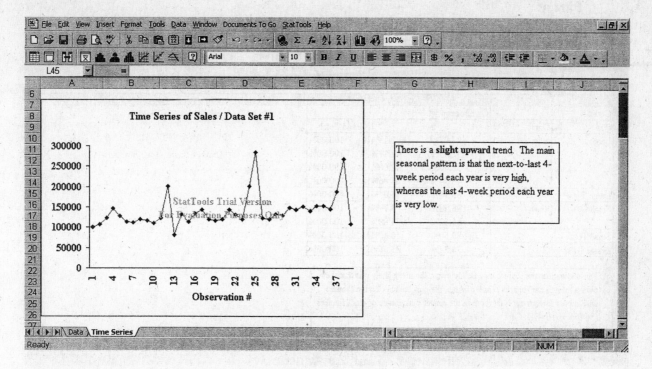

Problem 2_59

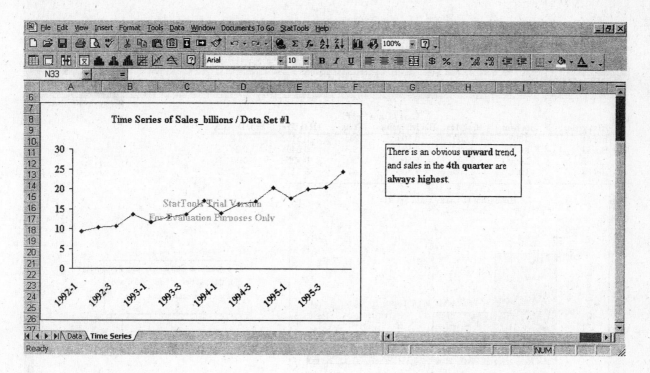

Problem 2_61

Part a:

		Count	OwnForeign		
Size	Cars		0	1	Grand Total
Large	1		97.87%	2.13%	100.00%
	2		52.83%	47.17%	100.00%
	3		58.00%	42.00%	100.00%
	4		48.94%	51.06%	100.00%
Large Total			63.96%	36.04%	100.00%
Small	1		96.23%	3.77%	100.00%
	2		65.12%	34.88%	100.00%
Small Total			89.60%	10.40%	100.00%
Grand Total			76.94%	23.06%	100.00%

This shows that the more cars a family owns, the more likely it is that they own a foreign car (makes sense!). Also, the percentage of large families who own a foreign car is larger than the similar percentage of small families (36.0% vs 10.4%).

Part b:

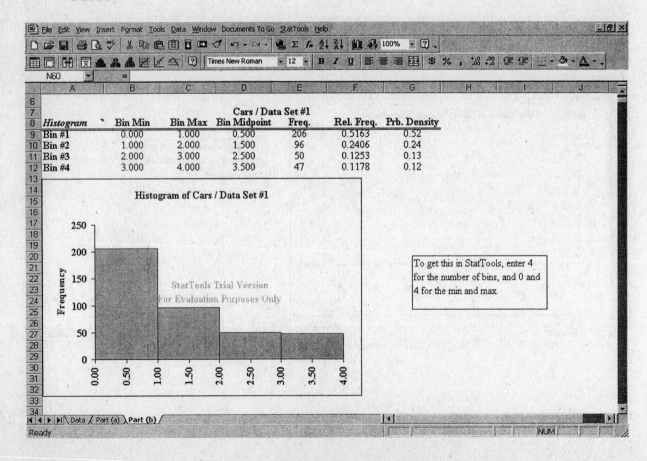

Histogram	Bin Min	Bin Max	Bin Midpoint	Freq.	Rel. Freq.	Prb. Density
			Cars / Data Set #1			
Bin #1	0.000	1.000	0.500	206	0.5163	0.52
Bin #2	1.000	2.000	1.500	96	0.2406	0.24
Bin #3	2.000	3.000	2.500	50	0.1253	0.13
Bin #4	3.000	4.000	3.500	47	0.1178	0.12

To get this in StatTools, enter 4 for the number of bins, and 0 and 4 for the min and max.

Problem 2_69

The scatterplots indicate the relationships between sales and price for the various products. All show the **negative relationship** we'd expect, although it's difficult to tell just by looking which product is most sensitive to price. One method is to fit a **power curve** (also called a constant elasticity curve) to the data, as shown on the last two graphs. (Use Excel's Chart-->Add Trendline menu item.) Then the exponent of the "X" variable (price) is the elasticity of sales to price. It is **higher** (in magnitude) for **Pepsi** than for Coke, indicating that Pepsi will lose a larger percentage of its sales for a given percentage increase in its price than Coke.

Coke

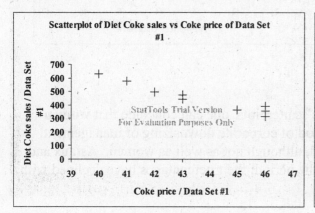
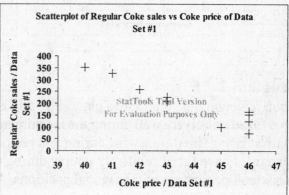

Pepsi

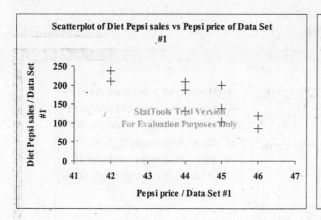
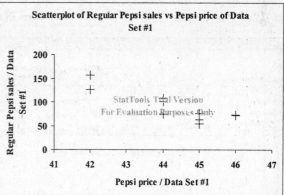

Power Curves

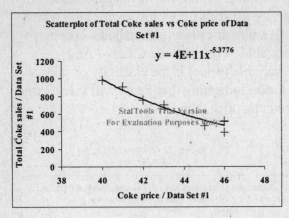

Scatterplot of Total Coke sales vs Coke price of Data Set #1

$y = 4E+11x^{-5.3776}$

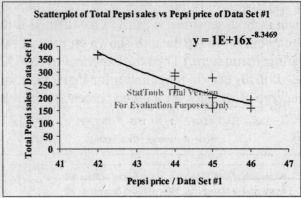

Scatterplot of Total Pepsi sales vs Pepsi price of Data Set #1

$y = 1E+16x^{-8.3469}$

Problem 2_75

Upon reviewing the time series plots and various scatterplots, one can conclude that **women** have **fared relatively well** during the recent period of corporate downsizing of management. **Blacks** have **gained** somewhat during this period, although not as well as women. **Asians** and **Hispanics** have **fared relatively poorly** during the period; their percentages have declined with the overall percentage of managerial positions.

Note: Men (that is, those who have traditionally managerial positions) have done extremely poorly during this period of downsizing.

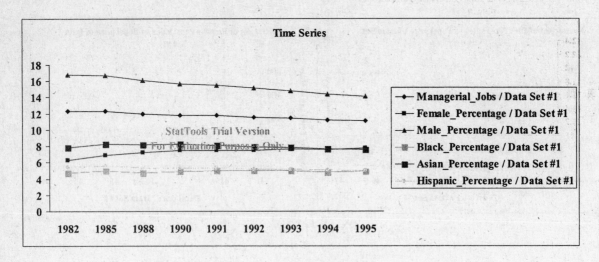

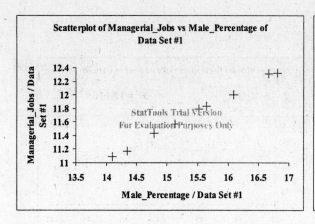

Scatterplot of Managerial_Jobs vs Male_Percentage of Data Set #1

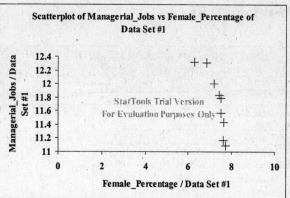

Scatterplot of Managerial_Jobs vs Female_Percentage of Data Set #1

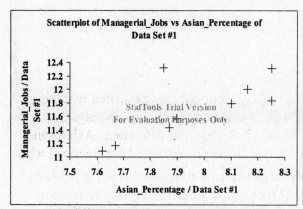

Scatterplot of Managerial_Jobs vs Asian_Percentage of Data Set #1

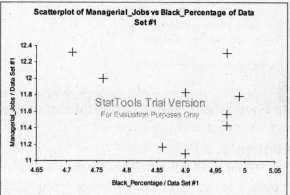

Scatterplot of Managerial_Jobs vs Black_Percentage of Data Set #1

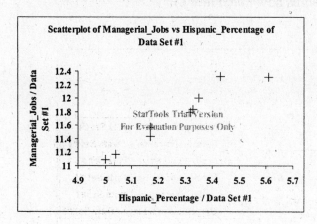

Scatterplot of Managerial_Jobs vs Hispanic_Percentage of Data Set #1

Problem 2_81

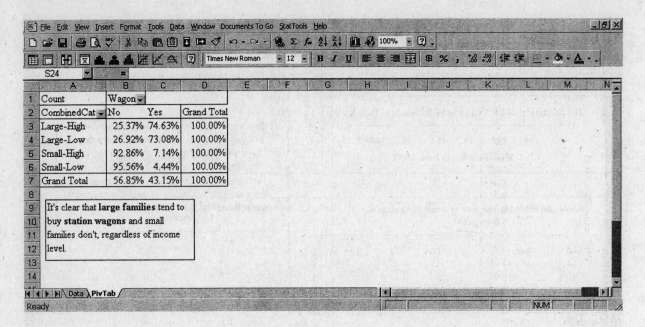

Problem 2_87
Part a: If this ratio is high, then a relatively large share of all income is being made by the people in the upper 10% -- hence "inequality". (Of course, by definition, they're making more than 10% of all income, but this ratio measures how much more.)

Part b:

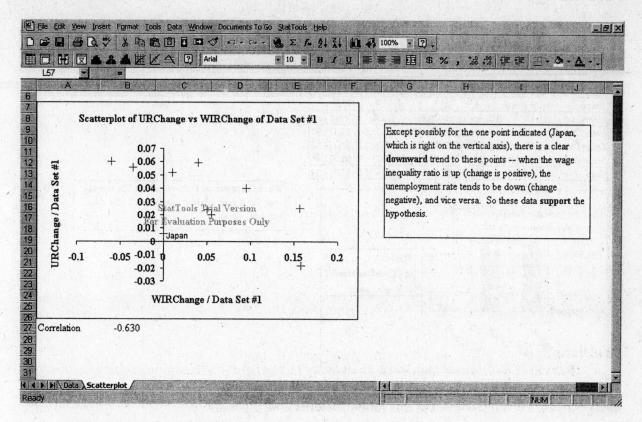

Part c: The ratio given here is only one measure of income inequality; others might shed more light on the issue. Also, these data are only for 10 countries and for one period of change (1980 to 1995). More data would be useful.

Problem 2_89

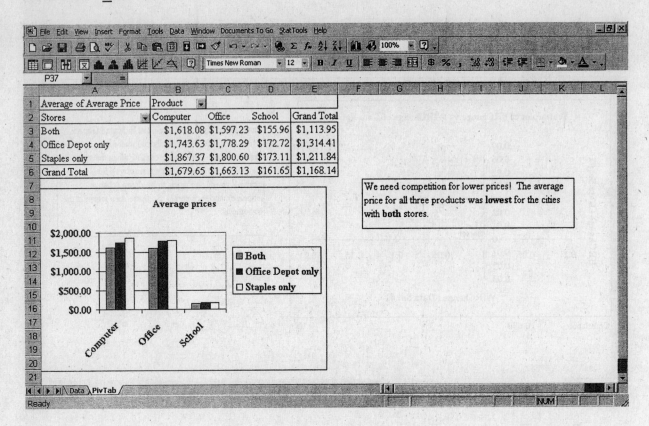

Problem 2_91

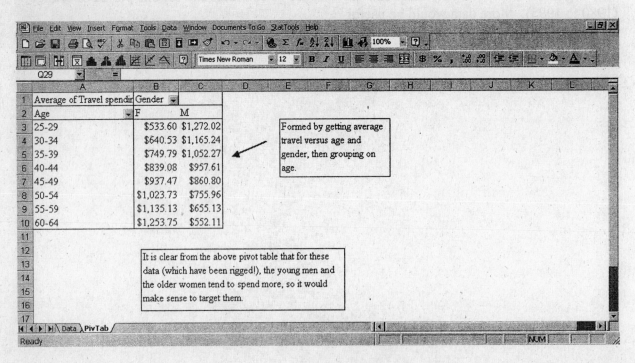

CHAPTER 3

Problem 3_1

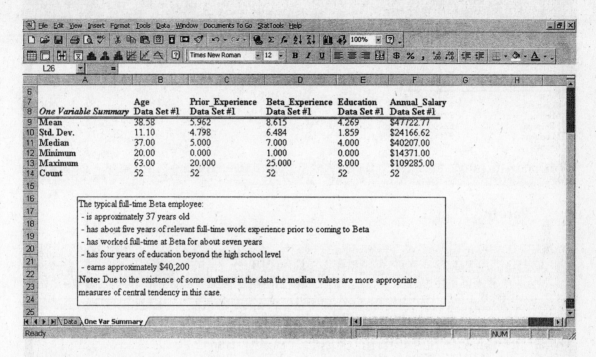

One Variable Summary	Age Data Set #1	Prior_Experience Data Set #1	Beta_Experience Data Set #1	Education Data Set #1	Annual_Salary Data Set #1
Mean	38.58	5.962	8.615	4.269	$47722.77
Std. Dev.	11.10	4.798	6.484	1.859	$24166.62
Median	37.00	5.000	7.000	4.000	$40207.00
Minimum	20.00	0.000	1.000	0.000	$14371.00
Maximum	63.00	20.000	25.000	8.000	$109285.00
Count	52	52	52	52	52

The typical full-time Beta employee:
- is approximately 37 years old
- has about five years of relevant full-time work experience prior to coming to Beta
- has worked full-time at Beta for about seven years
- has four years of education beyond the high school level
- earns approximately $40,200

Note: Due to the existence of some **outliers** in the data the **median** values are more appropriate measures of central tendency in this case.

Problem 3_3

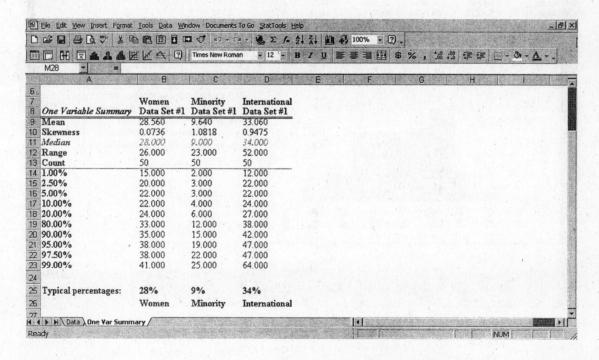

One Variable Summary	Women Data Set #1	Minority Data Set #1	International Data Set #1
Mean	28.560	9.640	33.060
Skewness	0.0736	1.0818	0.9475
Median	*28.000*	*9.000*	*34.000*
Range	26.000	23.000	52.000
Count	50	50	50
1.00%	15.000	2.000	12.000
2.50%	20.000	3.000	22.000
5.00%	22.000	3.000	22.000
10.00%	22.000	4.000	24.000
20.00%	24.000	6.000	27.000
80.00%	33.000	12.000	38.000
90.00%	35.000	15.000	42.000
95.00%	38.000	19.000	47.000
97.50%	38.000	22.000	47.000
99.00%	41.000	25.000	64.000
Typical percentages:	28%	9%	34%
	Women	Minority	International

Problem 3_5

Part a:

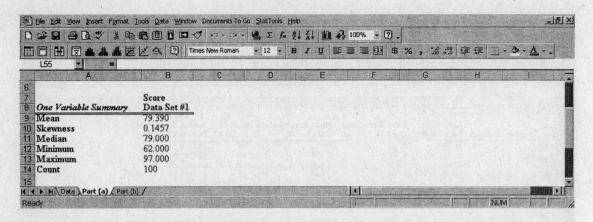

One Variable Summary — Score Data Set #1

One Variable Summary	Score Data Set #1
Mean	79.390
Skewness	0.1457
Median	79.000
Minimum	62.000
Maximum	97.000
Count	100

Part b:

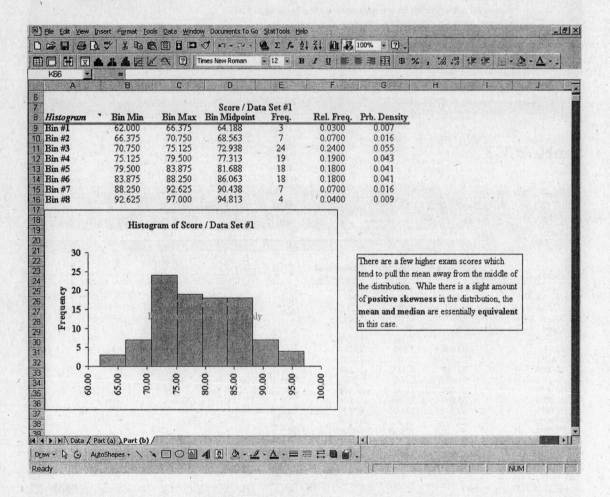

Score / Data Set #1

Histogram	Bin Min	Bin Max	Bin Midpoint	Freq.	Rel. Freq.	Prb. Density
Bin #1	62.000	66.375	64.188	3	0.0300	0.007
Bin #2	66.375	70.750	68.563	7	0.0700	0.016
Bin #3	70.750	75.125	72.938	24	0.2400	0.055
Bin #4	75.125	79.500	77.313	19	0.1900	0.043
Bin #5	79.500	83.875	81.688	18	0.1800	0.041
Bin #6	83.875	88.250	86.063	18	0.1800	0.041
Bin #7	88.250	92.625	90.438	7	0.0700	0.016
Bin #8	92.625	97.000	94.813	4	0.0400	0.009

There are a few higher exam scores which tend to pull the mean away from the middle of the distribution. While there is a slight amount of **positive skewness** in the distribution, the **mean and median** are essentially **equivalent** in this case.

Problem 3_7

Part a:

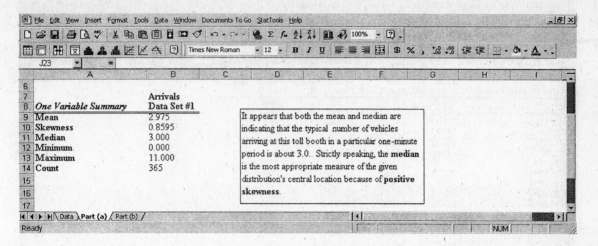

One Variable Summary	Arrivals Data Set #1
Mean	2.975
Skewness	0.8595
Median	3.000
Minimum	0.000
Maximum	11.000
Count	365

It appears that both the mean and median are indicating that the typical number of vehicles arriving at this toll booth in a particular one-minute period is about 3.0. Strictly speaking, the **median** is the most appropriate measure of the given distribution's central location because of **positive skewness**.

Part b:

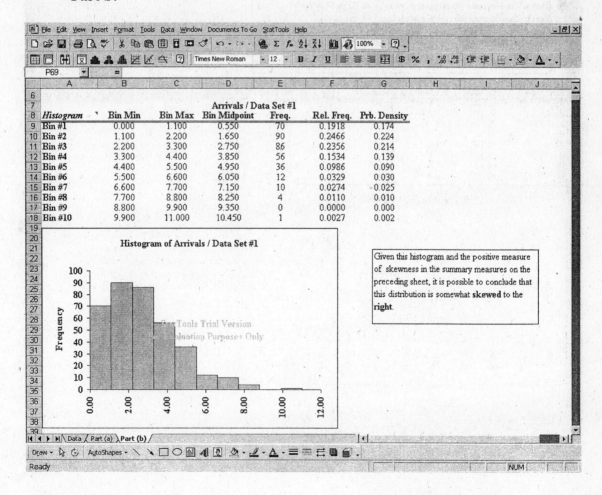

Histogram	Bin Min	Bin Max	Bin Midpoint	Freq.	Rel. Freq.	Prb. Density
Bin #1	0.000	1.100	0.550	70	0.1918	0.174
Bin #2	1.100	2.200	1.650	90	0.2466	0.224
Bin #3	2.200	3.300	2.750	86	0.2356	0.214
Bin #4	3.300	4.400	3.850	56	0.1534	0.139
Bin #5	4.400	5.500	4.950	36	0.0986	0.090
Bin #6	5.500	6.600	6.050	12	0.0329	0.030
Bin #7	6.600	7.700	7.150	10	0.0274	0.025
Bin #8	7.700	8.800	8.250	4	0.0110	0.010
Bin #9	8.800	9.900	9.350	0	0.0000	0.000
Bin #10	9.900	11.000	10.450	1	0.0027	0.002

Arrivals / Data Set #1

Histogram of Arrivals / Data Set #1

Given this histogram and the positive measure of skewness in the summary measures on the preceding sheet, it is possible to conclude that this distribution is somewhat **skewed** to the **right**.

Problem 3_11

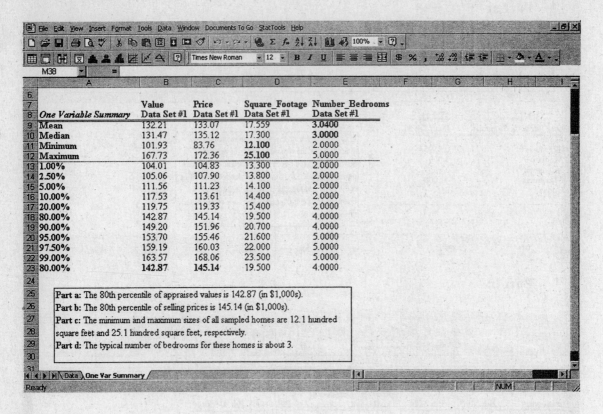

One Variable Summary	Value Data Set #1	Price Data Set #1	Square_Footage Data Set #1	Number_Bedrooms Data Set #1
Mean	132.21	133.07	17.559	3.0400
Median	131.47	135.12	17.300	3.0000
Minimum	101.93	83.76	12.100	2.0000
Maximum	167.73	172.36	25.100	5.0000
1.00%	104.01	104.83	13.300	2.0000
2.50%	105.06	107.90	13.800	2.0000
5.00%	111.56	111.23	14.100	2.0000
10.00%	117.53	113.61	14.400	2.0000
20.00%	119.75	119.33	15.400	2.0000
80.00%	142.87	145.14	19.500	4.0000
90.00%	149.20	151.96	20.700	4.0000
95.00%	153.70	155.46	21.600	5.0000
97.50%	159.19	160.03	22.000	5.0000
99.00%	163.57	168.06	23.500	5.0000
80.00%	142.87	145.14	19.500	4.0000

Part a: The 80th percentile of appraised values is 142.87 (in $1,000s).

Part b: The 80th percentile of selling prices is 145.14 (in $1,000s).

Part c: The minimum and maximum sizes of all sampled homes are 12.1 hundred square feet and 25.1 hundred square feet, respectively.

Part d: The typical number of bedrooms for these homes is about 3.

Problem 3_17

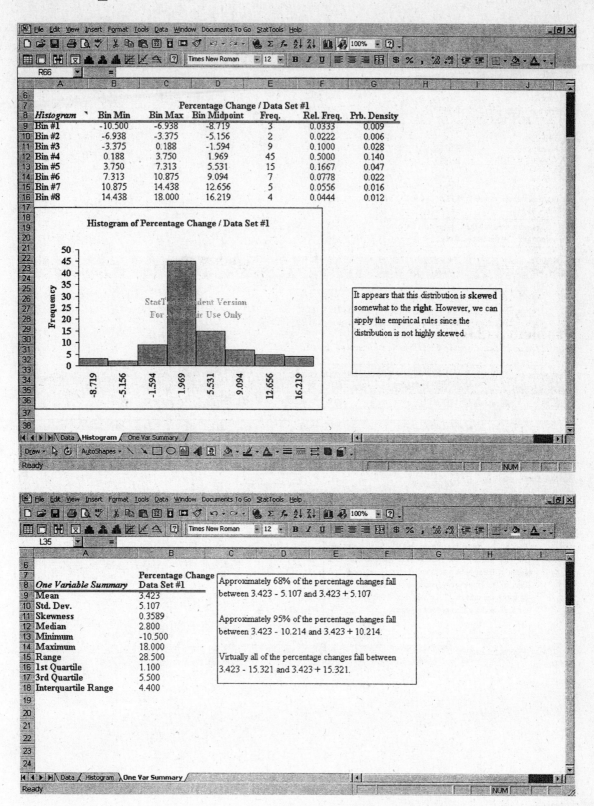

Problem 3_19

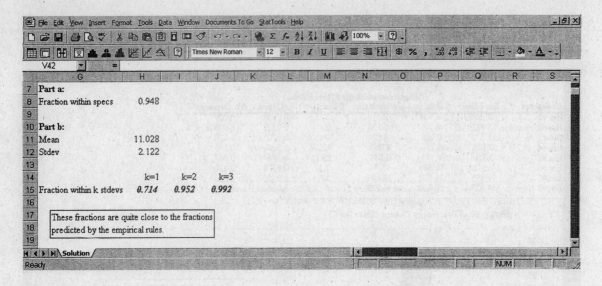

Problem 3_23

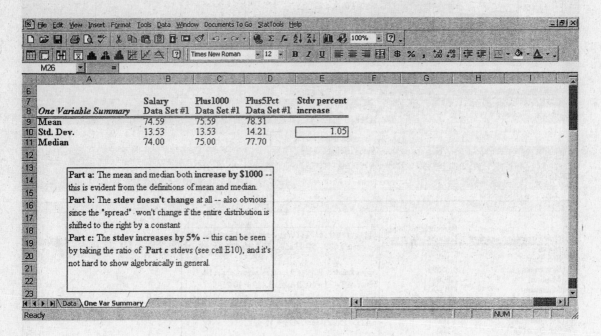

Problem 3_29

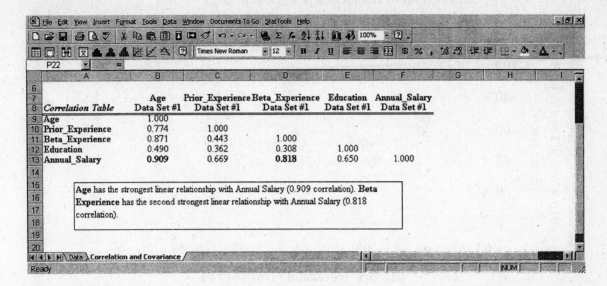

Correlation Table	Age Data Set #1	Prior_Experience Data Set #1	Beta_Experience Data Set #1	Education Data Set #1	Annual_Salary Data Set #1
Age	1.000				
Prior_Experience	0.774	1.000			
Beta_Experience	0.871	0.443	1.000		
Education	0.490	0.362	0.308	1.000	
Annual_Salary	**0.909**	0.669	**0.818**	0.650	1.000

Age has the strongest linear relationship with Annual Salary (0.909 correlation). **Beta Experience** has the second strongest linear relationship with Annual Salary (0.818 correlation).

Problem 3_33

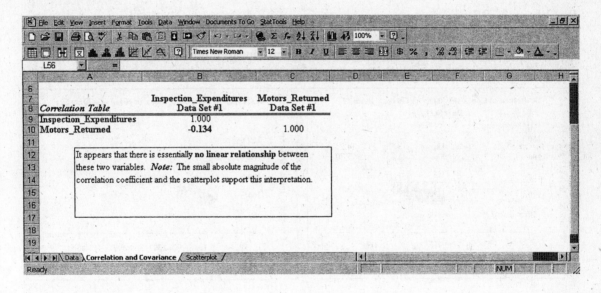

Correlation Table	Inspection_Expenditures Data Set #1	Motors_Returned Data Set #1
Inspection_Expenditures	1.000	
Motors_Returned	-0.134	1.000

It appears that there is essentially **no linear relationship** between these two variables. *Note:* The small absolute magnitude of the correlation coefficient and the scatterplot support this interpretation.

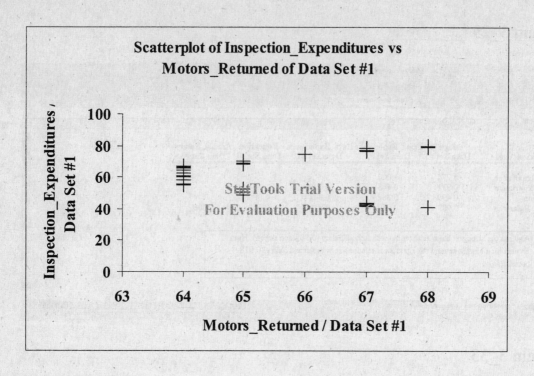

Problem 3_35

Part a: Housing has the **strongest relationship** with the **Composite Index.**
Part b: Utilities has the **weakest relationship** with the **Composite Index.**

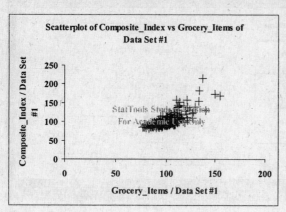

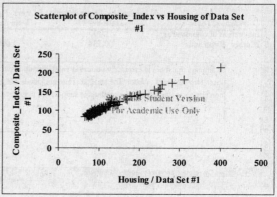

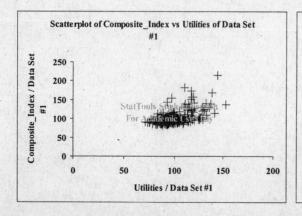

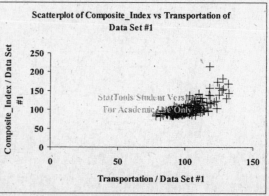

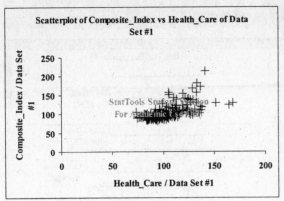

Scatterplot of Composite_Index vs Health_Care of Data Set #1

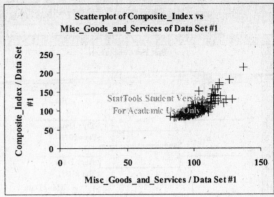

Scatterplot of Composite_Index vs Misc_Goods_and_Services of Data Set #1

Problem 3_43

There appears to be some downward trend in the averages from the early months to the later months. The trend probably was caused by an insufficient mixing of the balls.

Note: StatTools allows only 10 variables per boxplot. So I created two boxplots for each year and copied/pasted to get them both on the same sheet.

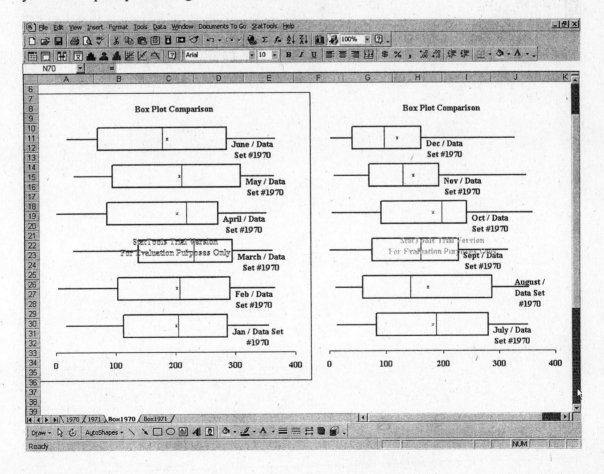

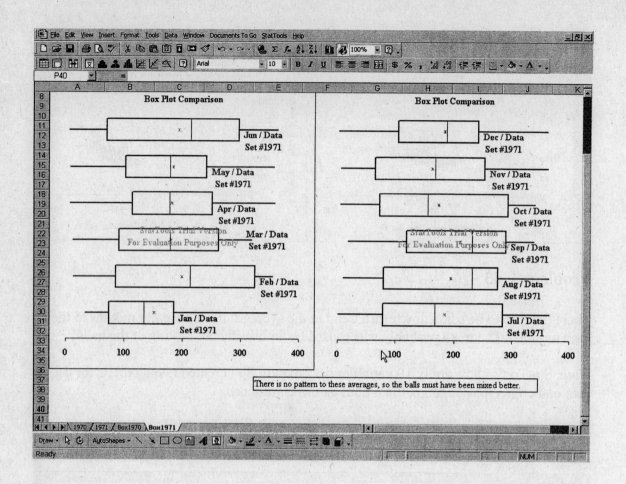

Problem 3_45

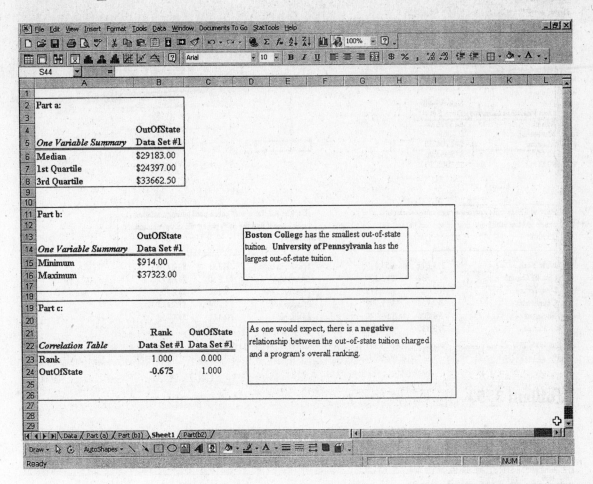

Problem 3_47

Part a: =PERCENTILE(B4:B37,0.85) = 111.115 This is the 85th percentile.

Part b: =PERCENTILE(B4:B37,0.4) = 92.38 This is the 40th percentile.

Part c: =MAX(B$:B37) = 136.1 This minimum corresponds to 1968.

Part d: =MIN(B$:B37) = 59.0 This minimum corresponds to 1982.

Problem 3_51

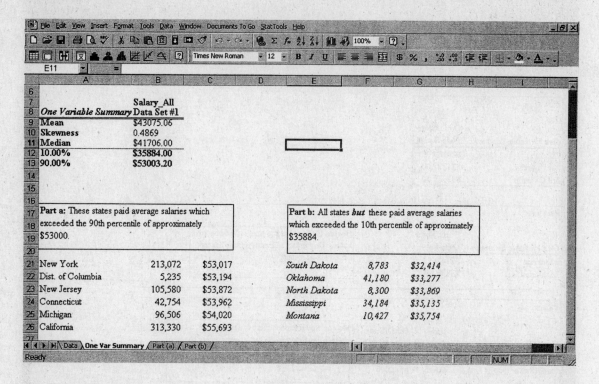

One Variable Summary | Salary_All Data Set #1
	Salary_All Data Set #1
Mean	$43075.06
Skewness	0.4869
Median	$41706.00
10.00%	$35884.00
90.00%	$53003.20

Part a: These states paid average salaries which exceeded the 90th percentile of approximately $53000.

New York	213,072	$53,017
Dist. of Columbia	5,235	$53,194
New Jersey	105,580	$53,872
Connecticut	42,754	$53,962
Michigan	96,506	$54,020
California	313,330	$55,693

Part b: All states *but* these paid average salaries which exceeded the 10th percentile of approximately $35884.

South Dakota	8,783	$32,414
Oklahoma	41,180	$33,277
North Dakota	8,300	$33,869
Mississippi	34,184	$35,135
Montana	10,427	$35,754

Problem 3_53

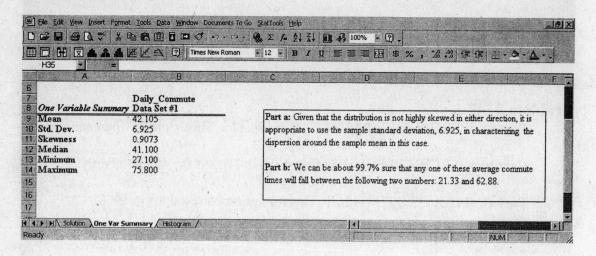

One Variable Summary	Daily_Commute Data Set #1
Mean	42.105
Std. Dev.	6.925
Skewness	0.9073
Median	41.100
Minimum	27.100
Maximum	75.800

Part a: Given that the distribution is not highly skewed in either direction, it is appropriate to use the sample standard deviation, 6.925, in characterizing the dispersion around the sample mean in this case.

Part b: We can be about 99.7% sure that any one of these average commute times will fall between the following two numbers: 21.33 and 62.88.

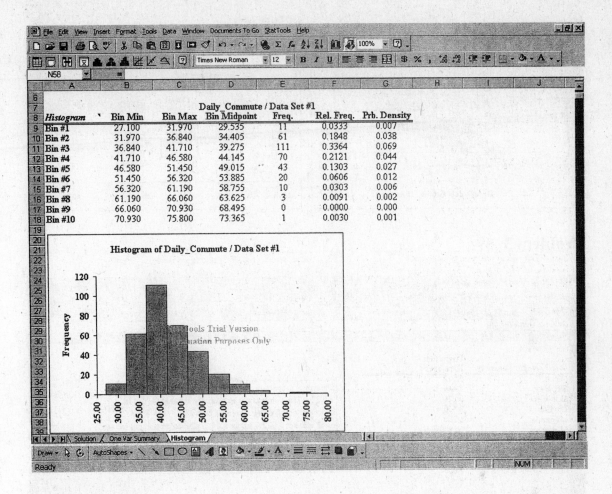

Problem 3_55

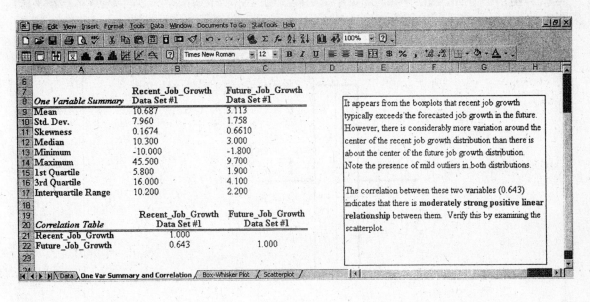

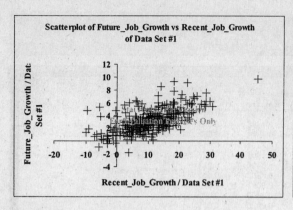

Scatterplot of Future_Job_Growth vs Recent_Job_Growth of Data Set #1

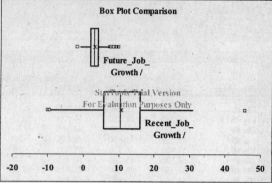

Box Plot Comparison

Problem 3_59

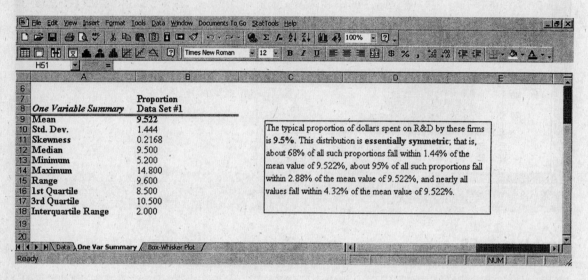

	Proportion Data Set #1
One Variable Summary	
Mean	9.522
Std. Dev.	1.444
Skewness	0.2168
Median	9.500
Minimum	5.200
Maximum	14.800
Range	9.600
1st Quartile	8.500
3rd Quartile	10.500
Interquartile Range	2.000

The typical proportion of dollars spent on R&D by these firms is **9.5%**. This distribution is **essentially symmetric**; that is, about 68% of all such proportions fall within 1.44% of the mean value of 9.522%, about 95% of all such proportions fall within 2.88% of the mean value of 9.522%, and nearly all values fall within 4.32% of the mean value of 9.522%.

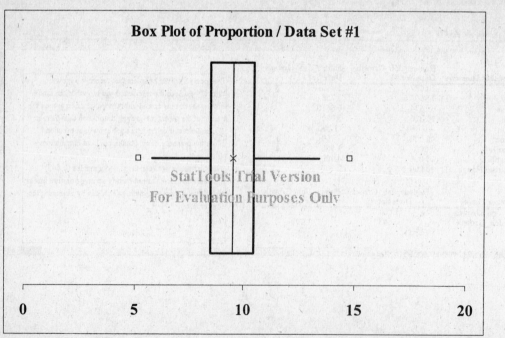

Box Plot of Proportion / Data Set #1

Problem 3_63
Part a:

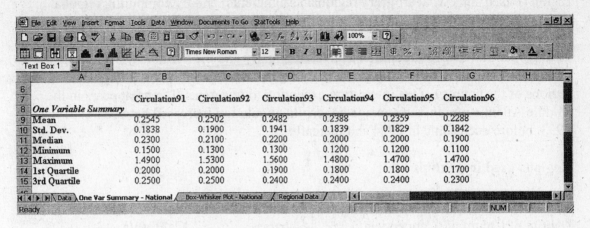

	Circulation91	Circulation92	Circulation93	Circulation94	Circulation95	Circulation96
One Variable Summary						
Mean	0.2545	0.2502	0.2482	0.2388	0.2359	0.2288
Std. Dev.	0.1838	0.1900	0.1941	0.1839	0.1829	0.1842
Median	0.2300	0.2100	0.2200	0.2000	0.2000	0.1900
Minimum	0.1500	0.1300	0.1300	0.1200	0.1200	0.1100
Maximum	1.4900	1.5300	1.5600	1.4800	1.4700	1.4700
1st Quartile	0.2000	0.2000	0.1900	0.1800	0.1800	0.1700
3rd Quartile	0.2500	0.2500	0.2400	0.2400	0.2400	0.2300

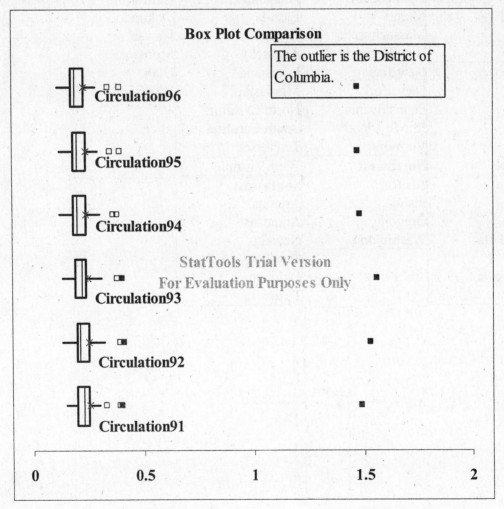

Part b: Nationally, the average value of per capita newspaper circulation **fell** between **1991** and **1996**. Regional trends can be identified by assigning each state to a region (I used somewhat arbitrary regional assignments) and by computing regional means and standard deviations (using built-in Excel functions) for each of the given years. In general, the regional trends reflect those at the national level; namely, the average per newspaper circulation decreased slightly and the variability of per capita circulation remained essentially stable over the given period in each of the various regions of the country. One interesting exception to this general trend appears in the Middle Atlantic region: the average per capita circulation increased between 1991 and 1993, before decreasing in 1994 and thereafter.

Regions used in analysis

Middle Atlantic	Northeast	Southeast	West
District of Columbia	Connecticut	Alabama	California
Maryland	Maine	Florida	Colorado
Virginia	Massachusetts	Georgia	Hawaii
Delaware	New Hampshire	Kentucky	Montana
Midwest	New Jersey	Louisiana	Utah
Illinois	New York	Mississippi	Wyoming
Indiana	Pennsylvania	North Carolina	
Iowa	Rhode Island	South Carolina	
Kansas	Vermont	Tennessee	
Michigan	**Northwest**	West Virginia	
Minnesota	Alaska	**Southwest**	
Missouri	Idaho	Arizona	
Nebraska	Oregon	Arkansas	
North Dakota	Washington	Nevada	
Ohio		New Mexico	
South Dakota		Oklahoma	
Wisconsin		Texas	

Problem 3_65

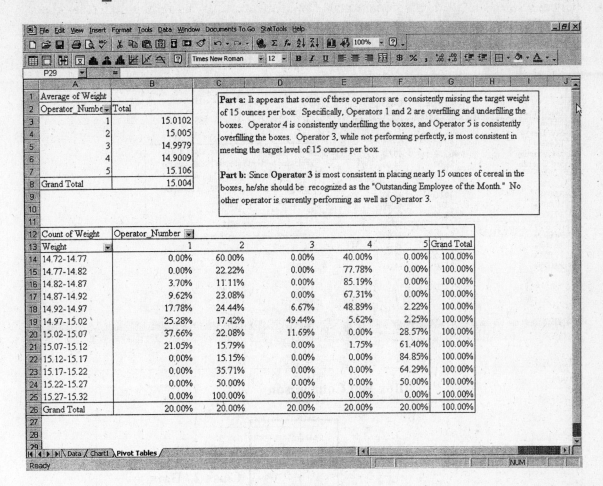

Average of Weight						
Operator_Number	Total					
1	15.0102					
2	15.005					
3	14.9979					
4	14.9009					
5	15.106					
Grand Total	15.004					

Part a: It appears that some of these operators are consistently missing the target weight of 15 ounces per box. Specifically, Operators 1 and 2 are overfilling and underfilling the boxes. Operator 4 is consistently underfilling the boxes, and Operator 5 is consistently overfilling the boxes. Operator 3, while not performing perfectly, is most consistent in meeting the target level of 15 ounces per box.

Part b: Since **Operator 3** is most consistent in placing nearly 15 ounces of cereal in the boxes, he/she should be recognized as the "Outstanding Employee of the Month." No other operator is currently performing as well as Operator 3.

Count of Weight	Operator_Number					
Weight	1	2	3	4	5	Grand Total
14.72-14.77	0.00%	60.00%	0.00%	40.00%	0.00%	100.00%
14.77-14.82	0.00%	22.22%	0.00%	77.78%	0.00%	100.00%
14.82-14.87	3.70%	11.11%	0.00%	85.19%	0.00%	100.00%
14.87-14.92	9.62%	23.08%	0.00%	67.31%	0.00%	100.00%
14.92-14.97	17.78%	24.44%	6.67%	48.89%	2.22%	100.00%
14.97-15.02	25.28%	17.42%	49.44%	5.62%	2.25%	100.00%
15.02-15.07	37.66%	22.08%	11.69%	0.00%	28.57%	100.00%
15.07-15.12	21.05%	15.79%	0.00%	1.75%	61.40%	100.00%
15.12-15.17	0.00%	15.15%	0.00%	0.00%	84.85%	100.00%
15.17-15.22	0.00%	35.71%	0.00%	0.00%	64.29%	100.00%
15.22-15.27	0.00%	50.00%	0.00%	0.00%	50.00%	100.00%
15.27-15.32	0.00%	100.00%	0.00%	0.00%	0.00%	100.00%
Grand Total	20.00%	20.00%	20.00%	20.00%	20.00%	100.00%

Problem 3_67

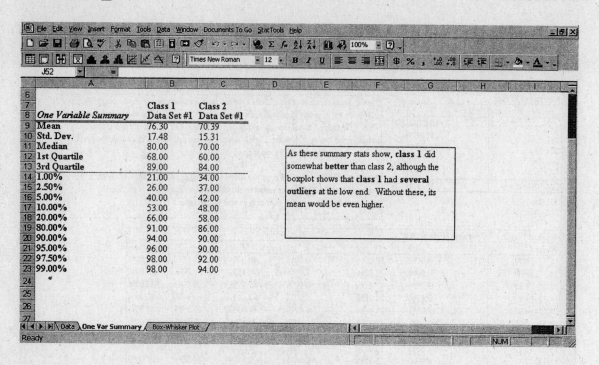

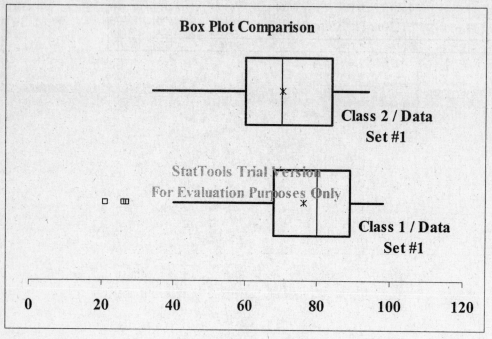

Problem 3_73

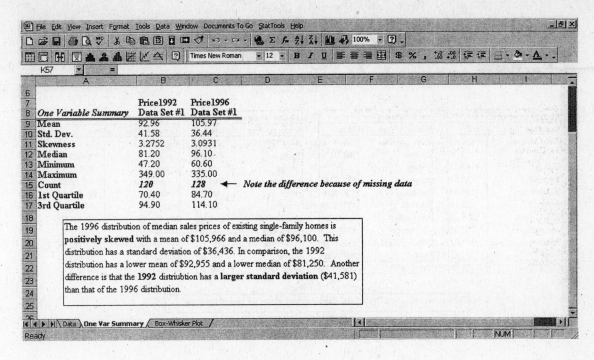

One Variable Summary	Price1992 Data Set #1	Price1996 Data Set #1	
Mean	92.96	105.97	
Std. Dev.	41.58	36.44	
Skewness	3.2752	3.0931	
Median	81.20	96.10	
Minimum	47.20	60.60	
Maximum	349.00	335.00	
Count	*120*	*128*	← Note the difference because of missing data
1st Quartile	70.40	84.70	
3rd Quartile	94.90	114.10	

The 1996 distribution of median sales prices of existing single-family homes is **positively skewed** with a mean of $105,966 and a median of $96,100. This distribution has a standard deviation of $36,436. In comparison, the 1992 distribution has a lower mean of $92,955 and a lower median of $81,250. Another difference is that the **1992** distriubtion has a **larger standard deviation** ($41,581) than that of the 1996 distribution.

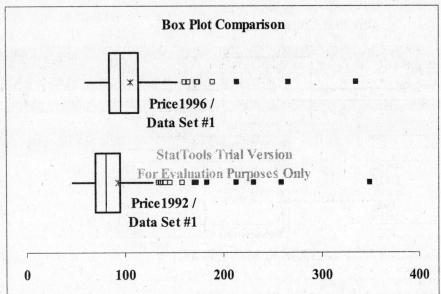

Box Plot Comparison

StatTools Trial Version
For Evaluation Purposes Only

Problem 3_77

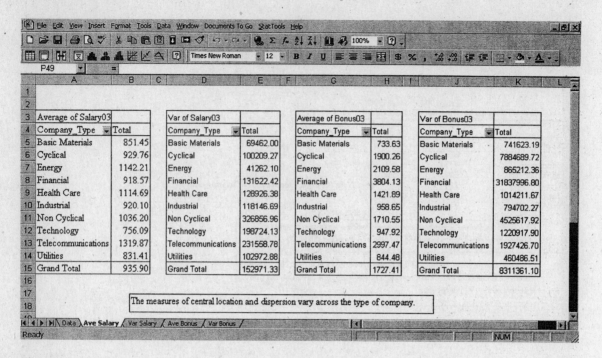

Average of Salary03				Var of Salary03				Average of Bonus03				Var of Bonus03		
Company_Type	Total			Company_Type	Total			Company_Type	Total			Company_Type	Total	
Basic Materials	851.45			Basic Materials	69462.00			Basic Materials	733.63			Basic Materials	741623.19	
Cyclical	929.76			Cyclical	100209.27			Cyclical	1900.26			Cyclical	7884689.72	
Energy	1142.21			Energy	41262.10			Energy	2109.58			Energy	865212.36	
Financial	918.57			Financial	131622.42			Financial	3804.13			Financial	31837996.80	
Health Care	1114.69			Health Care	128926.38			Health Care	1421.89			Health Care	1014211.67	
Industrial	920.10			Industrial	118146.69			Industrial	958.65			Industrial	794702.27	
Non Cyclical	1036.20			Non Cyclical	326856.96			Non Cyclical	1710.55			Non Cyclical	4525617.92	
Technology	756.09			Technology	198724.13			Technology	947.92			Technology	1220917.90	
Telecommunications	1319.87			Telecommunications	231558.78			Telecommunications	2997.47			Telecommunications	1927426.70	
Utilities	831.41			Utilities	102972.88			Utilities	844.48			Utilities	460486.51	
Grand Total	935.90			Grand Total	152971.33			Grand Total	1727.41			Grand Total	8311361.10	

The measures of central location and dispersion vary across the type of company.

Problem 3_81

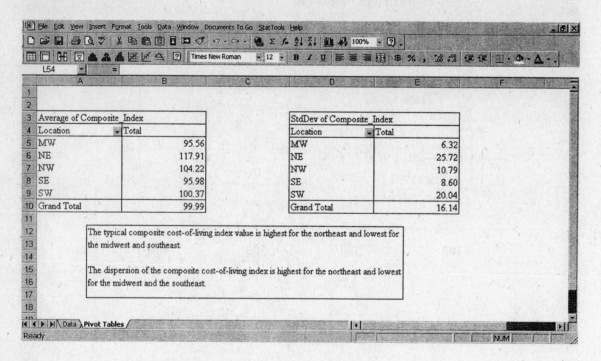

Average of Composite_Index				StdDev of Composite_Index	
Location	Total			Location	Total
MW	95.56			MW	6.32
NE	117.91			NE	25.72
NW	104.22			NW	10.79
SE	95.98			SE	8.60
SW	100.37			SW	20.04
Grand Total	99.99			Grand Total	16.14

The typical composite cost-of-living index value is highest for the northeast and lowest for the midwest and southeast.

The dispersion of the composite cost-of-living index is highest for the northeast and lowest for the midwest and the southeast.

Problem 3_87

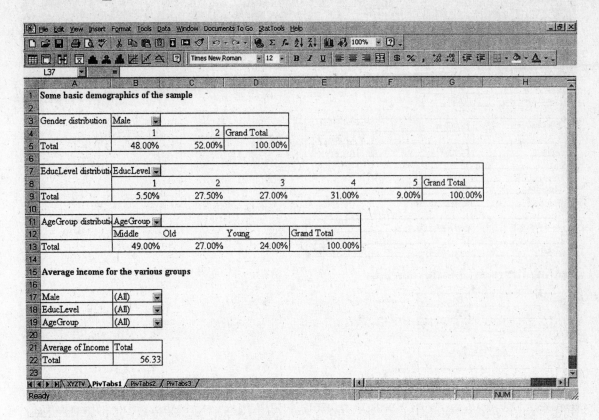

Some basic demographics of the sample							
Gender distribution	Male						
	1		2	Grand Total			
Total	48.00%	52.00%		100.00%			
EducLevel distributi	EducLevel						
	1	2	3	4	5	Grand Total	
Total	5.50%	27.50%	27.00%	31.00%	9.00%	100.00%	
AgeGroup distributi	AgeGroup						
	Middle	Old	Young	Grand Total			
Total	49.00%	27.00%	24.00%	100.00%			
Average income for the various groups							
Male	(All)						
EducLevel	(All)						
AgeGroup	(All)						
Average of Income	Total						
Total	56.33						

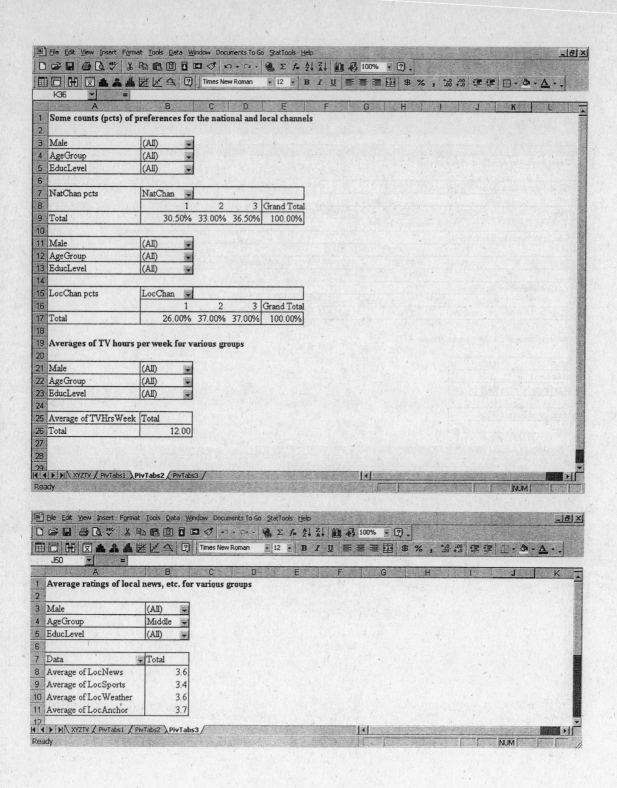

Excel window 1:

File Edit View Insert Format Tools Data Window Documents To Go StatTools Help

K36

	A	B	C	D	E	F	G	H	I	J	K	L
1	Some counts (pcts) of preferences for the national and local channels											
2												
3	Male	(All)										
4	AgeGroup	(All)										
5	EducLevel	(All)										
6												
7	NatChan pcts	NatChan										
8			1	2	3	Grand Total						
9	Total		30.50%	33.00%	36.50%	100.00%						
10												
11	Male	(All)										
12	AgeGroup	(All)										
13	EducLevel	(All)										
14												
15	LocChan pcts	LocChan										
16			1	2	3	Grand Total						
17	Total		26.00%	37.00%	37.00%	100.00%						
18												
19	Averages of TV hours per week for various groups											
20												
21	Male	(All)										
22	AgeGroup	(All)										
23	EducLevel	(All)										
24												
25	Average of TVHrsWeek	Total										
26	Total	12.00										
27												
28												
29												

XYZTV / PivTabs1 \ **PivTabs2** / PivTabs3 /

Ready   NUM

Excel window 2:

File Edit View Insert Format Tools Data Window Documents To Go StatTools Help

J50

	A	B	C	D	E	F	G	H	I	J	K
1	Average ratings of local news, etc. for various groups										
2											
3	Male	(All)									
4	AgeGroup	Middle									
5	EducLevel	(All)									
6											
7	Data	Total									
8	Average of LocNews	3.6									
9	Average of LocSports	3.4									
10	Average of LocWeather	3.6									
11	Average of LocAnchor	3.7									
12											

XYZTV / PivTabs1 / PivTabs2 \ **PivTabs3** /

Ready   NUM

CHAPTER 4

Problem 4_1
Part a:

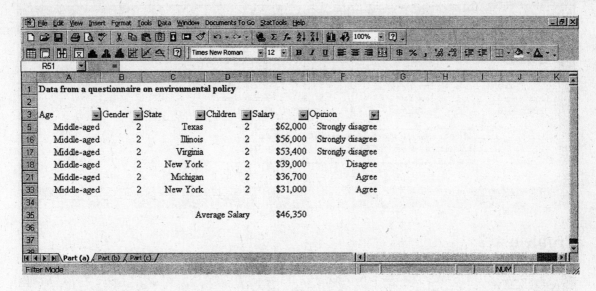

Part b:

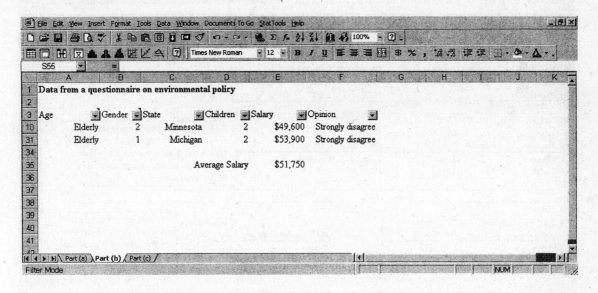

Part c:

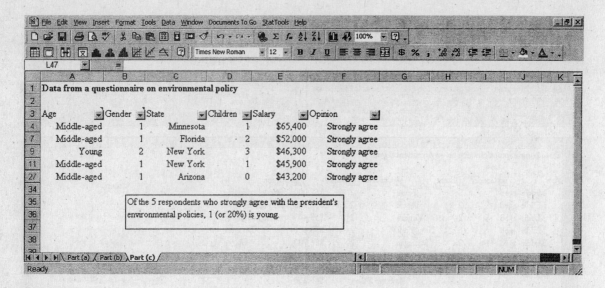

Problem 4_3

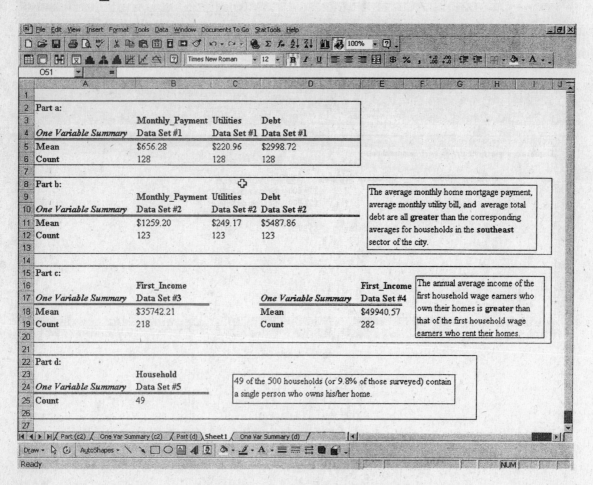

Problem 4_ 5

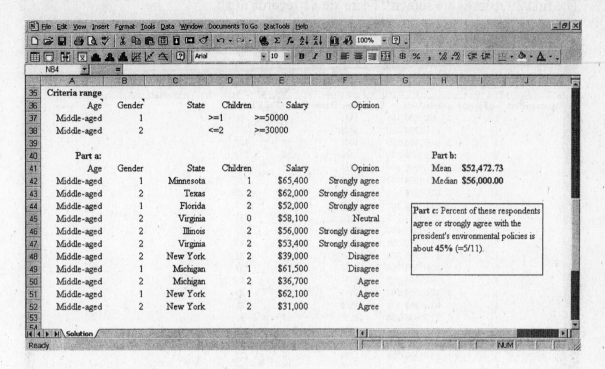

Problem 4_9

The first 29 records are shown. There are 81 records in all.

	File	Edit	View	Insert	Format	Tools	Data	Window	Documents To Go	StatTools	Help

M65

	A	B	C	D	E	F	G	H	I	J
1	CustomerNum	Discount	OrderDate	OrderNum	ProductNum	UnitsOrdered				
2	2	0	1/3/1998 0:00	1396	1	86				
3	1	0	1/11/1998 0:00	1403	1	94				
4	5	0	1/16/1998 0:00	1406	10	107				
5	1	0	1/18/1998 0:00	1409	10	109				
6	6	0.05	1/23/1998 0:00	1416	1	142				
7	3	0	1/29/1998 0:00	1425	1	78				
8	4	0	1/29/1998 0:00	1426	10	118				
9	1	0	1/31/1998 0:00	1427	1	131				
10	5	0	1/31/1998 0:00	1428	1	138				
11	2	0.05	2/5/1998 0:00	1434	1	87				
12	2	0.1	2/16/1998 0:00	1452	10	148				
13	1	0.15	2/18/1998 0:00	1456	10	81				
14	6	0	2/26/1998 0:00	1466	10	137				
15	4	0	3/7/1998 0:00	1474	1	90				
16	1	0	3/26/1998 0:00	1493	1	89				
17	4	0	4/18/1998 0:00	1520	1	81				
18	1	0	5/19/1998 0:00	1551	10	96				
19	6	0	5/23/1998 0:00	1559	1	139				
20	5	0.05	5/26/1998 0:00	1562	1	83				
21	5	0.1	5/31/1998 0:00	1568	10	122				
22	2	0	6/4/1998 0:00	1572	10	145				
23	5	0	6/10/1998 0:00	1577	1	125				
24	4	0.05	6/22/1998 0:00	1592	10	116				
25	5	0	7/11/1998 0:00	1617	1	123				
26	4	0.15	8/6/1998 0:00	1642	1	147				
27	4	0	8/6/1998 0:00	1643	10	103				
28	6	0	8/23/1998 0:00	1666	10	133				
29	2	0.05	9/15/1998 0:00	1689	10	108				
30	4		9/15/1998 0:00	1690	10	107				

Imported Data

Problem 4_11

The first 60 records are shown. There are 70 records in all.

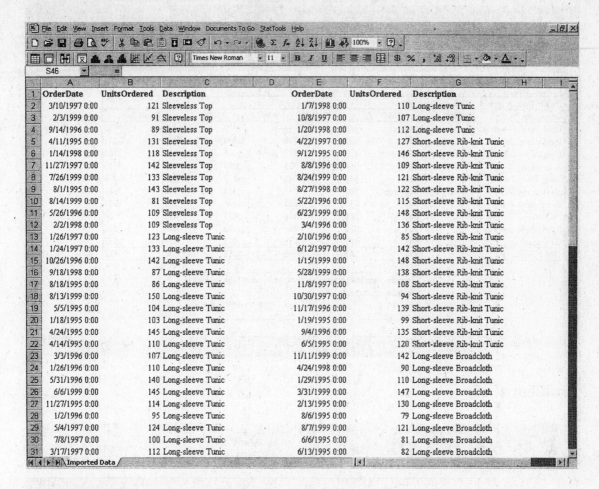

Problem 4_13

```
SELECT Orders.OrderDate, Orders.UnitsOrdered,
Orders.Discount
FROM `D:\Chapter 4 Data Sets\P04_09`.Orders Orders
WHERE (Orders.UnitsOrdered Between 50 And 100) AND
(Orders.CustomerNum=5) AND (Orders.ProductNum=2)
```

Note: The path to the file in the FROM line will depend on where your dataset is stored.

Problem 4_ 15

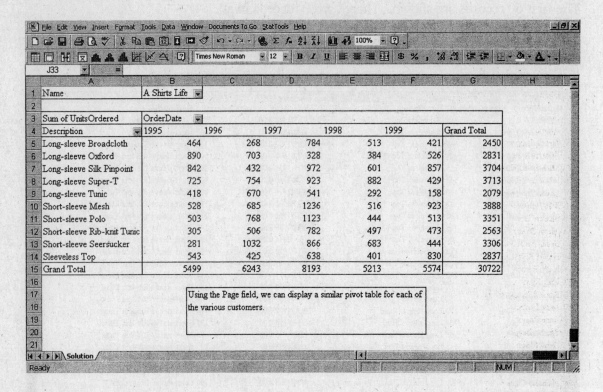

Problem 4_17

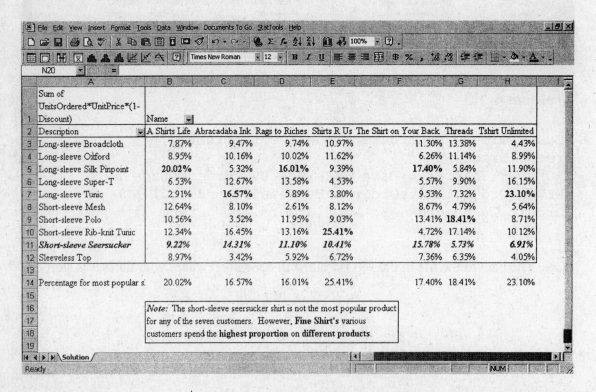

Problem 4_ 25

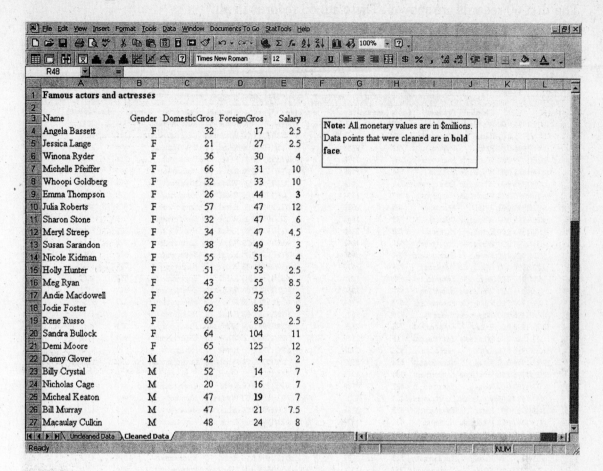

Name	Gender	DomesticGros	ForeignGros	Salary
Angela Bassett	F	32	17	2.5
Jessica Lange	F	21	27	2.5
Winona Ryder	F	36	30	4
Michelle Pfeiffer	F	66	31	10
Whoopi Goldberg	F	32	33	10
Emma Thompson	F	26	44	**3**
Julia Roberts	F	57	47	12
Sharon Stone	F	32	47	6
Meryl Streep	F	34	47	4.5
Susan Sarandon	F	38	49	3
Nicole Kidman	F	55	51	4
Holly Hunter	F	51	53	2.5
Meg Ryan	F	43	55	8.5
Andie Macdowell	F	26	75	2
Jodie Foster	F	62	85	9
Rene Russo	F	69	85	2.5
Sandra Bullock	F	64	104	11
Demi Moore	F	65	125	12
Danny Glover	M	42	4	2
Billy Crystal	M	52	14	7
Nicholas Cage	M	20	16	7
Micheal Keaton	M	47	**19**	7
Bill Murray	M	47	21	7.5
Macaulay Culkin	M	48	24	8

Note: All monetary values are in $millions. Data points that were cleaned are in **bold face**.

Problem 4_31

The first 60 records are shown. There are 63 records in all.

Date	Channel	Product	Units	AmountPaid	Date	Channel	Product	Units	AmountPaid
1/12/1995 0:00	Wholesale	Environment	685	1370	7/19/1997 0:00	Retail	Environment	753	3012
1/14/1995 0:00	Retail	Humorous	593	2372	8/3/1997 0:00	Wholesale	Environment	745	1490
1/18/1995 0:00	Retail	Political	722	2888	9/16/1997 0:00	Retail	Environment	694	2776
2/15/1995 0:00	Wholesale	Humorous	569	1138	10/13/1997 0:00	Retail	Humorous	716	2864
2/16/1995 0:00	Wholesale	Political	594	1188	11/13/1997 0:00	Retail	Humorous	867	3468
4/9/1995 0:00	Wholesale	Environment	714	1428	1/2/1998 0:00	Wholesale	Humorous	979	1958
4/26/1995 0:00	Wholesale	Humorous	797	1594	1/5/1998 0:00	Retail	Humorous	570	2280
6/11/1995 0:00	Retail	Humorous	668	2672	1/22/1998 0:00	Retail	Environment	964	3856
6/23/1995 0:00	Wholesale	Political	733	1466	2/3/1998 0:00	Wholesale	Environment	919	1838
11/2/1995 0:00	Retail	Humorous	720	2880	2/15/1998 0:00	Retail	Humorous	571	2284
1/1/1996 0:00	Wholesale	Environment	521	1042	3/10/1998 0:00	Wholesale	Environment	978	1956
5/19/1996 0:00	Retail	Environment	864	3456	3/11/1998 0:00	Retail	Environment	522	2088
5/27/1996 0:00	Wholesale	Humorous	785	1570	3/17/1998 0:00	Wholesale	Humorous	929	1858
6/9/1996 0:00	Wholesale	Environment	639	1278	4/5/1998 0:00	Retail	Environment	652	2608
6/14/1996 0:00	Wholesale	Humorous	530	1060	4/21/1998 0:00	Wholesale	Environment	913	1826
7/1/1996 0:00	Wholesale	Environment	677	1354	4/30/1998 0:00	Wholesale	Humorous	927	1854
8/14/1996 0:00	Wholesale	Humorous	986	1972	5/12/1998 0:00	Retail	Humorous	658	2632
10/27/1996 0:00	Retail	Environment	706	2824	5/20/1998 0:00	Wholesale	Humorous	521	1042
11/12/1996 0:00	Wholesale	Environment	915	1830	5/24/1998 0:00	Wholesale	Environment	984	1968
11/25/1996 0:00	Retail	Humorous	932	3728	6/26/1998 0:00	Retail	Humorous	1012	4048
12/14/1996 0:00	Retail	Environment	658	2632	7/6/1998 0:00	Wholesale	Environment	710	1420
12/20/1996 0:00	Wholesale	Environment	988	1976	7/14/1998 0:00	Retail	Humorous	1124	4271
1/8/1997 0:00	Retail	Environment	627	2508	7/19/1998 0:00	Retail	Environment	611	2444
2/15/1997 0:00	Wholesale	Environment	863	1726	7/23/1998 0:00	Wholesale	Humorous	1061	2122
3/20/1997 0:00	Retail	Environment	832	3328	8/9/1998 0:00	Wholesale	Humorous	646	1292
4/19/1997 0:00	Wholesale	Humorous	689	1378	8/23/1998 0:00	Retail	Environment	651	2604
4/24/1997 0:00	Wholesale	Environment	699	1398	9/7/1998 0:00	Wholesale	Humorous	651	1302
5/18/1997 0:00	Retail	Environment	502	2008	9/28/1998 0:00	Retail	Environment	970	3880
5/29/1997 0:00	Retail	Environment	823	3292	10/12/1998 0:00	Retail	Environment	1036	4144
7/5/1997 0:00	Wholesale	Environment	757	1514	10/12/1998 0:00	Wholesale	Environment	936	1872

Problem 4_33

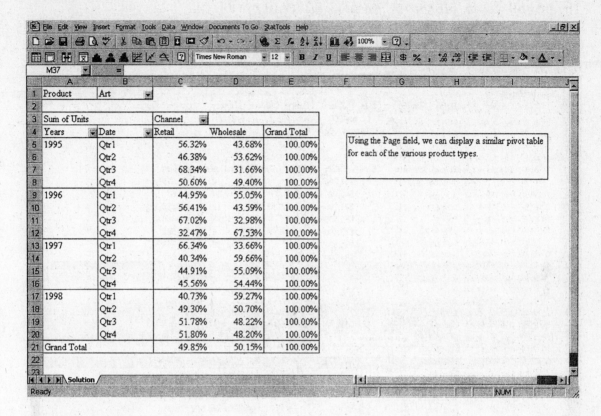

Using the Page field, we can display a similar pivot table for each of the various product types.

		Channel		
Sum of Units				
Years	Date	Retail	Wholesale	Grand Total
1995	Qtr1	56.32%	43.68%	100.00%
	Qtr2	46.38%	53.62%	100.00%
	Qtr3	68.34%	31.66%	100.00%
	Qtr4	50.60%	49.40%	100.00%
1996	Qtr1	44.95%	55.05%	100.00%
	Qtr2	56.41%	43.59%	100.00%
	Qtr3	67.02%	32.98%	100.00%
	Qtr4	32.47%	67.53%	100.00%
1997	Qtr1	66.34%	33.66%	100.00%
	Qtr2	40.34%	59.66%	100.00%
	Qtr3	44.91%	55.09%	100.00%
	Qtr4	45.56%	54.44%	100.00%
1998	Qtr1	40.73%	59.27%	100.00%
	Qtr2	49.30%	50.70%	100.00%
	Qtr3	51.78%	48.22%	100.00%
	Qtr4	51.80%	48.20%	100.00%
Grand Total		49.85%	50.15%	100.00%

Product: Art

Problem 4_35

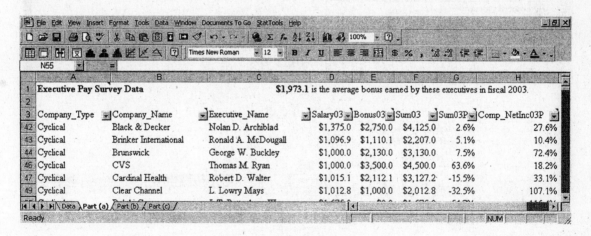

Executive Pay Survey Data $1,973.1 is the average bonus earned by these executives in fiscal 2003.

Company_Type	Company_Name	Executive_Name	Salary03	Bonus03	Sum03	Sum03P	Comp_NetInc03P
Cyclical	Black & Decker	Nolan D. Archiblad	$1,375.0	$2,750.0	$4,125.0	2.6%	27.6%
Cyclical	Brinker International	Ronald A. McDougall	$1,096.9	$1,110.1	$2,207.0	5.1%	10.4%
Cyclical	Brunswick	George W. Buckley	$1,000.0	$2,130.0	$3,130.0	7.5%	72.4%
Cyclical	CVS	Thomas M. Ryan	$1,000.0	$3,500.0	$4,500.0	63.6%	18.2%
Cyclical	Cardinal Health	Robert D. Walter	$1,015.1	$2,112.1	$3,127.2	-15.5%	33.1%
Cyclical	Clear Channel	L. Lowry Mays	$1,012.8	$1,000.0	$2,012.8	-32.5%	107.1%

Problem 4_ 37

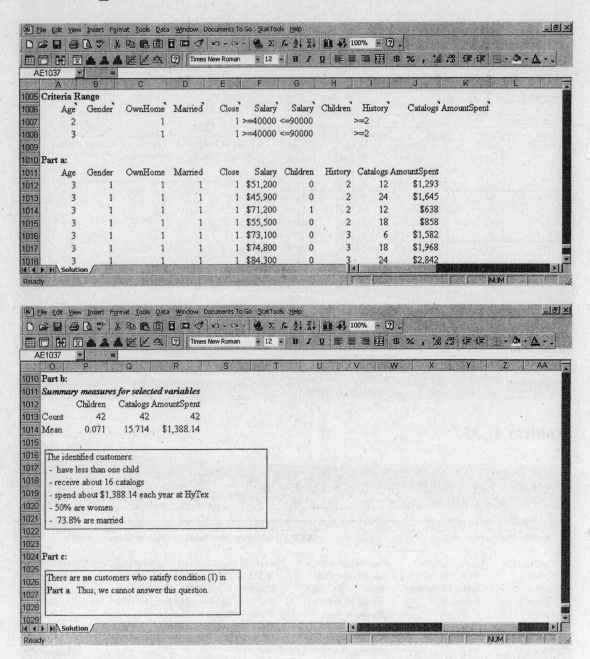

CHAPTER 5

Problem 5_1

Part a: The probability that a randomly selected household from this suburb has not installed an electronic security system is 1-0.30 = **0.70** (using the *complement rule*).

Part b: The probability that neither of two randomly selected households has installed an electronic security system is (0.70)*(0.70) = **0.49** (using the *multiplication rule for independent events*).

Problem 5_3

Given that P(number < 3000) = 0.25 and P(3000 <= number <= 5000) = 1/3, we know that P(number > 5000) = 1 - 1/4 - 1/3 = 5/12 from the *Addition Rule*.

Thus, using the Addition Rule once again, we know that the P(number < 3000 or number > 5000) = 1/4 + 5/12 = or **2/3**.

Problem 5_7

Given: P(MBA) = 0.35, P(<5) = 0.45
  P(MBA and >=5) = 0.75 * P(no MBA and <5).

Thus, we know that
  P(>=5) = 1 - P(<5) = 1 - 0.45 = 0.55
  P(no MBA) = 1 - P(MBA) = 1 - 0.35 = 0.65.

So, the desired probability is the sum of P(MBA and <5) + P(no MBA and >=5).

Let's concentrate on finding the P(no MBA and >=5).
  First, we know that P(MBA and >=5) + P(no MBA and >=5) = P(>=5) = 0.55.
  Alternatively, we have P(MBA and >=5) = 0.55 - P(no MBA and >=5).

Furthermore, we know that
  P(no MBA and <5) + P(no MBA and >=5) = P(no MBA) = 0.65.

But we know from the given information that
  P(no MBA and <5) = 4/3*P(MBA and >=5).

This gives us
  4/3*P(MBA and >= 5) + P(no MBA and >= 5) = 0.65.
Alternatively, we have
  P(MBA and >=5) = 3/4[0.65 - P(no MBA and >=5)] = 3/4(0.65) - 3/4P(no MBA and >=5).

Thus, we can use these relationships to find that

0.55 - P(no MBA and >=5) = 3/4(0.65) - 3/4P(no MBA and >=5).
0.55 - 0.75(0.65) = 0.25P(no MBA and >=5)
0.25 = P(no MBA and >=5)

which implies that

P(MBA and >=5) = 0.55 - 0.25 = 0.30.

But *P(MBA and <5)* = P(MBA) - P(MBA and >=5) = 0.35 - 0.30 = *0.05*.

Finally, we can find the desired probability to be
P(MBA and <5) + P(no MBA and >=5) = *0.05 + 0.25* = **0.30**.

Problem 5_11

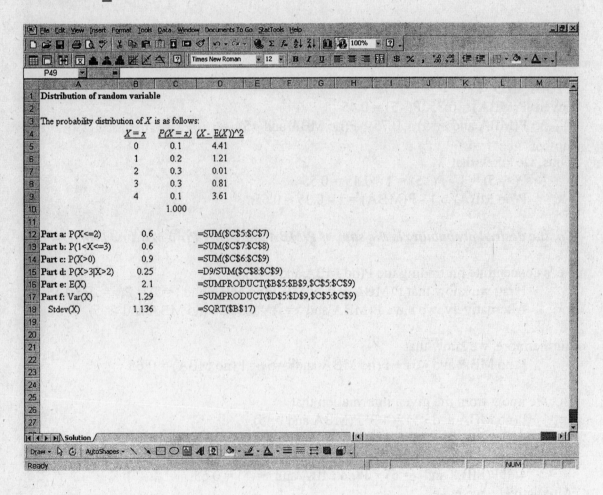

Problem 5_13

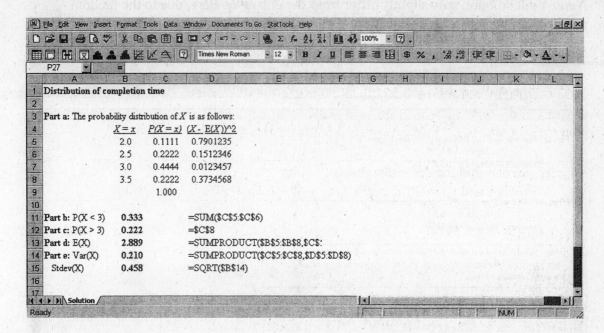

Problem 5_17

Note: Your solution may slightly differ from the one given here, due to the random numbers generated. Only results from part b will be shown.

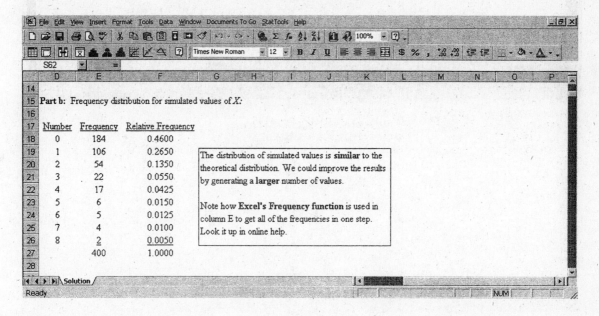

Problem 5_19

Note: Your solution may slightly differ from the one given here, due to the random numbers generated. Only results from part b and c will be shown.

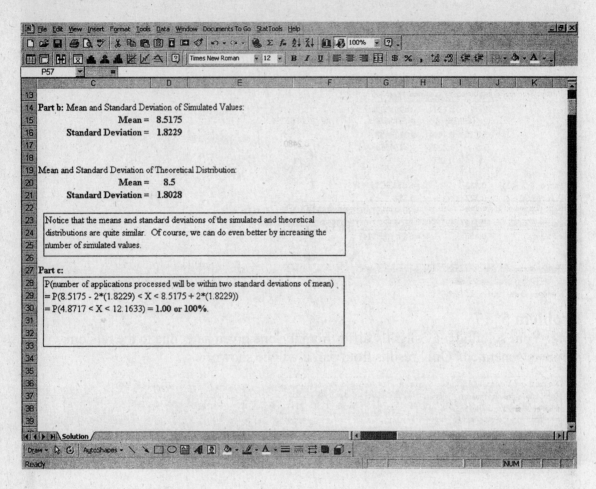

Part b: Mean and Standard Deviation of Simulated Values:

Mean = 8.5175

Standard Deviation = 1.8229

Mean and Standard Deviation of Theoretical Distribution:

Mean = 8.5

Standard Deviation = 1.8028

Notice that the means and standard deviations of the simulated and theoretical distributions are quite similar. Of course, we can do even better by increasing the number of simulated values.

Part c:

P(number of applications processed will be within two standard deviations of mean)
= P(8.5175 - 2*(1.8229) < X < 8.5175 + 2*(1.8229))
= P(4.8717 < X < 12.1633) = 1.00 or 100%.

Problem 5_21

Note: Your solution may slightly differ from the one given here, due to the random numbers generated. Only results from part b and c will be shown.

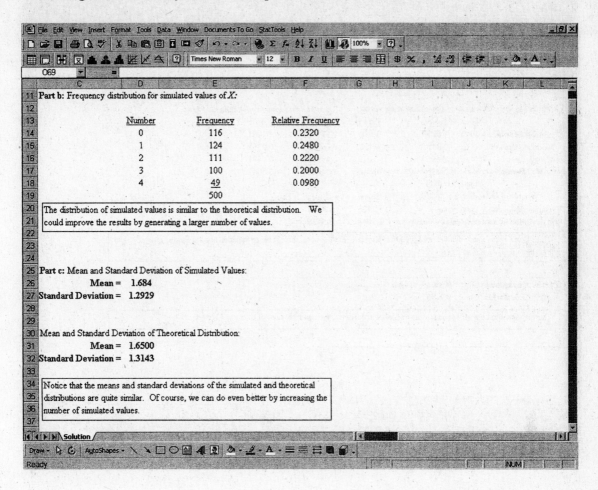

Part b: Frequency distribution for simulated values of *X*:

Number	Frequency	Relative Frequency
0	116	0.2320
1	124	0.2480
2	111	0.2220
3	100	0.2000
4	49	0.0980
	500	

The distribution of simulated values is similar to the theoretical distribution. We could improve the results by generating a larger number of values.

Part c: Mean and Standard Deviation of Simulated Values:

Mean = 1.684
Standard Deviation = 1.2929

Mean and Standard Deviation of Theoretical Distribution:

Mean = 1.6500
Standard Deviation = 1.3143

Notice that the means and standard deviations of the simulated and theoretical distributions are quite similar. Of course, we can do even better by increasing the number of simulated values.

Problem 5_23

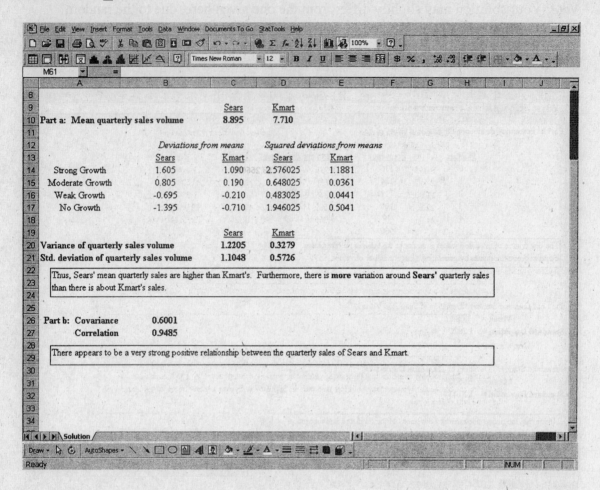

		Sears	Kmart
Part a: Mean quarterly sales volume		8.895	7.710

	Deviations from means		Squared deviations from means	
	Sears	Kmart	Sears	Kmart
Strong Growth	1.605	1.090	2.576025	1.1881
Moderate Growth	0.805	0.190	0.648025	0.0361
Weak Growth	-0.695	-0.210	0.483025	0.0441
No Growth	-1.395	-0.710	1.946025	0.5041

	Sears	Kmart
Variance of quarterly sales volume	1.2205	0.3279
Std. deviation of quarterly sales volume	1.1048	0.5726

Thus, Sears' mean quarterly sales are higher than Kmart's. Furthermore, there is **more** variation around **Sears'** quarterly sales than there is about Kmart's sales.

Part b: Covariance	0.6001
Correlation	0.9485

There appears to be a very strong positive relationship between the quarterly sales of Sears and Kmart.

Problem 5_25

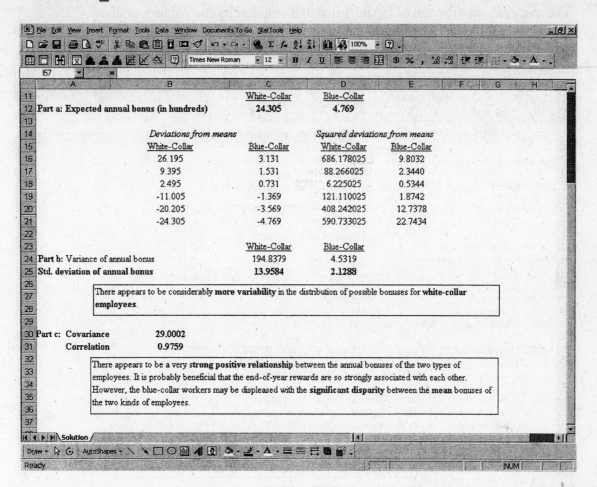

		White-Collar	Blue-Collar
Part a: Expected annual bonus (in hundreds)		24.305	4.769

	Deviations from means		*Squared deviations from means*	
	White-Collar	Blue-Collar	White-Collar	Blue-Collar
	26.195	3.131	686.178025	9.8032
	9.395	1.531	88.266025	2.3440
	2.495	0.731	6.225025	0.5344
	-11.005	-1.369	121.110025	1.8742
	-20.205	-3.569	408.242025	12.7378
	-24.305	-4.769	590.733025	22.7434

	White-Collar	Blue-Collar
Part b: Variance of annual bonus	194.8379	4.5319
Std. deviation of annual bonus	13.9584	2.1288

> There appears to be considerably **more variability** in the distribution of possible bonuses for **white-collar employees**.

Part c: Covariance   29.0002
Correlation   0.9759

> There appears to be a very **strong positive relationship** between the annual bonuses of the two types of employees. It is probably beneficial that the end-of-year rewards are so strongly associated with each other. However, the blue-collar workers may be displeased with the **significant disparity** between the **mean** bonuses of the two kinds of employees.

Problem 5_29

The marginal distribution of Brand 1 demand is given by the column total of probabilities. The marginal distribution of Brand 2 demand is given by the row total of probabilities.

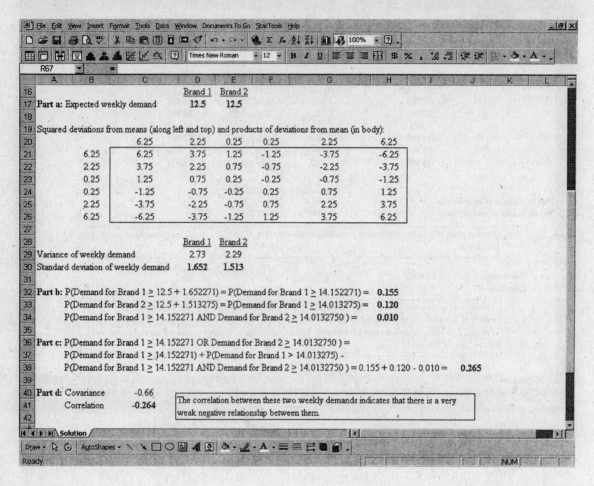

Problem 5_33

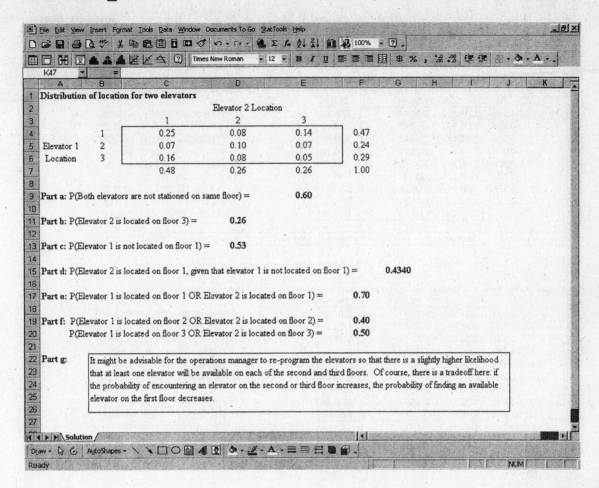

Distribution of location for two elevators

		Elevator 2 Location			
		1	2	3	
	1	0.25	0.08	0.14	0.47
Elevator 1	2	0.07	0.10	0.07	0.24
Location	3	0.16	0.08	0.05	0.29
		0.48	0.26	0.26	1.00

Part a: P(Both elevators are not stationed on same floor) = **0.60**

Part b: P(Elevator 2 is located on floor 3) = **0.26**

Part c: P(Elevator 1 is not located on floor 1) = **0.53**

Part d: P(Elevator 2 is located on floor 1, given that elevator 1 is not located on floor 1) = **0.4340**

Part e: P(Elevator 1 is located on floor 1 OR Elevator 2 is located on floor 1) = **0.70**

Part f: P(Elevator 1 is located on floor 2 OR Elevator 2 is located on floor 2) = **0.40**

P(Elevator 1 is located on floor 3 OR Elevator 2 is located on floor 3) = **0.50**

Part g: It might be advisable for the operations manager to re-program the elevators so that there is a slightly higher likelihood that at least one elevator will be available on each of the second and third floors. Of course, there is a tradeoff here: if the probability of encountering an elevator on the second or third floor increases, the probability of finding an available elevator on the first floor decreases.

Problem 5_39

	A	B	C	D	E	F	G	H	I
20	**Part a:**	Down payment		$0					
21									
22	Monthly payment for each combination of change in rate and increase in price						Squared deviations from mean		
23		$0	$5,000	$10,000					
24	-1.00%	$719.46	$749.44	$779.42			15216.14563	8719.12	4019.39
25	-0.75%	$738.86	$769.65	$800.43			10806.3783	5353.54	1796.23
26	-0.50%	$758.48	$790.09	$821.69			7112.011686	2780.38	446.305
27	-0.25%	$778.32	$810.75	$843.18			4159.818657	1028.28	0.13188
28	0.00%	$798.36	$831.63	$864.89			1975.924991	125.132	487.477
29	0.25%	$818.61	$852.72	$886.83			585.7772695	98.1284	1937.3
30	0.50%	$839.06	$874.02	$908.98			14.11476185	973.675	4377.74
31	0.75%	$859.69	$895.52	$931.34			284.9452919	2777.39	7836.06
32	1.00%	$880.52	$917.21	$953.89			1421.525002	5534.07	12338.7
33									
34	Expected payment	**$842.81**		Variance of payment	**1655.14**		Stdev of payment	**$40.68**	
35									
36	**Part b:**	Down payment		10% of price of house (which depends on the increase in price in one year)					
37									
38	Monthly payment for each combination of change in rate and increase in price						Squared deviations from mean		
39		$0	$5,000	$10,000					
40	-1.00%	$647.51	$674.49	$701.47			12325.07796	7062.49	3255.71
41	-0.75%	$664.97	$692.68	$720.39			8753.166423	4336.37	1454.95
42	-0.50%	$682.63	$711.08	$739.52			5760.729466	2252.11	361.507
43	-0.25%	$700.49	$729.67	$758.86			3369.453112	832.904	0.10682
44	0.00%	$718.53	$748.47	$778.40			1600.499243	101.357	394.856
45	0.25%	$736.75	$767.45	$798.15			474.4795883	79.484	1569.21
46	0.50%	$755.15	$786.62	$818.08			11.43295709	788.677	3545.97
47	0.75%	$773.73	$805.96	$838.20			230.8056864	2249.68	6347.21
48	1.00%	$792.47	$825.49	$858.50			1151.435252	4482.6	9994.32
49									
50	Expected payment	**$758.53**		Variance of payment	**1340.66**		Stdev of payment	**$36.62**	

Problem 5_41

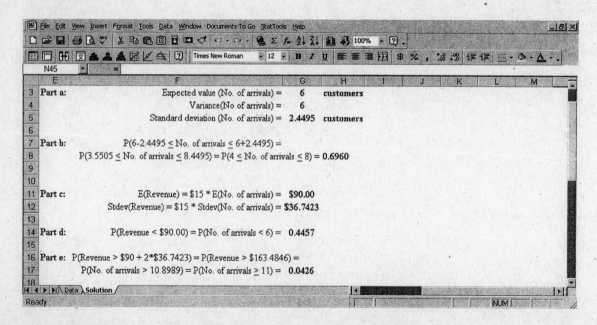

	E	F	G	H	I	J	K	L	M
3	**Part a:**	Expected value (No. of arrivals) =	6	customers					
4		Variance(No of arrivals) =	6						
5		Standard deviation (No. of arrivals) =	**2.4495**	customers					
6									
7	**Part b:**	P(6-2.4495 ≤ No. of arrivals ≤ 6+2.4495) =							
8		P(3.5505 ≤ No. of arrivals ≤ 8.4495) = P(4 ≤ No. of arrivals ≤ 8) = **0.6960**							
9									
10									
11	**Part c:**	E(Revenue) = $15 * E(No. of arrivals) = **$90.00**							
12		Stdev(Revenue) = $15 * Stdev(No. of arrivals) = **$36.7423**							
13									
14	**Part d:**	P(Revenue < $90.00) = P(No. of arrivals < 6) = **0.4457**							
15									
16	**Part e:**	P(Revenue > $90 + 2*$36.7423) = P(Revenue > $163.4846) =							
17		P(No. of arrivals > 10.8989) = P(No. of arrivals ≥ 11) = **0.0426**							

Problem 5_43

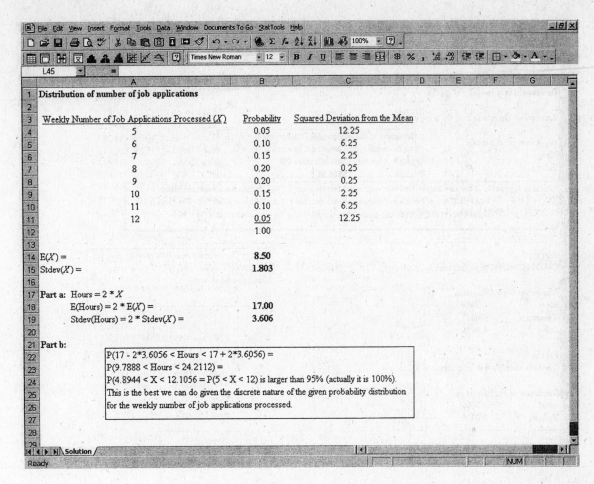

Spreadsheet contents:

Distribution of number of job applications

Weekly Number of Job Applications Processed (X)	Probability	Squared Deviation from the Mean
5	0.05	12.25
6	0.10	6.25
7	0.15	2.25
8	0.20	0.25
9	0.20	0.25
10	0.15	2.25
11	0.10	6.25
12	0.05	12.25
	1.00	

$E(X)$ = 8.50

Stdev(X) = 1.803

Part a: Hours = 2 * X

E(Hours) = 2 * E(X) = 17.00

Stdev(Hours) = 2 * Stdev(X) = 3.606

Part b:

P(17 - 2*3.6056 < Hours < 17 + 2*3.6056) =

P(9.7888 < Hours < 24.2112) =

P(4.8944 < X < 12.1056 = P(5 < X < 12) is larger than 95% (actually it is 100%).
This is the best we can do given the discrete nature of the given probability distribution
for the weekly number of job applications processed.

Problem 5_47

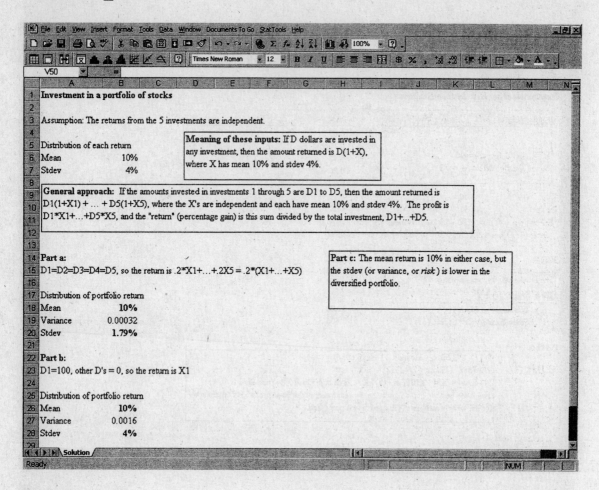

Problem 5_51

We assume the lengths of the four parts are *independent random variables*. In this case, if the standard deviation of each of the four parts is 0.01/sqrt(4), then the variance of each of the parts is .0001/4. The variance of the assembly is sum of the 4 variances (because of independence), or 4*(0.0001/4) = 0.0001, and the standard deviation is the square root of this, or 0.01, the desired value. *So Peter is correct, except that he's asking for much more precision on the individual parts than is actually required.*

Problem 5_53

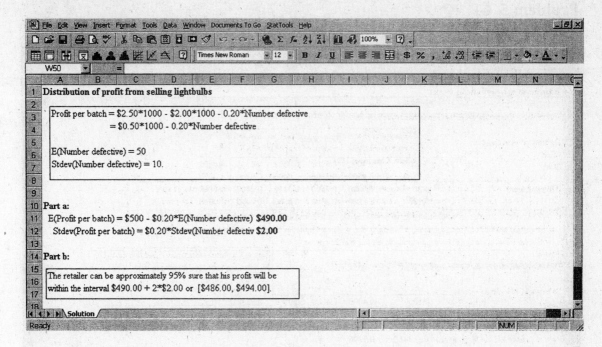

Problem 5_55

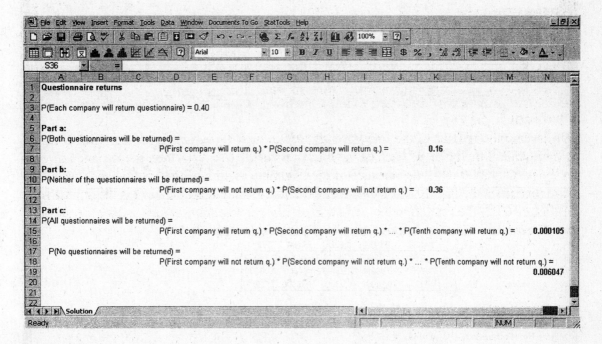

Problem 5_61

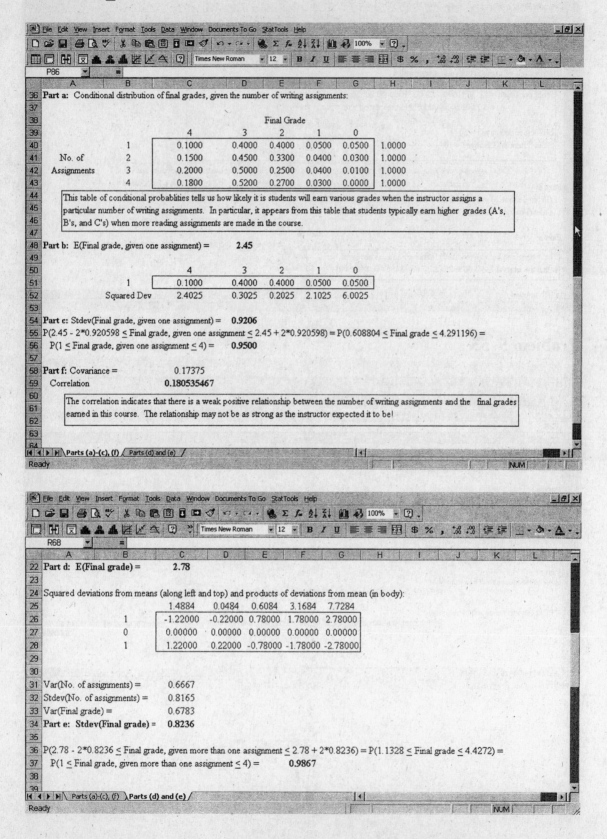

Part a: Conditional distribution of final grades, given the number of writing assignments:

		Final Grade					
		4	3	2	1	0	
No. of	1	0.1000	0.4000	0.4000	0.0500	0.0500	1.0000
Assignments	2	0.1500	0.4500	0.3300	0.0400	0.0300	1.0000
	3	0.2000	0.5000	0.2500	0.0400	0.0100	1.0000
	4	0.1800	0.5200	0.2700	0.0300	0.0000	1.0000

This table of conditional probablities tells us how likely it is students will earn various grades when the instructor assigns a particular number of writing assignments. In particular, it appears from this table that students typically earn higher grades (A's, B's, and C's) when more reading assignments are made in the course.

Part b: E(Final grade, given one assignment) = **2.45**

	4	3	2	1	0
1	0.1000	0.4000	0.4000	0.0500	0.0500
Squared Dev	2.4025	0.3025	0.2025	2.1025	6.0025

Part c: Stdev(Final grade, given one assignment) = **0.9206**

P(2.45 - 2*0.920598 ≤ Final grade, given one assignment ≤ 2.45 + 2*0.920598) = P(0.608804 ≤ Final grade ≤ 4.291196) =

P(1 ≤ Final grade, given one assignment ≤ 4) = **0.9500**

Part f: Covariance = 0.17375

Correlation **0.180535467**

The correlation indicates that there is a weak positive relationship between the number of writing assignments and the final grades earned in this course. The relationship may not be as strong as the instructor expected it to be!

Part d: E(Final grade) = **2.78**

Squared deviations from means (along left and top) and products of deviations from mean (in body):

	1.4884	0.0484	0.6084	3.1684	7.7284
1	-1.22000	-0.22000	0.78000	1.78000	2.78000
0	0.00000	0.00000	0.00000	0.00000	0.00000
1	1.22000	0.22000	-0.78000	-1.78000	-2.78000

Var(No. of assignments) = 0.6667

Stdev(No. of assignments) = 0.8165

Var(Final grade) = 0.6783

Part e: Stdev(Final grade) = **0.8236**

P(2.78 - 2*0.8236 ≤ Final grade, given more than one assignment ≤ 2.78 + 2*0.8236) = P(1.1328 ≤ Final grade ≤ 4.4272) =

P(1 ≤ Final grade, given more than one assignment ≤ 4) = **0.9867**

Problem 5_63

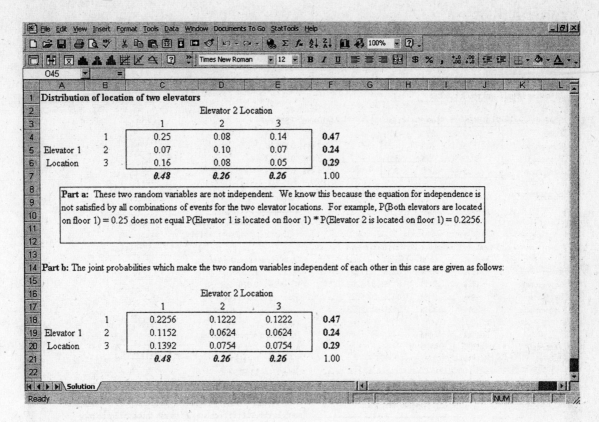

Problem 5_65

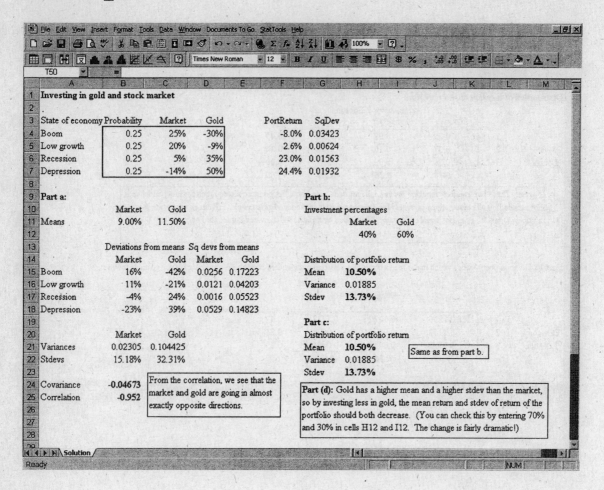

Problem 5_67

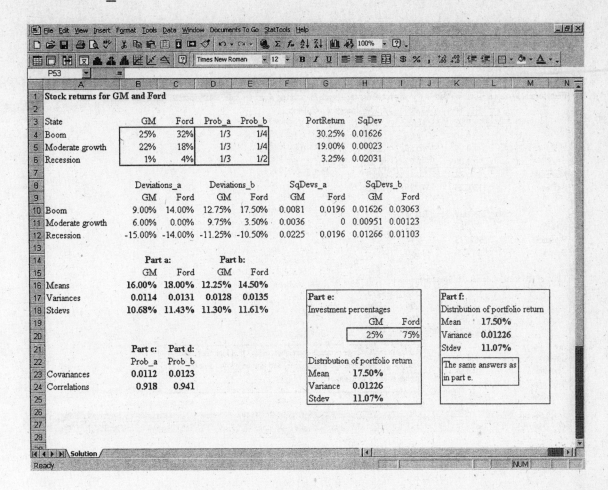

Stock returns for GM and Ford

State	GM	Ford	Prob_a	Prob_b		PortReturn	SqDev
Boom	25%	32%	1/3	1/4		30.25%	0.01626
Moderate growth	22%	18%	1/3	1/4		19.00%	0.00023
Recession	1%	4%	1/3	1/2		3.25%	0.02031

	Deviations_a		Deviations_b		SqDevs_a		SqDevs_b	
	GM	Ford	GM	Ford	GM	Ford	GM	Ford
Boom	9.00%	14.00%	12.75%	17.50%	0.0081	0.0196	0.01626	0.03063
Moderate growth	6.00%	0.00%	9.75%	3.50%	0.0036	0	0.00951	0.00123
Recession	-15.00%	-14.00%	-11.25%	-10.50%	0.0225	0.0196	0.01266	0.01103

	Part a:		Part b:	
	GM	Ford	GM	Ford
Means	16.00%	18.00%	12.25%	14.50%
Variances	0.0114	0.0131	0.0128	0.0135
Stdevs	10.68%	11.43%	11.30%	11.61%

	Part c:	Part d:
	Prob_a	Prob_b
Covariances	0.0112	0.0123
Correlations	0.918	0.941

Part e:

Investment percentages

	GM	Ford
	25%	75%

Distribution of portfolio return

Mean	17.50%
Variance	0.01226
Stdev	11.07%

Part f:

Distribution of portfolio return

Mean	17.50%
Variance	0.01226
Stdev	11.07%

The same answers as in part e.

Problem 5_71

Times New Roman   12   B I U

P63   =

17 First, for convenience, put these data in a joint probability table, with merit rating along the side, salary increase along the top

		$0	$2,000	$4,500	Marginal	SqDevs
18						
19	0	0.08	0.06	0.01	0.15	1.96
20	1	0.10	0.20	0.10	0.40	0.16
21	2	0.05	0.20	0.10	0.35	0.36
22	3	0.00	0.02	0.08	0.10	2.56
23	Marginal	0.23	0.48	0.29		
24	SqDevs	5130225	70225	4995225		

		Salary Increase	Merit Rating
26		Salary Increase	Merit Rating
27	Means	$2,265	1.4
28	Variances	2662275	0.74
29	Stdevs	$1,632	0.860

31 Table of products of deviations from means

32	3171	371	-3129
33	906	106	-894
34	-1359	-159	1341
35	-3624	-424	3576

37	Covariance	579
38	Correlation	0.413

This moderately large positive correlation means that high merit ratings tend to go with high salary increases, and low with low. But the relationship is far from perfect.

Solution

Ready

Problem 5_75

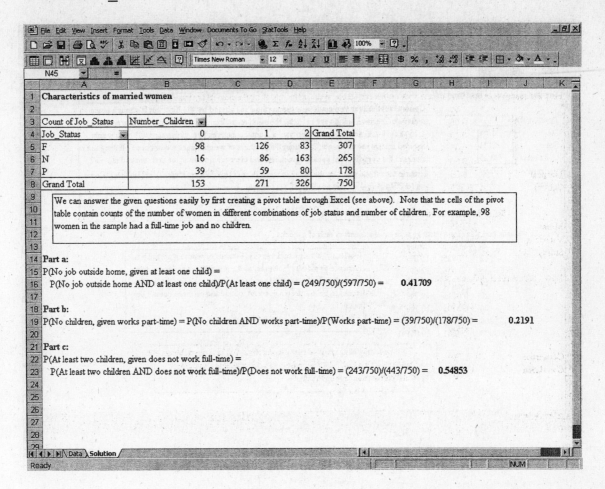

Characteristics of married women

Count of Job_Status	Number_Children			
Job_Status	0	1	2	Grand Total
F	98	126	83	307
N	16	86	163	265
P	39	59	80	178
Grand Total	153	271	326	750

We can answer the given questions easily by first creating a pivot table through Excel (see above). Note that the cells of the pivot table contain counts of the number of women in different combinations of job status and number of children. For example, 98 women in the sample had a full-time job and no children.

Part a:

P(No job outside home, given at least one child) =

  P(No job outside home AND at least one child)/P(At least one child) = (249/750)/(597/750) = **0.41709**

Part b:

P(No children, given works part-time) = P(No children AND works part-time)/P(Works part-time) = (39/750)/(178/750) = **0.2191**

Part c:

P(At least two children, given does not work full-time) =

  P(At least two children AND does not work full-time)/P(Does not work full-time) = (243/750)/(443/750) = **0.54853**

Problem 5_79

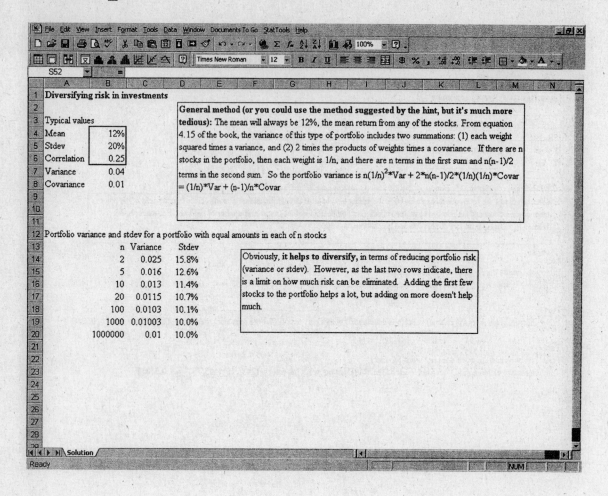

General method (or you could use the method suggested by the hint, but it's much more tedious): The mean will always be 12%, the mean return from any of the stocks. From equation 4.15 of the book, the variance of this type of portfolio includes two summations: (1) each weight squared times a variance, and (2) 2 times the products of weights times a covariance. If there are n stocks in the portfolio, then each weight is 1/n, and there are n terms in the first sum and n(n-1)/2 terms in the second sum. So the portfolio variance is $n(1/n)^2*Var + 2*n(n-1)/2*(1/n)(1/n)*Covar = (1/n)*Var + (n-1)/n*Covar$

Diversifying risk in investments

Typical values

Mean	12%
Stdev	20%
Correlation	0.25
Variance	0.04
Covariance	0.01

Portfolio variance and stdev for a portfolio with equal amounts in each of n stocks

n	Variance	Stdev
2	0.025	15.8%
5	0.016	12.6%
10	0.013	11.4%
20	0.0115	10.7%
100	0.0103	10.1%
1000	0.01003	10.0%
1000000	0.01	10.0%

Obviously, **it helps to diversify**, in terms of reducing portfolio risk (variance or stdev). However, as the last two rows indicate, there is a limit on how much risk can be eliminated. Adding the first few stocks to the portfolio helps a lot, but adding on more doesn't help much.

Problem 5_81

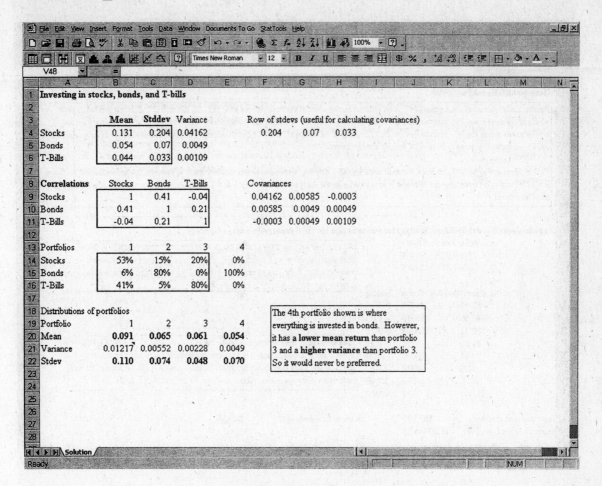

	Mean	Stddev	Variance		Row of stdevs (useful for calculating covariances)		
Stocks	0.131	0.204	0.04162		0.204	0.07	0.033
Bonds	0.054	0.07	0.0049				
T-Bills	0.044	0.033	0.00109				

Investing in stocks, bonds, and T-bills

Correlations	Stocks	Bonds	T-Bills		Covariances		
Stocks	1	0.41	-0.04		0.04162	0.00585	-0.0003
Bonds	0.41	1	0.21		0.00585	0.0049	0.00049
T-Bills	-0.04	0.21	1		-0.0003	0.00049	0.00109

Portfolios	1	2	3	4
Stocks	53%	15%	20%	0%
Bonds	6%	80%	0%	100%
T-Bills	41%	5%	80%	0%

Distributions of portfolios

Portfolio	1	2	3	4
Mean	0.091	0.065	0.061	0.054
Variance	0.01217	0.00552	0.00228	0.0049
Stdev	0.110	0.074	0.048	0.070

The 4th portfolio shown is where everything is invested in bonds. However, it has a **lower mean return** than portfolio 3 and a **higher variance** than portfolio 3. So it would never be preferred.

Problem 5_83

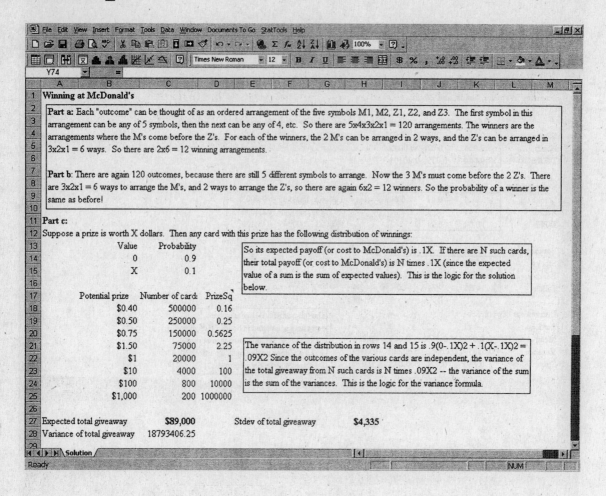

File Edit View Insert Format Tools Data Window Documents To Go StatTools Help

Times New Roman ▾ 12 ▾ B I U

Y74 =

	A	B	C	D	E	F	G	H	I	J	K	L	M

1 Winning at McDonald's

2-6 Part a: Each "outcome" can be thought of as an ordered arrangement of the five symbols M1, M2, Z1, Z2, and Z3. The first symbol in this arrangement can be any of 5 symbols, then the next can be any of 4, etc. So there are 5x4x3x2x1 = 120 arrangements. The winners are the arrangements where the M's come before the Z's. For each of the winners, the 2 M's can be arranged in 2 ways, and the Z's can be arranged in 3x2x1 = 6 ways. So there are 2x6 = 12 winning arrangements.

7-9 Part b: There are again 120 outcomes, because there are still 5 different symbols to arrange. Now the 3 M's must come before the 2 Z's. There are 3x2x1 = 6 ways to arrange the M's, and 2 ways to arrange the Z's, so there are again 6x2 = 12 winners. So the probability of a winner is the same as before!

11 Part c:

12 Suppose a prize is worth X dollars. Then any card with this prize has the following distribution of winnings:

	Value	Probability
13		
14	0	0.9
15	X	0.1

So its expected payoff (or cost to McDonald's) is .1X. If there are N such cards, their total payoff (or cost to McDonald's) is N times .1X (since the expected value of a sum is the sum of expected values). This is the logic for the solution below.

	Potential prize	Number of cards	PrizeSq
17			
18	$0.40	500000	0.16
19	$0.50	250000	0.25
20	$0.75	150000	0.5625
21	$1.50	75000	2.25
22	$1	20000	1
23	$10	4000	100
24	$100	800	10000
25	$1,000	200	1000000

The variance of the distribution in rows 14 and 15 is $.9(0-.1X)2 + .1(X-.1X)2 = .09X2$ Since the outcomes of the various cards are independent, the variance of the total giveaway from N such cards is N times .09X2 -- the variance of the sum is the sum of the variances. This is the logic for the variance formula.

27	Expected total giveaway	$89,000	Stdev of total giveaway $4,335
28	Variance of total giveaway	18793406.25	

Solution

Ready   NUM

CHAPTER 6

Problem 6_1

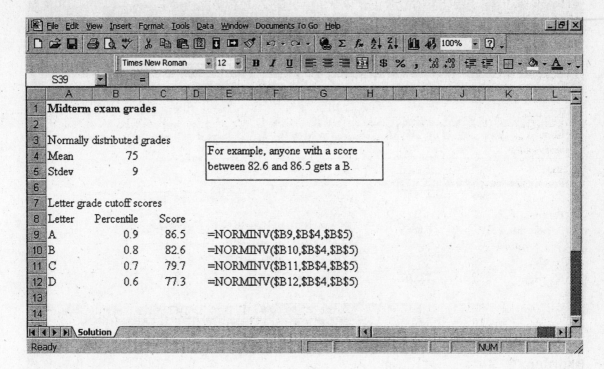

Problem 6_3

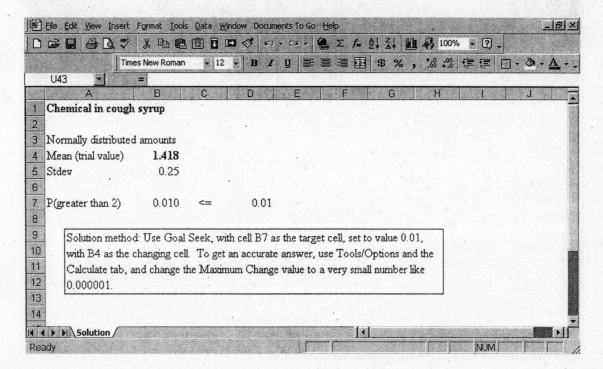

Problem 6_7

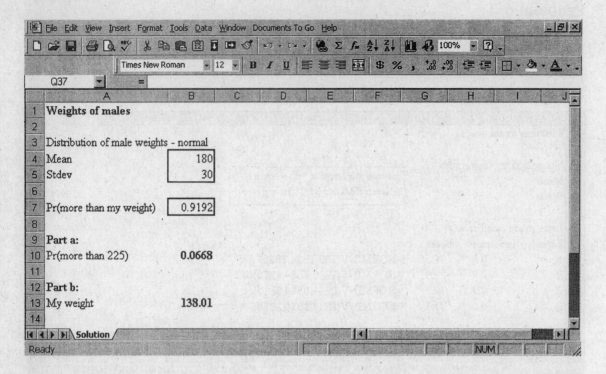

Problem 6_9

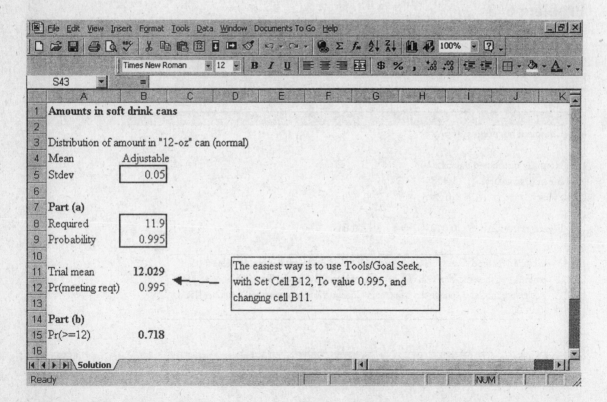

Problem 6_11

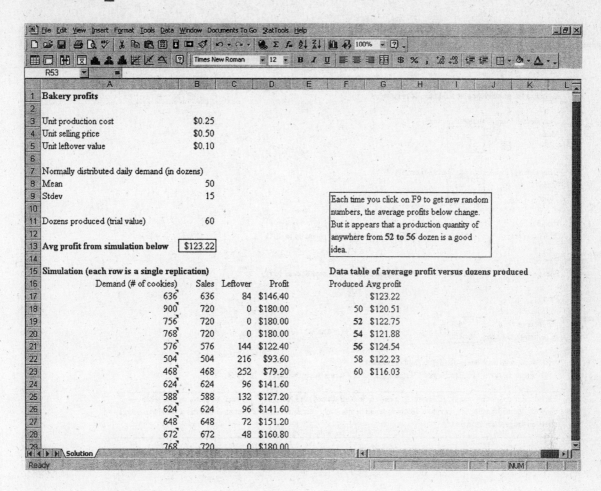

Problem 6_17

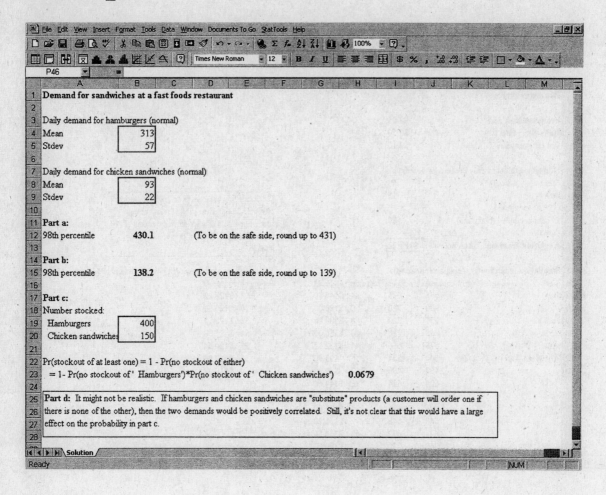

File Edit View Insert Format Tools Data Window Documents To Go StatTools Help

P46

	A	B	C	D	E	F	G	H	I	J	K	L	M
1	**Demand for sandwiches at a fast foods restaurant**												
2													
3	Daily demand for hamburgers (normal)												
4	Mean	313											
5	Stdev	57											
6													
7	Daily demand for chicken sandwiches (normal)												
8	Mean	93											
9	Stdev	22											
10													
11	**Part a:**												
12	98th percentile	**430.1**			(To be on the safe side, round up to 431)								
13													
14	**Part b:**												
15	98th percentile	**138.2**			(To be on the safe side, round up to 139)								
16													
17	**Part c:**												
18	Number stocked:												
19	Hamburgers	400											
20	Chicken sandwiches	150											
21													
22	Pr(stockout of at least one) = 1 - Pr(no stockout of either)												
23	= 1- Pr(no stockout of ' Hamburgers')*Pr(no stockout of ' Chicken sandwiches')						**0.0679**						
24													
25	**Part d:** It might not be realistic. If hamburgers and chicken sandwiches are "substitute" products (a customer will order one if												
26	there is none of the other), then the two demands would be positively correlated. Still, it's not clear that this would have a large												
27	effect on the probability in part c.												
28													

Solution

Ready   NUM

Problem 6_19

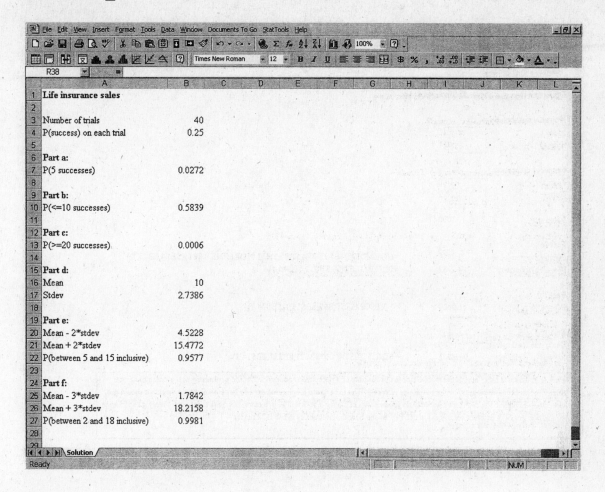

	A	B
1	**Life insurance sales**	
2		
3	Number of trials	40
4	P(success) on each trial	0.25
5		
6	**Part a:**	
7	P(5 successes)	0.0272
8		
9	**Part b:**	
10	P(<=10 successes)	0.5839
11		
12	**Part c:**	
13	P(>=20 successes)	0.0006
14		
15	**Part d:**	
16	Mean	10
17	Stdev	2.7386
18		
19	**Part e:**	
20	Mean - 2*stdev	4.5228
21	Mean + 2*stdev	15.4772
22	P(between 5 and 15 inclusive)	0.9577
23		
24	**Part f:**	
25	Mean - 3*stdev	1.7842
26	Mean + 3*stdev	18.2158
27	P(between 2 and 18 inclusive)	0.9981

Problem 6_23

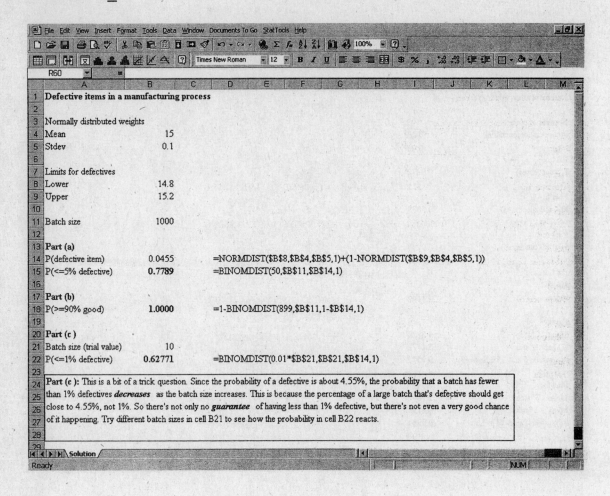

Problem 6_25

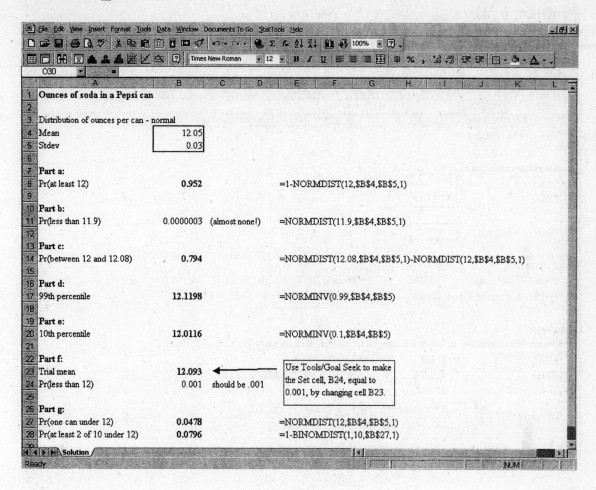

File Edit View Insert Format Tools Data Window Documents To Go StatTools Help

Times New Roman | 12 |

O30

	A	B	C	D	E	F	G	H	I	J	K	L
1	**Ounces of soda in a Pepsi can**											
2												
3	Distribution of ounces per can - normal											
4	Mean	12.05										
5	Stdev	0.03										
6												
7	**Part a:**											
8	Pr(at least 12)	**0.952**			=1-NORMDIST(12,$B$4,$B$5,1)							
9												
10	**Part b:**											
11	Pr(less than 11.9)	0.0000003	(almost none!)		=NORMDIST(11.9,$B$4,$B$5,1)							
12												
13	**Part c:**											
14	Pr(between 12 and 12.08)	**0.794**			=NORMDIST(12.08,$B$4,$B$5,1)-NORMDIST(12,$B$4,$B$5,1)							
15												
16	**Part d:**											
17	99th percentile	**12.1198**			=NORMINV(0.99,$B$4,$B$5)							
18												
19	**Part e:**											
20	10th percentile	**12.0116**			=NORMINV(0.1,$B$4,$B$5)							
21												
22	**Part f:**											
23	Trial mean	**12.093**	←		Use Tools/Goal Seek to make							
24	Pr(less than 12)	0.001	should be .001		the Set cell, B24, equal to							
25					0.001, by changing cell B23.							
26	**Part g:**											
27	Pr(one can under 12)	**0.0478**			=NORMDIST(12,$B$4,$B$5,1)							
28	Pr(at least 2 of 10 under 12)	**0.0796**			=1-BINOMDIST(1,10,$B$27,1)							

Solution

Ready

NUM

Problem 6_31

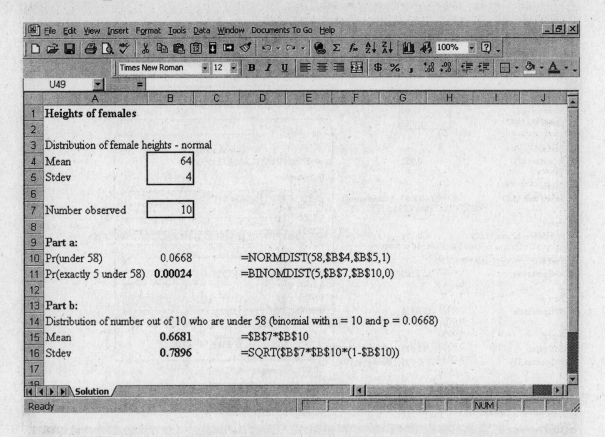

Problem 6_33

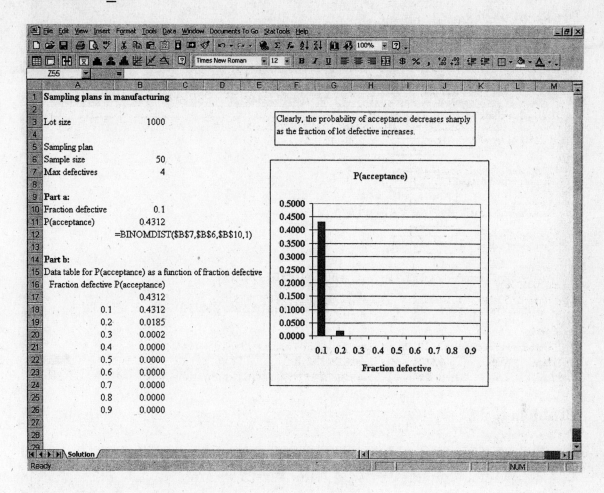

Problem 6_35

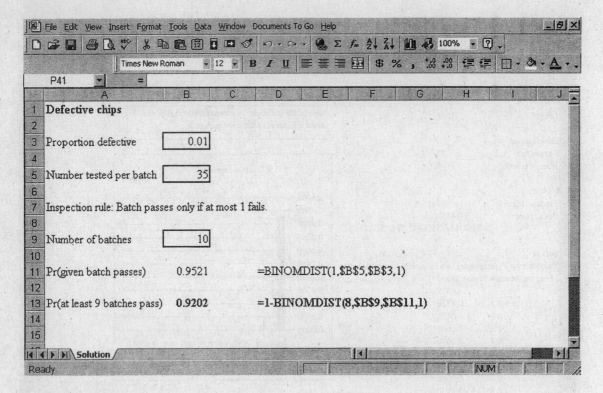

Problem 6_37

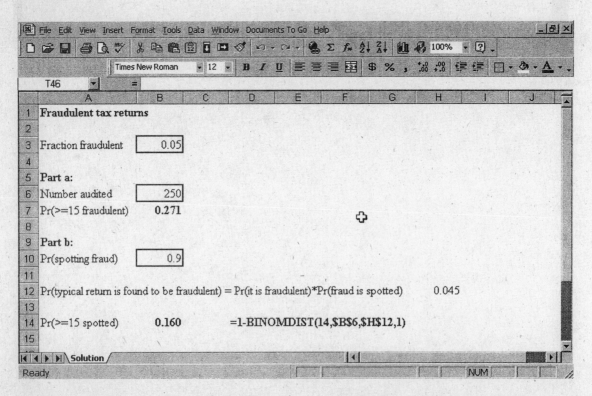

Problem 6_43

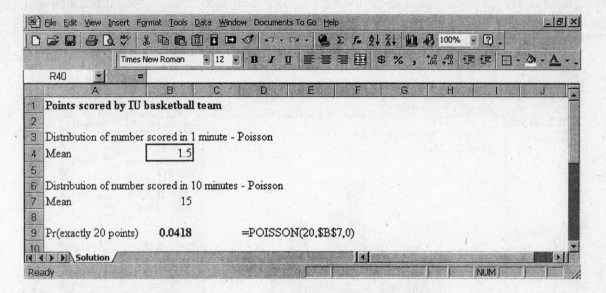

Problem 6_45

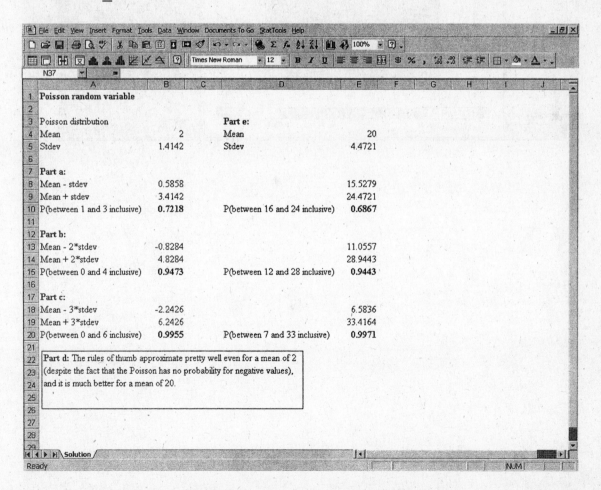

Problem 6_47

First specify bounded, but unknown, limits. I could have also chosen fixed limits of 0 and 1 (because these are proportions), but then BestFit has problems with BetaGeneral if any data values are exactly equal to 0 or 1. BestFit picks a "Beta" distribution as the best fitting of the three families of distributions listed.

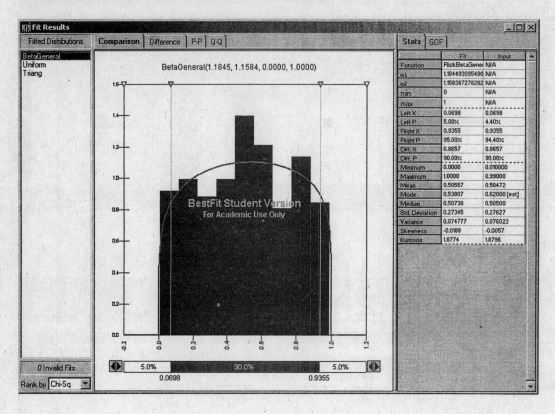

Problem 6_49

First specify a discrete distribution (from the Fitting/Input Data Options menu). Best Fit picks a Binomial distribution as the best fitting of the families of distributions listed. *Note*: A binomial distribution can provide a good fit, even though the data do not come from a "binomial model" of successes and failures.

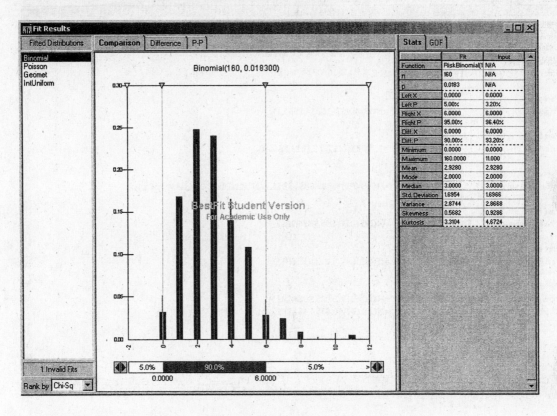

Problem 6_51

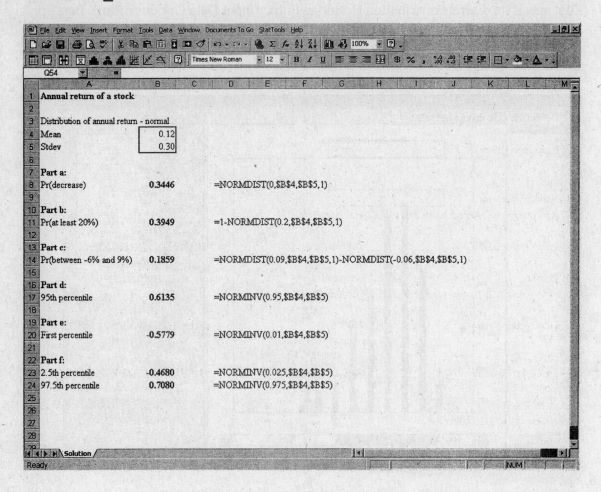

Problem 6_53

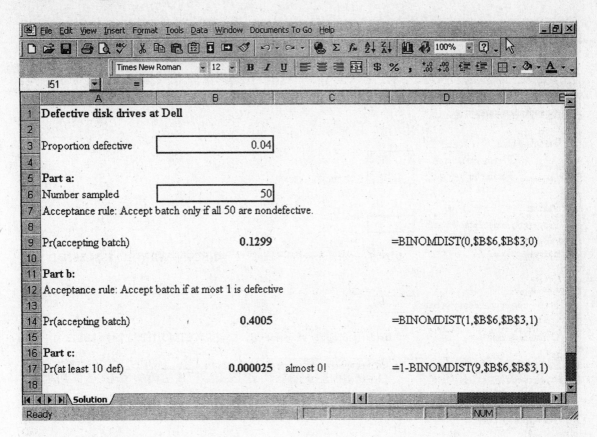

Problem 6_55

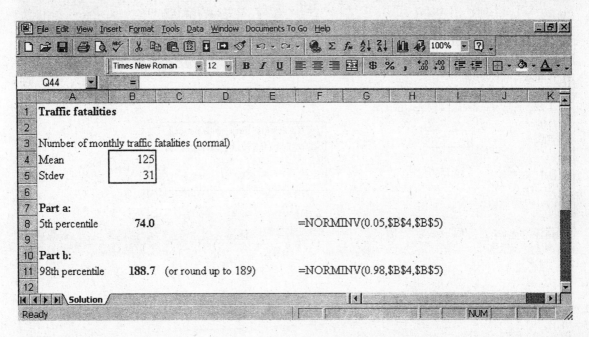

Problem 6_59

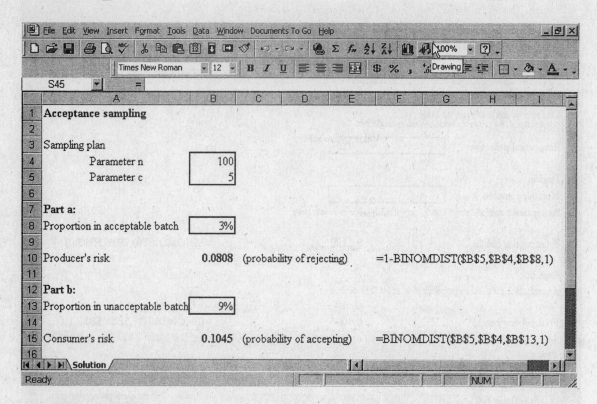

Problem 6_61

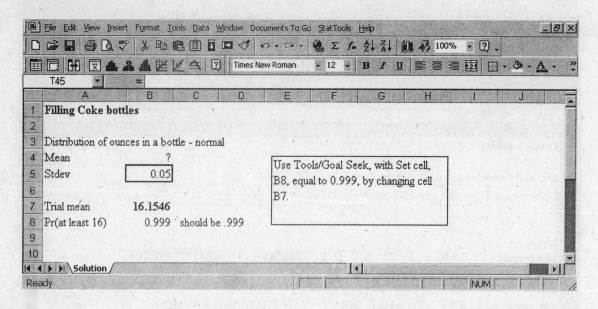

Problem 6_65

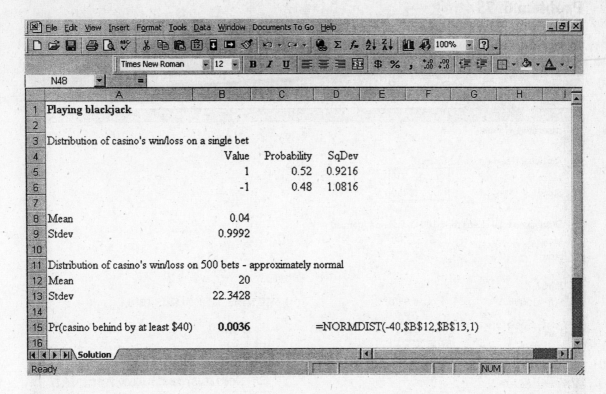

	A	B	C	D	E	F	G	H	I
1	Playing blackjack								
2									
3	Distribution of casino's win/loss on a single bet								
4		Value	Probability	SqDev					
5		1	0.52	0.9216					
6		-1	0.48	1.0816					
7									
8	Mean	0.04							
9	Stdev	0.9992							
10									
11	Distribution of casino's win/loss on 500 bets - approximately normal								
12	Mean	20							
13	Stdev	22.3428							
14									
15	Pr(casino behind by at least $40)	**0.0036**		=NORMDIST(-40,$B$12,$B$13,1)					
16									

Problem 6_71

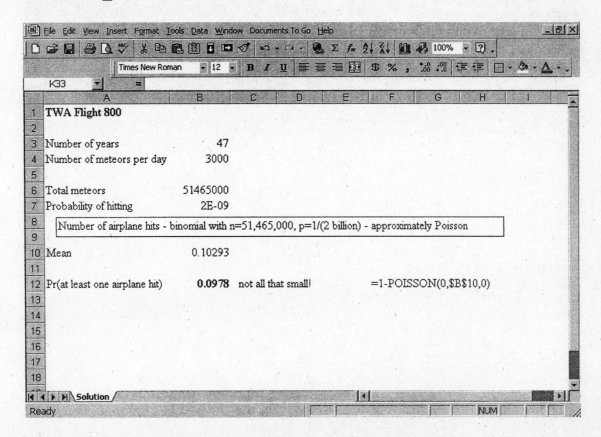

	A	B	C	D	E	F	G	H	I
1	TWA Flight 800								
2									
3	Number of years	47							
4	Number of meteors per day	3000							
5									
6	Total meteors	51465000							
7	Probability of hitting	2E-09							
8	Number of airplane hits - binomial with n=51,465,000, p=1/(2 billion) - approximately Poisson								
9									
10	Mean	0.10293							
11									
12	Pr(at least one airplane hit)	**0.0978**	not all that small!			=1-POISSON(0,$B$10,0)			
13									

Problem 6_73

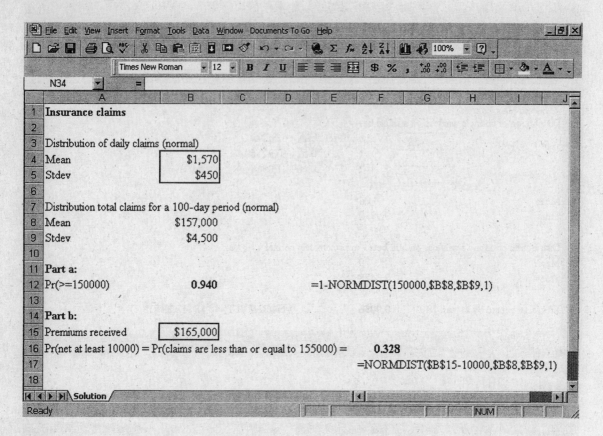

Problem 6_79

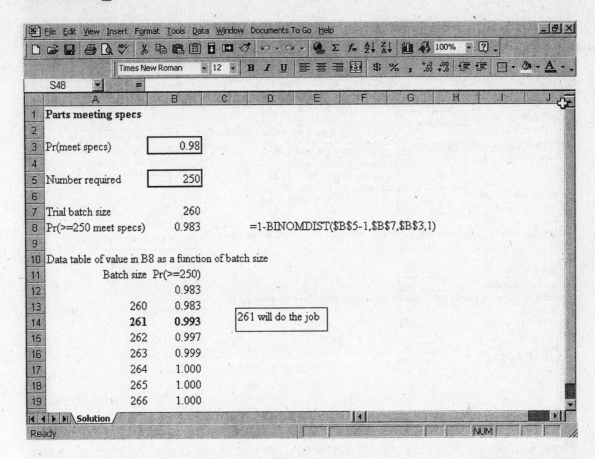

Problem 6_81

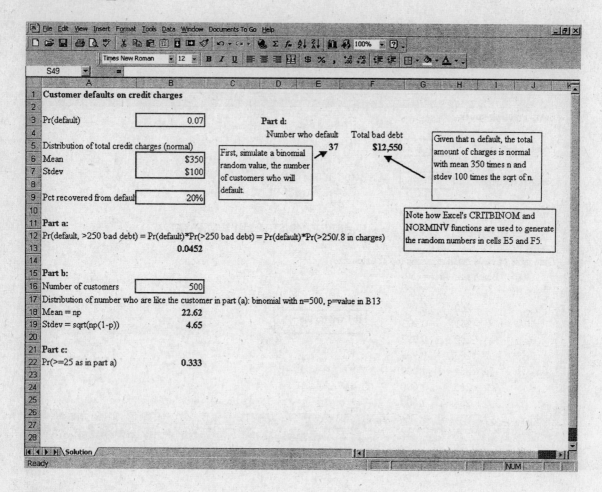

Problem 6_83

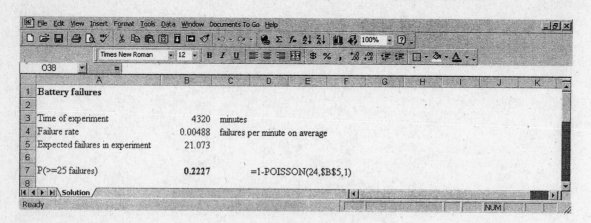

CHAPTER 7

Problem 7_1

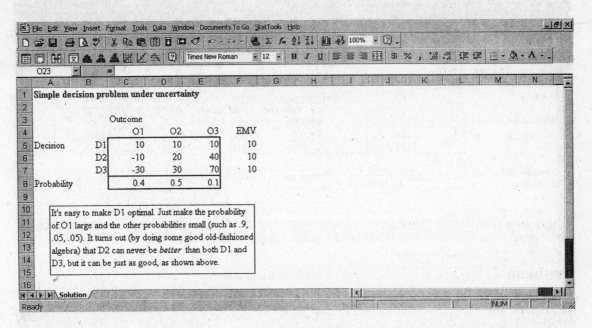

Simple decision problem under uncertainty

		Outcome			EMV
		O1	O2	O3	
Decision	D1	10	10	10	10
	D2	-10	20	40	10
	D3	-30	30	70	10
Probability		0.4	0.5	0.1	

It's easy to make D1 optimal. Just make the probability of O1 large and the other probabilities small (such as .9, .05, .05). It turns out (by doing some good old-fashioned algebra) that D2 can never be *better* than both D1 and D3, but it can be just as good, as shown above.

Problem 7_3

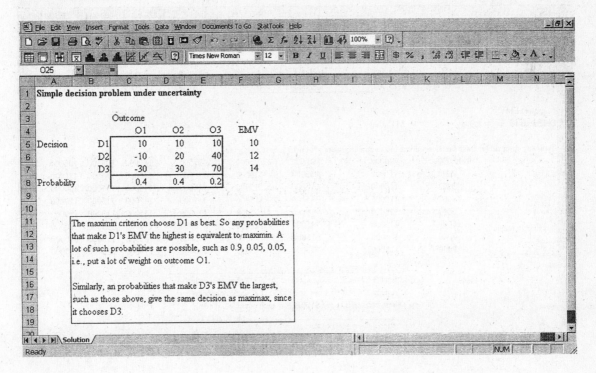

Simple decision problem under uncertainty

		Outcome			EMV
		O1	O2	O3	
Decision	D1	10	10	10	10
	D2	-10	20	40	12
	D3	-30	30	70	14
Probability		0.4	0.4	0.2	

The maximin criterion choose D1 as best. So any probabilities that make D1's EMV the highest is equivalent to maximin. A lot of such probabilities are possible, such as 0.9, 0.05, 0.05, i.e., put a lot of weight on outcome O1.

Similarly, an probabilities that make D3's EMV the largest, such as those above, give the same decision as maximax, since it chooses D3.

Problem 7_5

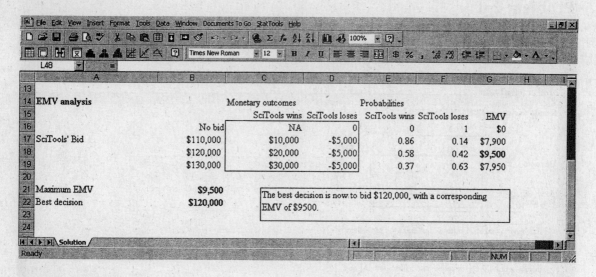

		Monetary outcomes		Probabilities		
EMV analysis		SciTools wins	SciTools loses	SciTools wins	SciTools loses	EMV
	No bid	NA	0	0	1	$0
SciTools' Bid	$110,000	$10,000	-$5,000	0.86	0.14	$7,900
	$120,000	$20,000	-$5,000	0.58	0.42	$9,500
	$130,000	$30,000	-$5,000	0.37	0.63	$7,950
Maximum EMV	$9,500					
Best decision	$120,000					

The best decision is now to bid $120,000, with a corresponding EMV of $9500.

Problem 7_7

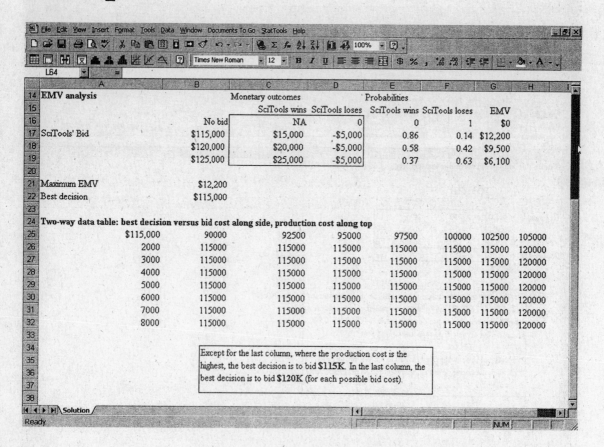

		Monetary outcomes		Probabilities		
EMV analysis		SciTools wins	SciTools loses	SciTools wins	SciTools loses	EMV
	No bid	NA	0	0	1	$0
SciTools' Bid	$115,000	$15,000	-$5,000	0.86	0.14	$12,200
	$120,000	$20,000	-$5,000	0.58	0.42	$9,500
	$125,000	$25,000	-$5,000	0.37	0.63	$6,100
Maximum EMV	$12,200					
Best decision	$115,000					

Two-way data table: best decision versus bid cost along side, production cost along top

$115,000	90000	92500	95000	97500	100000	102500	105000
2000	115000	115000	115000	115000	115000	115000	120000
3000	115000	115000	115000	115000	115000	115000	120000
4000	115000	115000	115000	115000	115000	115000	120000
5000	115000	115000	115000	115000	115000	115000	120000
6000	115000	115000	115000	115000	115000	115000	120000
7000	115000	115000	115000	115000	115000	115000	120000
8000	115000	115000	115000	115000	115000	115000	120000

Except for the last column, where the production cost is the highest, the best decision is to bid $115K. In the last column, the best decision is to bid $120K (for each possible bid cost).

Problem 7_9

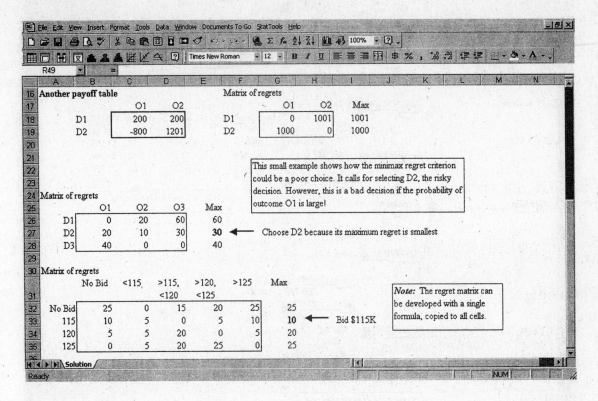

Problem 7_11

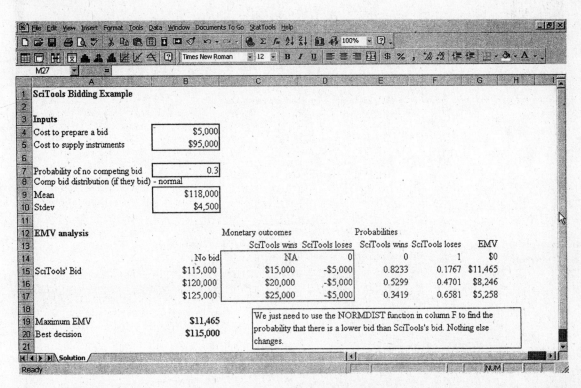

Problem 7_13

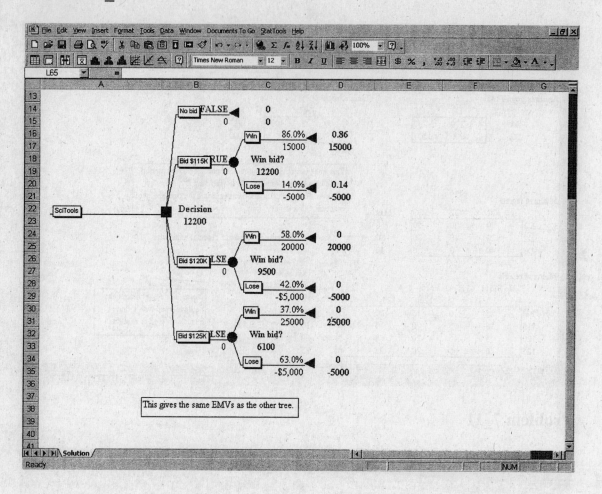

Problem 7_15

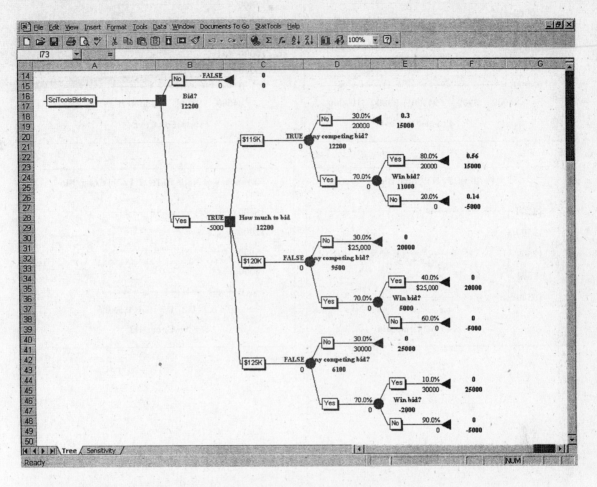

Compare the two graphs below. The line in the left chart is really the same as the top line on the right (with a different scale). It shows how the EMV for the optimal decision from the tree varies with the input. The chart on the right shows such a line for every decision. Therefore, if the lines cross, we know that another decision becomes optimal.

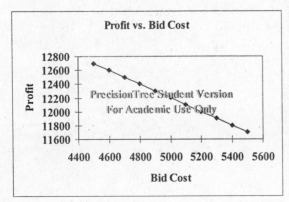

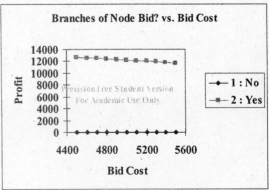

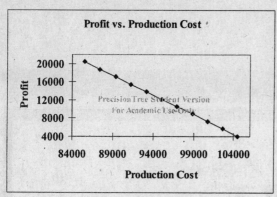

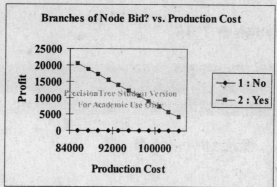

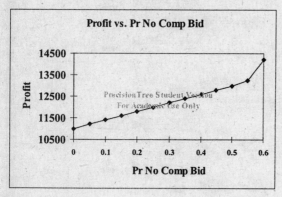

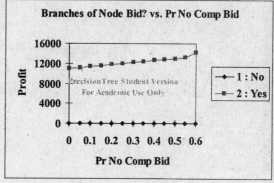

Problem 7_17

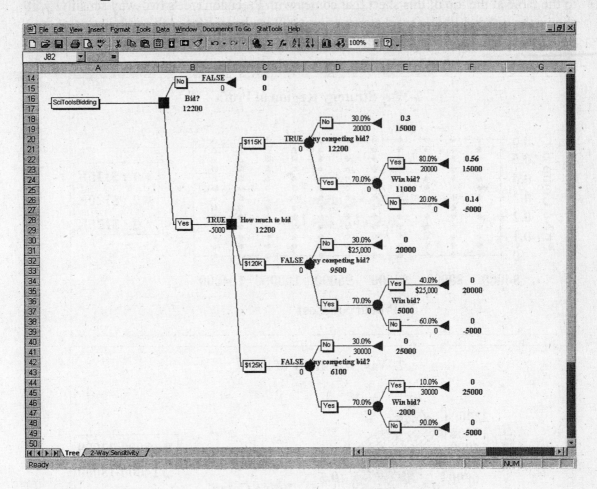

The chart on the top is probably easier to understand. It shows which decision is optimal for each point in the grid. The two-way data table, created on the first sheet, is equivalent to the table at the top of this sheet that comes with PrecisionTree's two-way sensitivity. It shows the optimal EMV (or whatever output cell is chosen) for each combination of the two inputs. The chart on the bottom attempts to graph this in three dimensions.

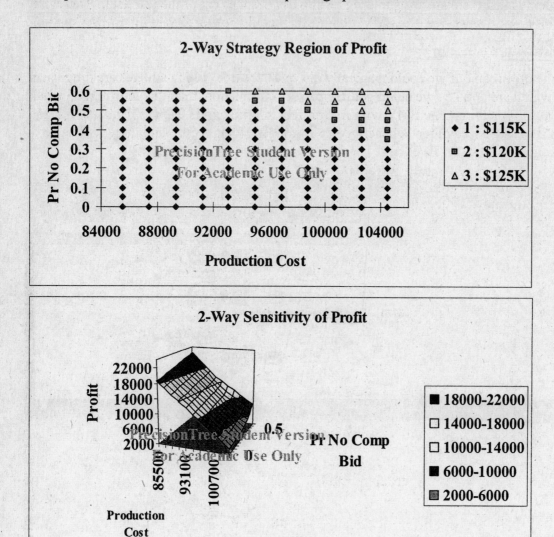

Problem 7_23

The way we would normally calculate EVSI doesn't make sense in this example. The problem is that there are costs to drug testing besides the cost of the test itself. Therefore, even if the test were free, the EMV from testing would be worse than the EMV from not testing.

On the other hand, if we could magically discover, for free, which athletes are drug users and which are not, i.e., we could get free perfect information, then this information would be worth something. The EMV with free perfect information is 0.05(25)+0.95(0) = 1.25. This is because we will get a benefit of 25 from identifying a user, and there will be no costs for nonusers. So EVPI = 1.

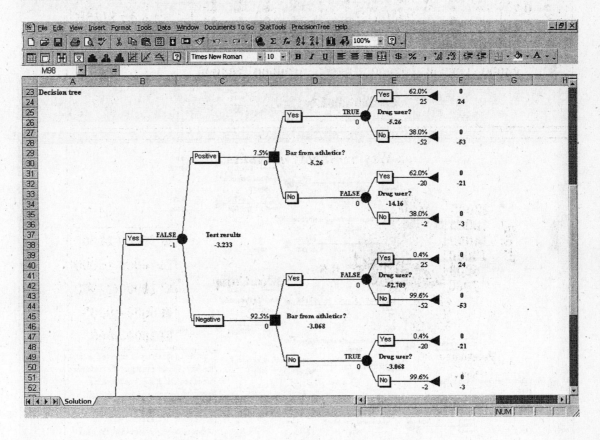

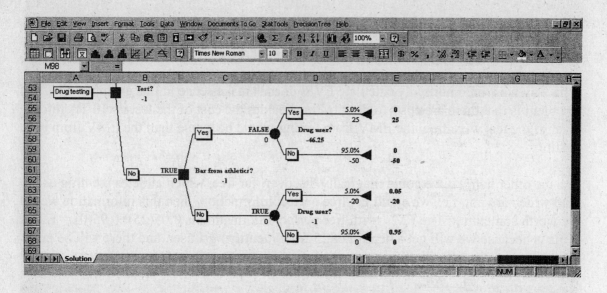

Problem 7_29

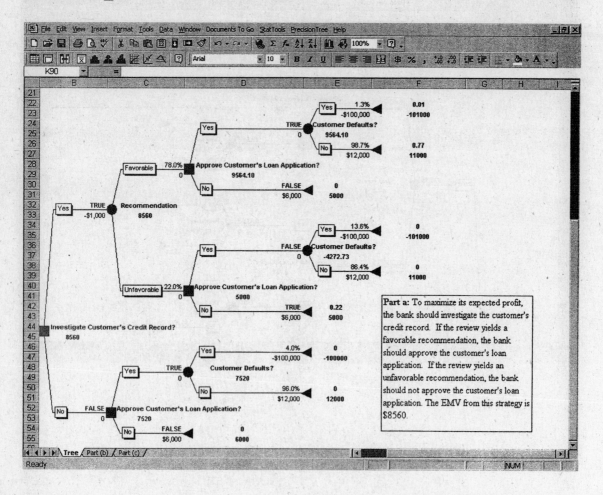

Part a: To maximize its expected profit, the bank should investigate the customer's credit record. If the review yields a favorable recommendation, the bank should approve the customer's loan application. If the review yields an unfavorable recommendation, the bank should not approve the customer's loan application. The EMV from this strategy is $8560.

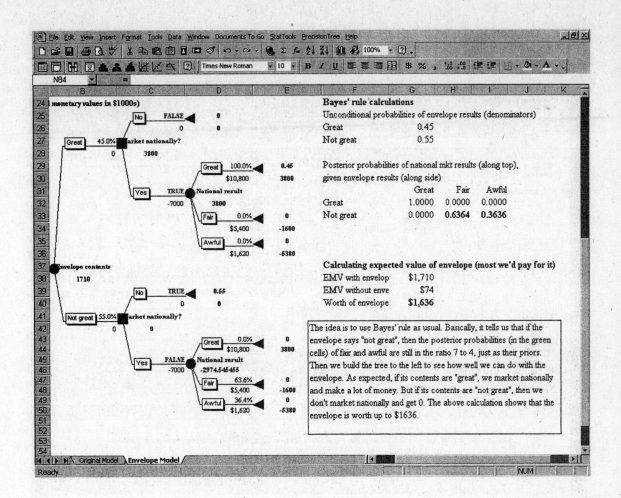

The idea is to use Bayes' rule as usual. Basically, it tells us that if the envelope says "not great", then the posterior probabilities (in the green cells) of fair and awful are still in the ratio 7 to 4, just as their priors. Then we build the tree to the left to see how well we can do with the envelope. As expected, if its contents are "great", we market nationally and make a lot of money. But if its contents are "not great", then we don't market nationally and get 0. The above calculation shows that the envelope is worth up to $1636.

Problem 7_31

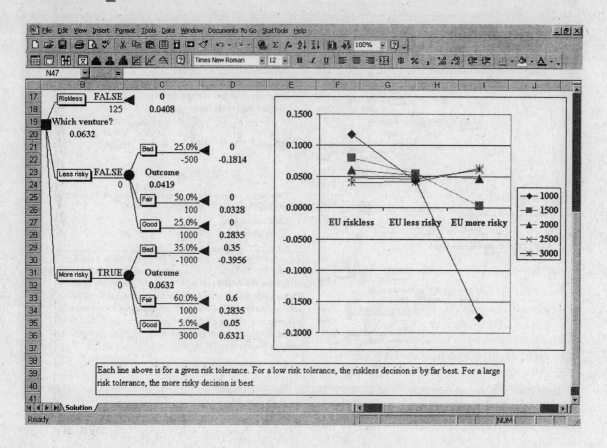

Problem 7_37

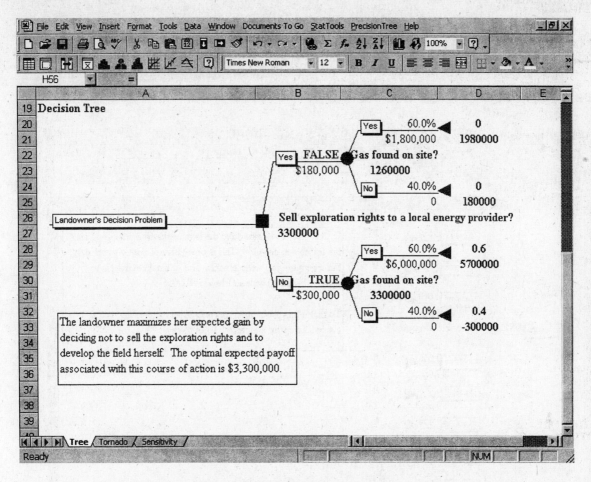

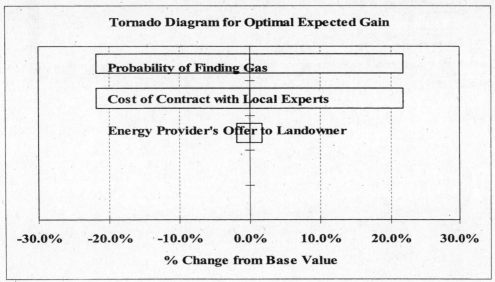

The tornado diagram indicates that the probability of finding gas on the site and the landowner's net profit (if she develops the field herself and gas is found) are the most influential model inputs. To a lesser extent, the cost of contracting with local experts (if she decides to develop the field herself) also has a nontrivial impact on the optimal expected gain.

The sensitivity graphs reveal, + 20% changes in the values of each of the model inputs lead to no changes in the landowner's optimal decision to develop the field herself.

Problem 7_41

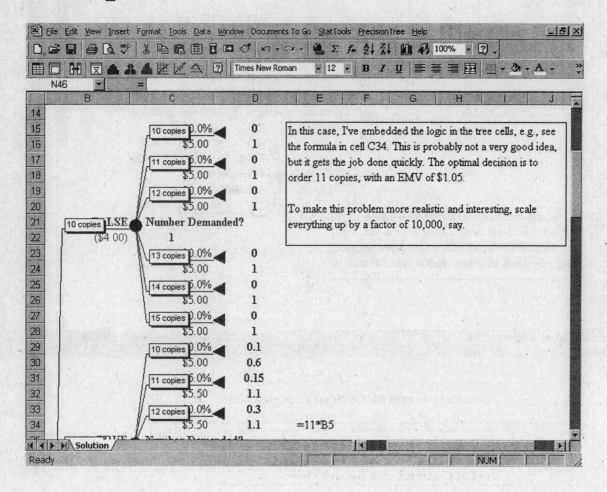

Problem 7_43

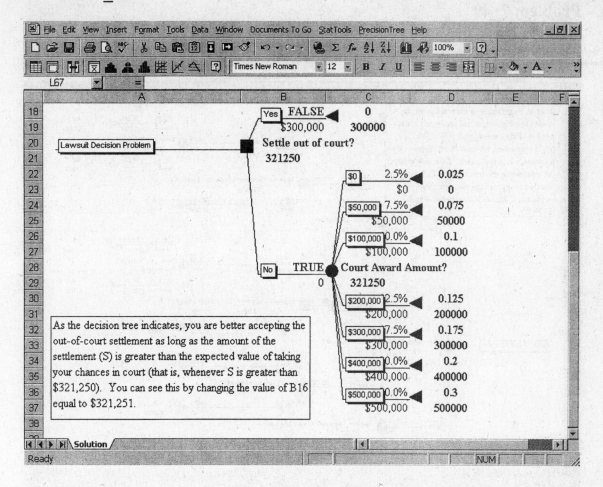

Problem 7_49

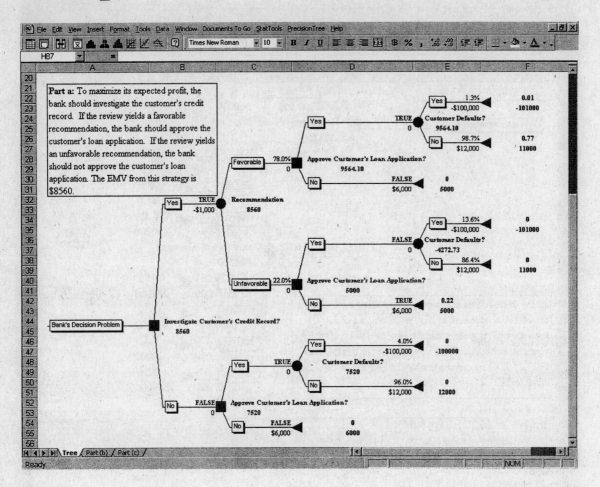

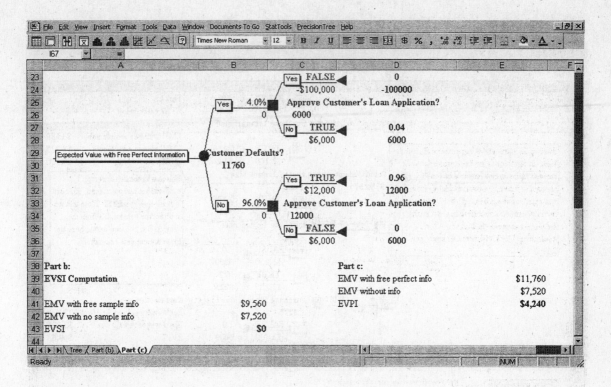

Problem 7_53

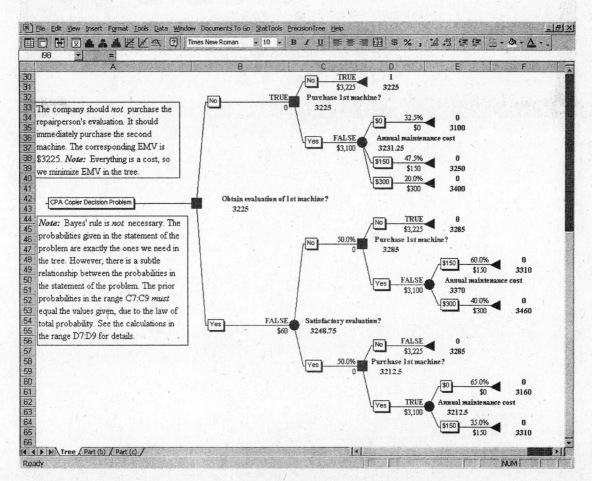

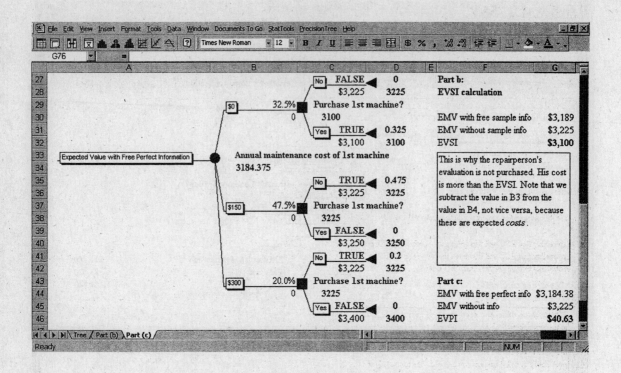

Problem 7_55

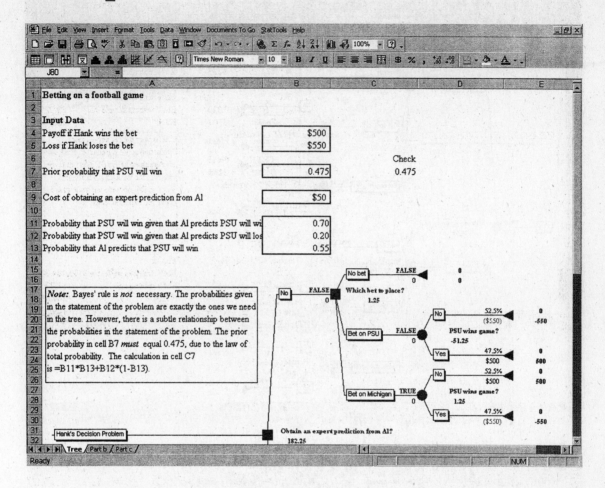

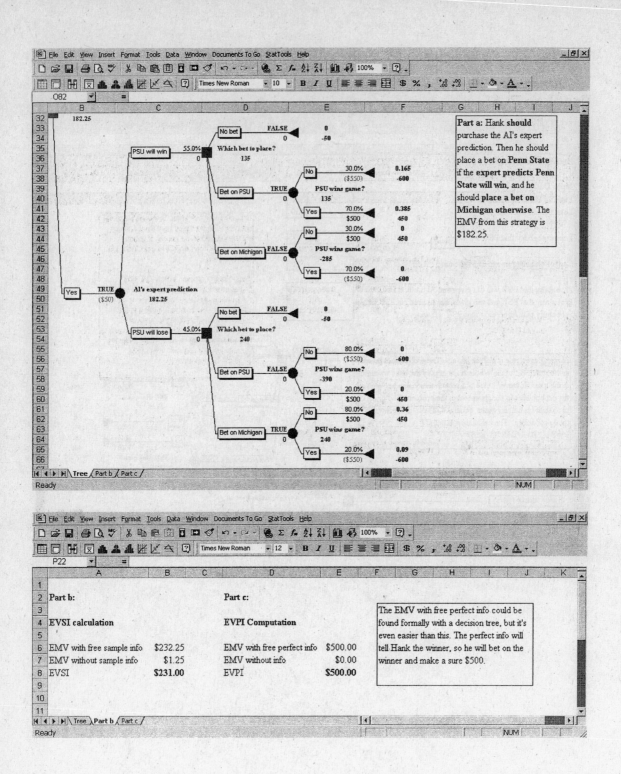

Part a: Hank should purchase the AI's expert prediction. Then he should place a bet on Penn State if the expert predicts Penn State will win, and he should place a bet on Michigan otherwise. The EMV from this strategy is $182.25.

Part b:

EVSI calculation

EMV with free sample info	$232.25
EMV without sample info	$1.25
EVSI	$231.00

Part c:

EVPI Computation

EMV with free perfect info	$500.00
EMV without info	$0.00
EVPI	$500.00

The EMV with free perfect info could be found formally with a decision tree, but it's even easier than this. The perfect info will tell Hank the winner, so he will bet on the winner and make a sure $500.

Problem 7_61
Part a:

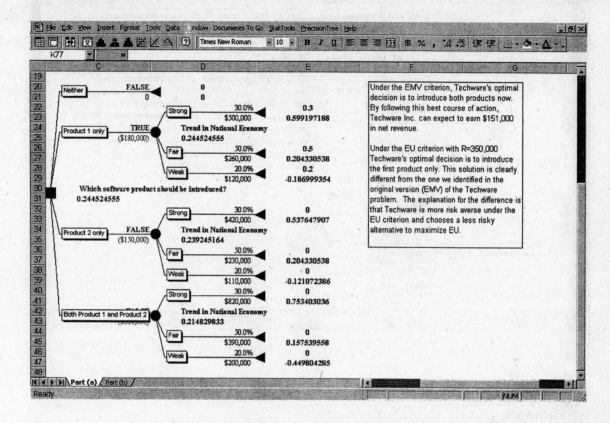

Under the EMV criterion, Techware's optimal decision is to introduce both products now. By following this best course of action, Techware Inc. can expect to earn $151,000 in net revenue.

Under the EU criterion with R=350,000 Techware's optimal decision is to introduce the first product only. This solution is clearly different from the one we identified in the original version (EMV) of the Techware problem. The explanation for the difference is that Techware is more risk averse under the EU criterion and chooses a less risky alternative to maximize EU.

Part b:

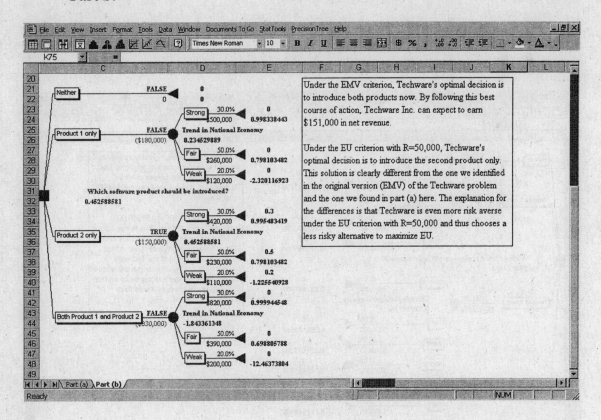

Problem 7_63

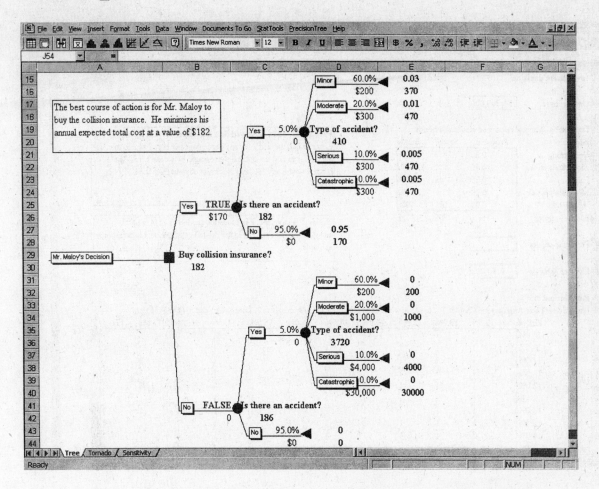

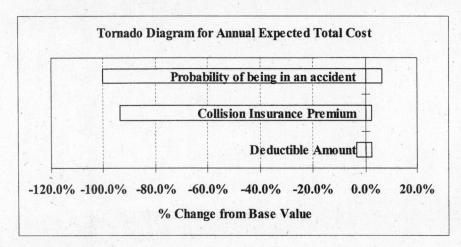

This tornado diagram indicates that the probability of being in an accident and the collision insurance premium are relatively influential in the determination of annual expected total cost. The optimal expected total cost is only slightly sensitive to changes in the deductible amount.

As the probability of being in an accident falls slightly below 5%, Mr. Maloy would prefer not to purchase the collision insurance.

Problem 7_67

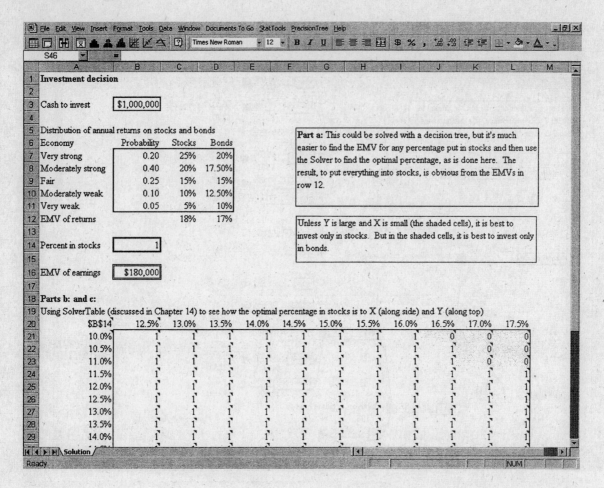

Problem 7_73

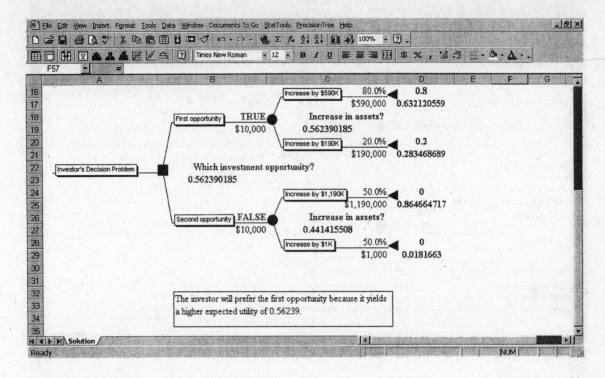

The investor will prefer the first opportunity because it yields a higher expected utility of 0.56239.

Problem 7_79

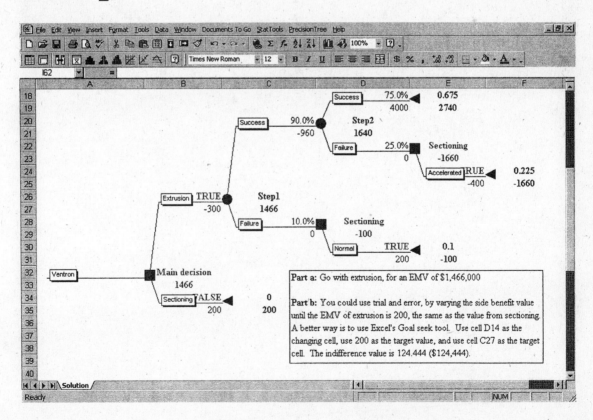

Part a: Go with extrusion, for an EMV of $1,466,000

Part b: You could use trial and error, by varying the side benefit value until the EMV of extrusion is 200, the same as the value from sectioning. A better way is to use Excel's Goal seek tool. Use cell D14 as the changing cell, use 200 as the target value, and use cell C27 as the target cell. The indifference value is 124.444 ($124,444).

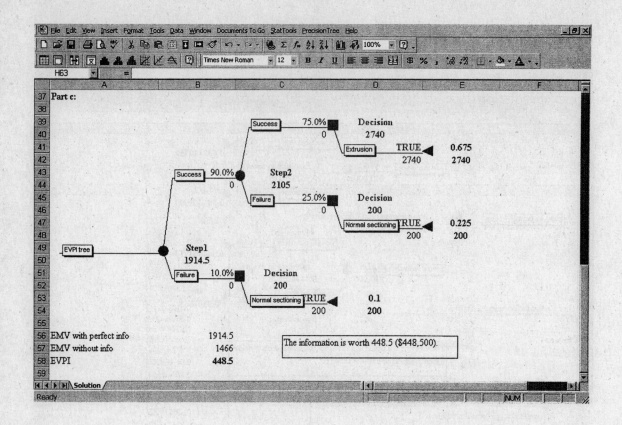

CHAPTER 8

Problem 8_3
The exact solution depends on the random sample generated. Your solution may differ.

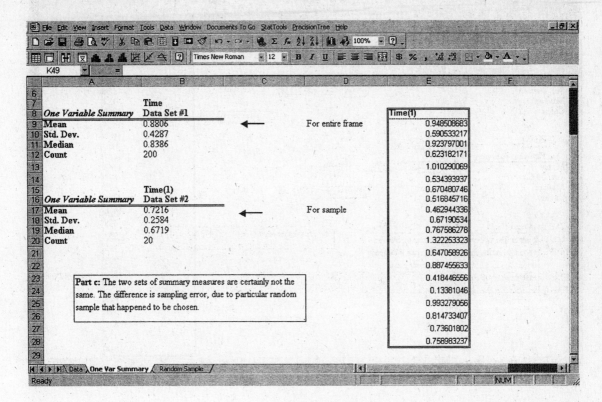

Problem 8_5

The exact solution depends on the random sample generated. Your solution may differ.

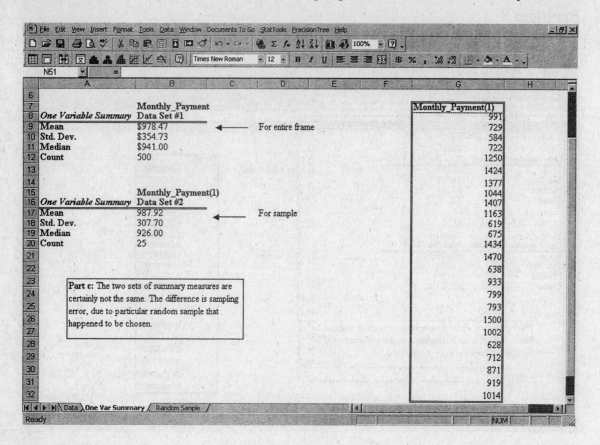

Problem 8_9

The exact solution depends on the random sample generated. Your solution may differ.

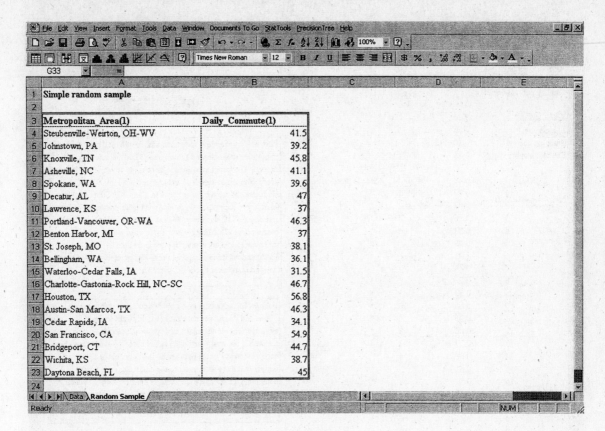

Problem 8_11

The exact solution depends on the random sample generated. Your solution may differ.

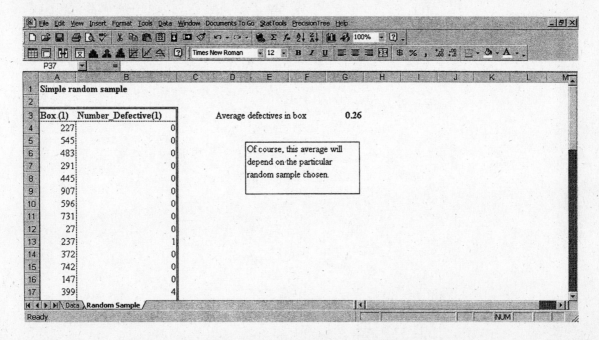

Problem 8_13

The exact solution depends on the random sample generated. Your solution may differ.

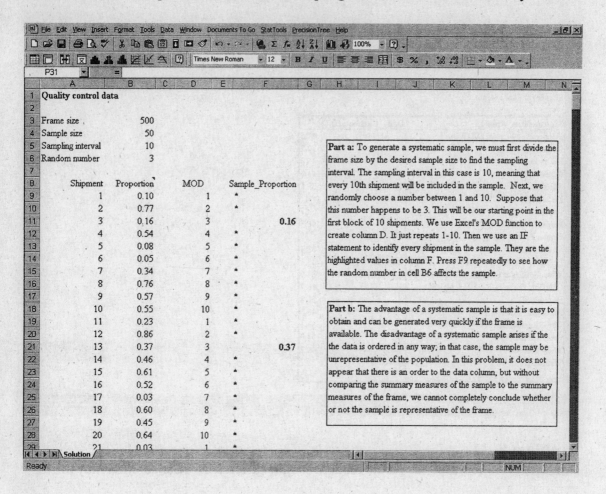

Problem 8_15

The exact solution depends on the random sample generated. Your solution may differ.

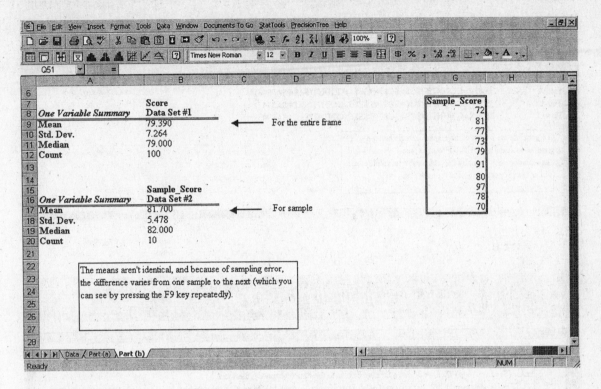

Problem 8_17

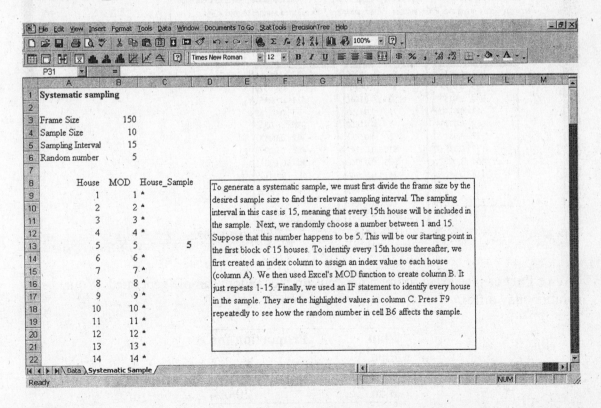

Problem 8_25

Part a:

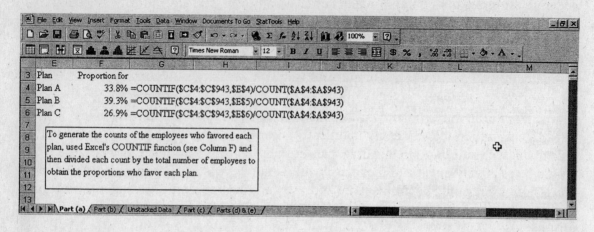

	Plan	Proportion for	
3	Plan	Proportion for	
4	Plan A	33.8%	=COUNTIF($C$4:$C$943,$E$4)/COUNT($A$4:$A$943)
5	Plan B	39.3%	=COUNTIF($C$4:$C$943,$E$5)/COUNT($A$4:$A$943)
6	Plan C	26.9%	=COUNTIF($C$4:$C$943,$E$6)/COUNT($A$4:$A$943)

To generate the counts of the employees who favored each plan, used Excel's COUNTIF function (see Column F) and then divided each count by the total number of employees to obtain the proportions who favor each plan.

Part b:

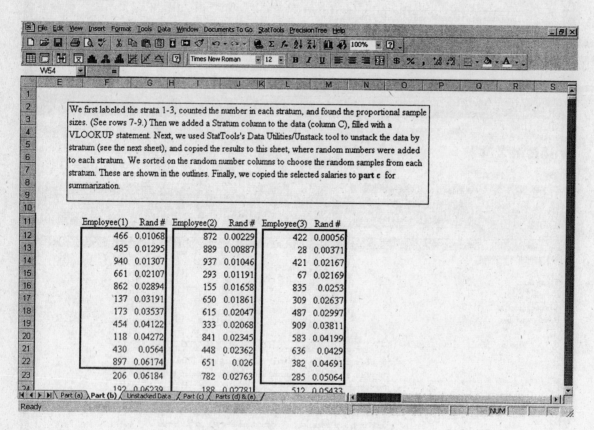

We first labeled the strata 1-3, counted the number in each stratum, and found the proportional sample sizes. (See rows 7-9.) Then we added a Stratum column to the data (column C), filled with a VLOOKUP statement. Next, we used StatTools's Data Utilities/Unstack tool to unstack the data by stratum (see the next sheet), and copied the results to this sheet, where random numbers were added to each stratum. We sorted on the random number columns to choose the random samples from each stratum. These are shown in the outlines. Finally, we copied the selected salaries to **part c** for summarization.

Employee(1)	Rand #	Employee(2)	Rand #	Employee(3)	Rand #
466	0.01068	872	0.00229	422	0.00056
485	0.01295	889	0.00887	28	0.00371
940	0.01307	937	0.01046	421	0.02167
661	0.02107	293	0.01191	67	0.02169
862	0.02894	155	0.01658	835	0.0253
137	0.03191	650	0.01861	309	0.02637
173	0.03537	615	0.02047	487	0.02997
454	0.04122	333	0.02068	909	0.03811
118	0.04272	841	0.02345	583	0.04199
430	0.0564	448	0.02362	636	0.0429
897	0.06174	651	0.026	382	0.04691
206	0.06184	782	0.02763	285	0.05064
192	0.06239	188	0.02781	512	0.05433

Part c: The exact solution depends on the random sample generated. Your solution may differ.

Plan	Proportion for
Plan A	33.3%
Plan B	46.7%
Plan C	20.0%

Part d: The main advantage of stratified sampling is that it generally produces accurate estimates of one or more population parameters. The key to this is selecting appropriate strata. On the other hand, as shown in this problem, the main disadvantage is **not selecting** the proper strata and still using the sample information obtained from the poorly chosen strata. In this case, the stratified sample found in part b **did not** adequately estimate the true proportions of employees who favor each type of health plan.

Part e: In this problem, the benefit managers could have selected a few departments within the university in order to select the sample data; this method would be called **cluster sampling**. In this case, cluster sampling may be a good idea because it would be relatively quick and inexpensive to sample from a few departments. However, cluster sampling could be problematic because the clusters that are selected **may not be completely representative** of the entire frame of university employees.

Problem 8_31
The exact solution depends on the random sample generated. Your solution may differ.

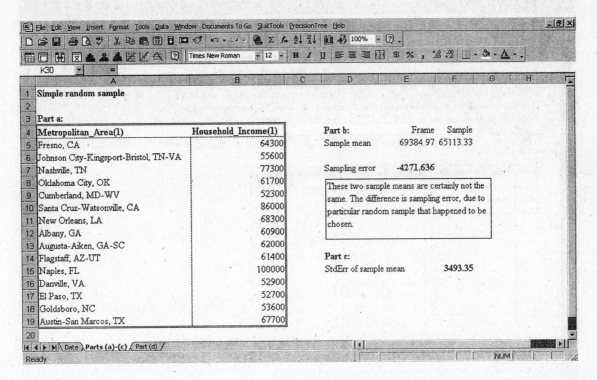

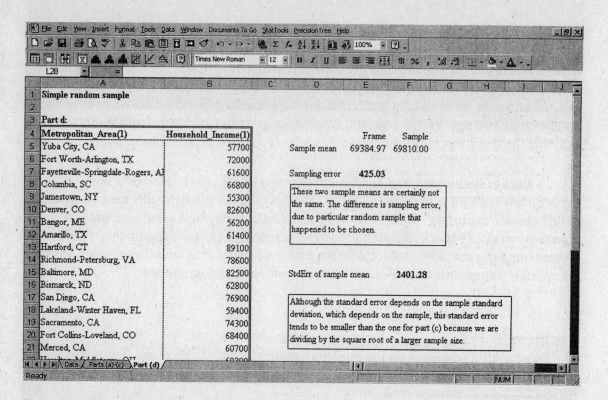

Problem 8_33

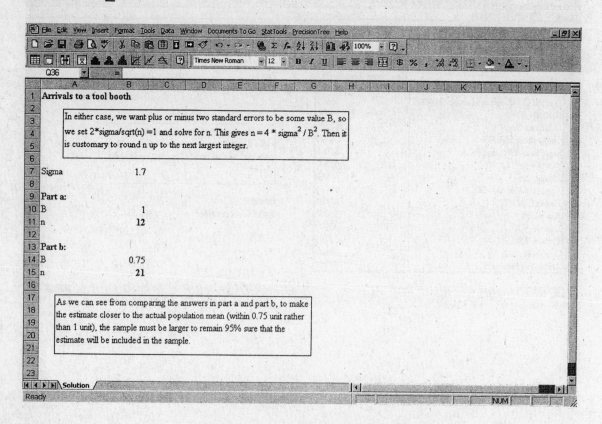

Problem 8_35

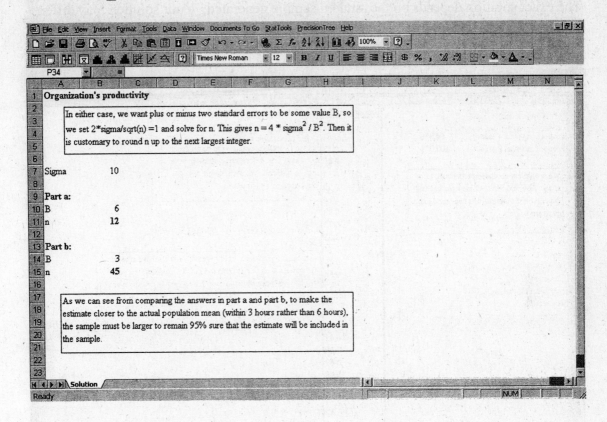

Problem 8_37

The exact solution depends on the random sample generated. Your solution may differ.

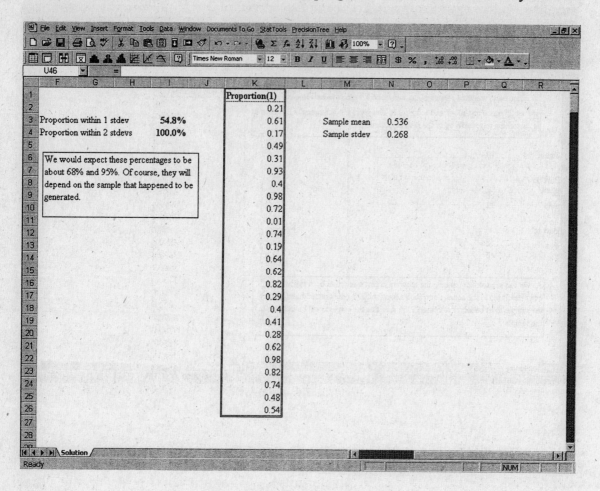

Problem 8_39

The exact solution depends on the random sample generated. Your solution may differ.

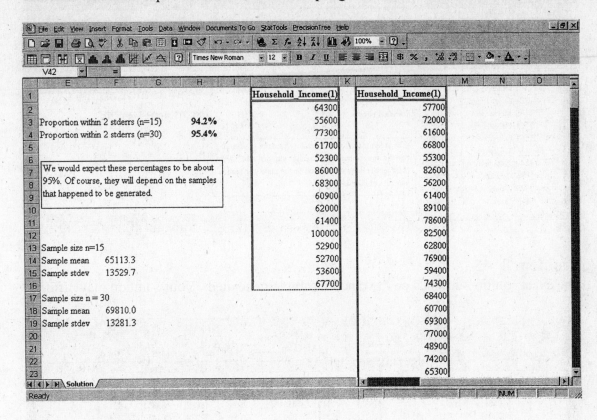

Problem 8_41

The exact solution depends on the random sample generated. Your solution may differ.

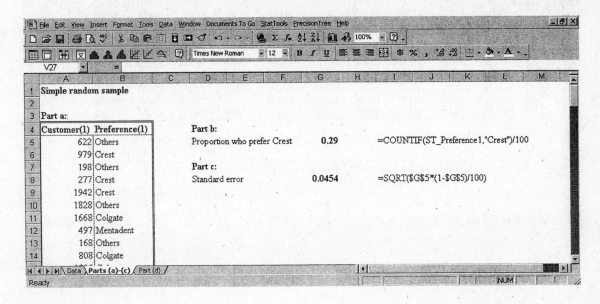

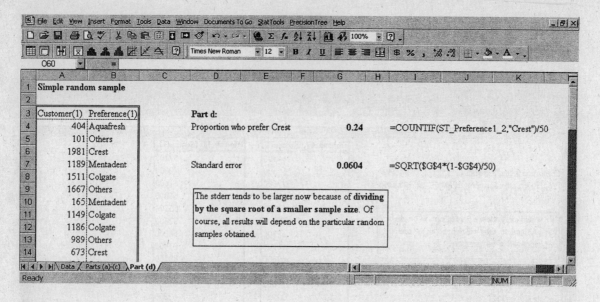

The spreadsheet shows:

Simple random sample

Customer(1)	Preference(1)
404	Aquafresh
101	Others
1981	Crest
1189	Mentadent
1511	Colgate
1667	Others
165	Mentadent
1149	Colgate
1186	Colgate
989	Others
673	Crest

Part d:

Proportion who prefer Crest	0.24	=COUNTIF(ST_Preference1_2,"Crest")/50
Standard error	0.0604	=SQRT($G$4*(1-$G$4)/50)

The stderr tends to be larger now because of **dividing by the square root of a smaller sample size**. Of course, all results will depend on the particular random samples obtained.

Problem 8_45

The exact solution depends on the random sample generated. Your solution may differ.

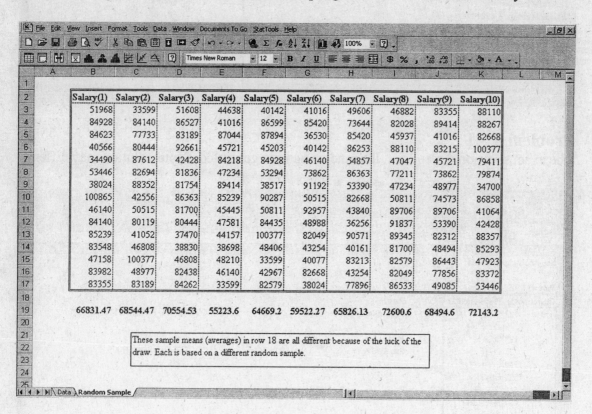

Salary(1)	Salary(2)	Salary(3)	Salary(4)	Salary(5)	Salary(6)	Salary(7)	Salary(8)	Salary(9)	Salary(10)
51968	33599	51608	44638	40142	41016	49606	46882	83355	88110
84928	84140	86527	41016	86599	85420	73644	82028	89414	88267
84623	77733	83189	87044	87894	36530	85420	45937	41016	82668
40566	80444	92661	45721	45203	40142	86253	88110	83215	100377
34490	87612	42428	84218	84928	46140	54857	47047	45721	79411
53446	82694	81836	47234	53294	73862	86363	77211	73862	79874
38024	88352	81754	89414	38517	91192	53390	47234	48977	34700
100865	42556	86363	85239	90287	50515	82668	50811	74573	86858
46140	50515	81700	45445	50811	92957	43840	89706	89706	41064
84140	80119	80444	47581	84435	48988	36256	91837	53390	42428
85239	41052	37470	44157	100377	82049	90571	89345	82312	88357
83548	46808	38830	38698	48406	43254	40161	81700	48494	85293
47158	100377	46808	48210	33599	40077	83213	82579	86443	47923
83982	48977	82438	46140	42967	82668	43254	82049	77856	83372
83355	83189	84262	33599	82579	38024	77896	86533	49085	53446
66831.47	68544.47	70554.53	55223.6	64669.2	59522.27	65826.13	72600.6	68494.6	72143.2

These sample means (averages) in row 18 are all different because of the luck of the draw. Each is based on a different random sample.

Problem 8_53

The exact solution depends on the random sample generated. Your solution may differ.

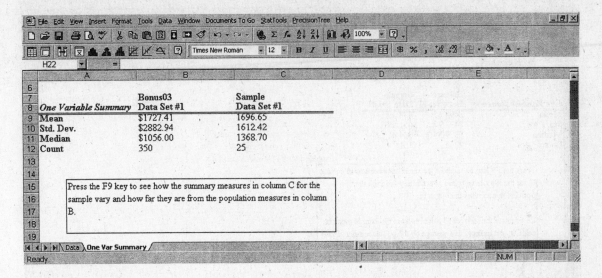

Cells shown in the spreadsheet:

	A	B	C
7		Bonus03	Sample
8	*One Variable Summary*	Data Set #1	Data Set #1
9	Mean	$1727.41	1696.65
10	Std. Dev.	$2882.94	1612.42
11	Median	$1056.00	1368.70
12	Count	350	25

Press the F9 key to see how the summary measures in column C for the sample vary and how far they are from the population measures in column B.

Problem 8_55

The exact solution depends on the random sample generated. Your solution may differ.

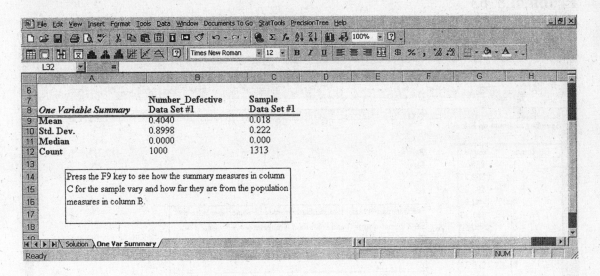

Cells shown in the spreadsheet:

	A	B	C
7		Number_Defective	Sample
8	*One Variable Summary*	Data Set #1	Data Set #1
9	Mean	0.4040	0.018
10	Std. Dev.	0.8998	0.222
11	Median	0.0000	0.000
12	Count	1000	1313

Press the F9 key to see how the summary measures in column C for the sample vary and how far they are from the population measures in column B.

Problem 8_59

The exact solution depends on the random sample generated. Your solution may differ.

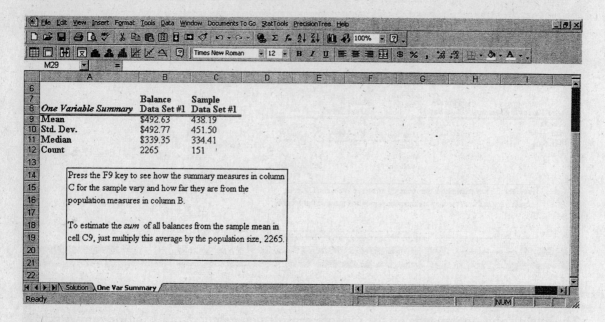

Problem 8_63

The exact solution depends on the random sample generated. Your solution may differ.

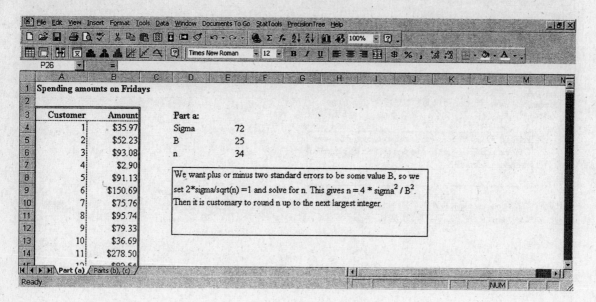

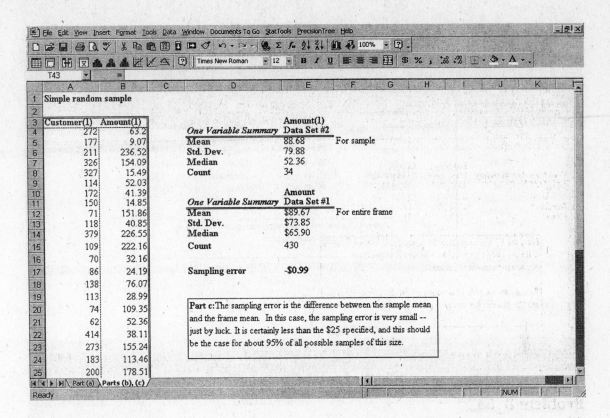

The spreadsheet shows:

Simple random sample

Customer(1)	Amount(1)
272	63.2
177	9.07
211	236.52
326	154.09
327	15.49
114	52.03
172	41.39
150	14.85
71	151.86
118	40.85
379	226.55
109	222.16
70	32.16
86	24.19
138	76.07
113	28.99
74	109.35
62	52.36
414	38.11
273	155.24
183	113.46
200	178.51

	Amount(1)
One Variable Summary	Data Set #2
Mean	88.68
Std. Dev.	79.88
Median	52.36
Count	34

For sample

	Amount
One Variable Summary	Data Set #1
Mean	$89.67
Std. Dev.	$73.85
Median	$65.90
Count	430

For entire frame

Sampling error   -$0.99

Part c: The sampling error is the difference between the sample mean and the frame mean. In this case, the sampling error is very small -- just by luck. It is certainly less than the $25 specified, and this should be the case for about 95% of all possible samples of this size.

Problem 8_67

The exact solution depends on the random sample generated. Your solution may differ.

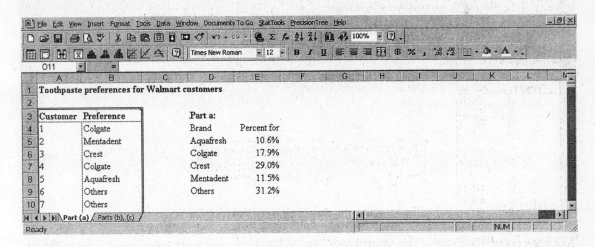

Toothpaste preferences for Walmart customers

Customer	Preference
1	Colgate
2	Mentadent
3	Crest
4	Colgate
5	Aquafresh
6	Others
7	Others

Part a:

Brand	Percent for
Aquafresh	10.6%
Colgate	17.9%
Crest	29.0%
Mentadent	11.5%
Others	31.2%

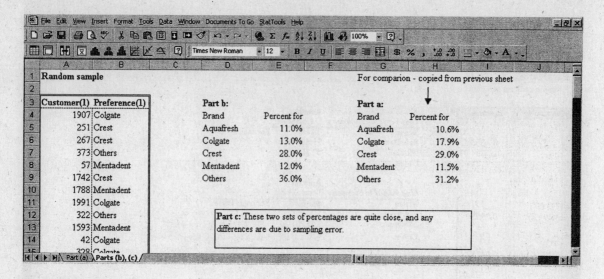

Problem 8_73

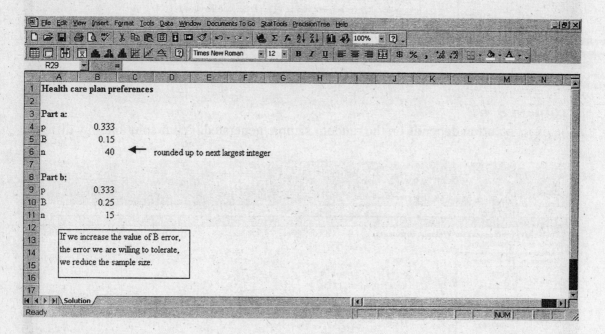

Problem 8_75

Suppose one home had billings of $1 million. We select a $1 invoice and determine That Nurseco overbilled 40%. We would then make Nurseco pay back $400,000. The problem is, of course, that the $1 invoice is only $1 out of $1,000,000. If we made each invoice's chance of being chosen proportional to its dollar size, then each dollar would have the same chance of being chosen, and we would have done an simple random sample of dollars. An alternative would be to randomly choose, say, 70 invoices over all homes and make Nurseco pay back a percentage equal to the percentage overbilled in the sample. For example, if Nurseco overbilled in the sample $4000 out of $40,000, they should have to pay back 10% of what they collected.

CHAPTER 9

Problem 9_1

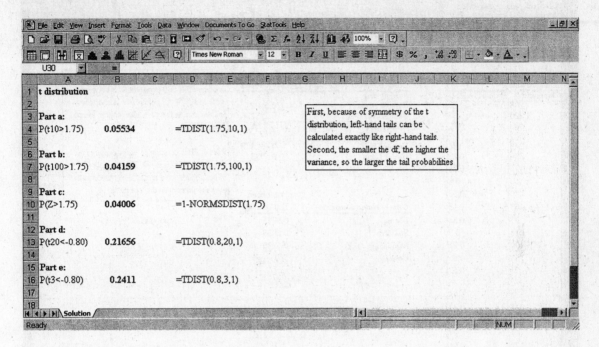

Problem 9_3

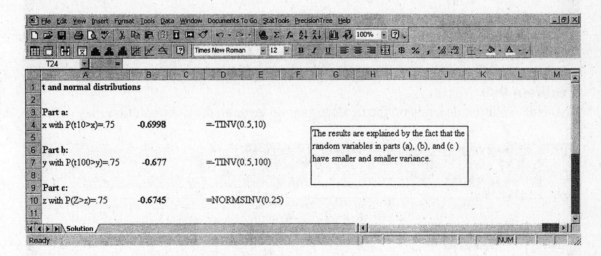

Problem 9_5

The exact solution depends on the random sample generated. Your solution may differ.

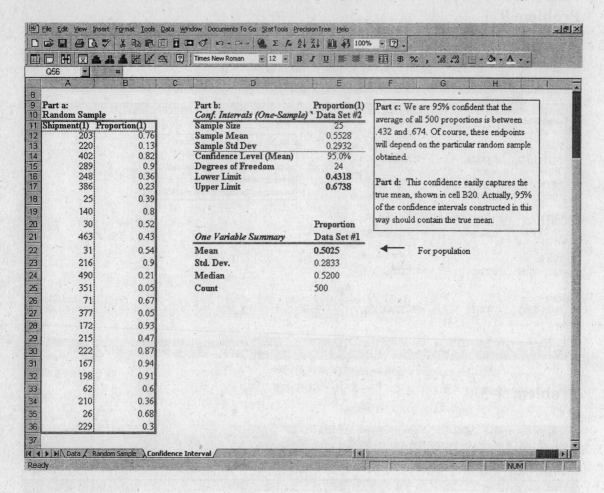

Problem 9_9

The exact solution depends on the random sample generated. Your solution may differ.

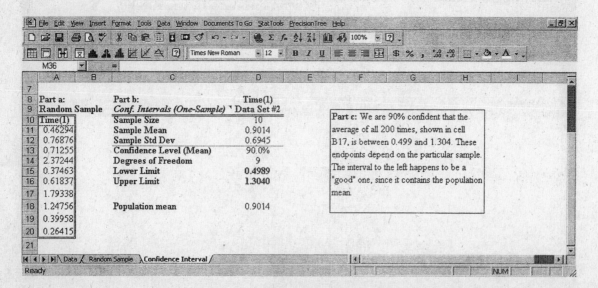

Problem 9_11

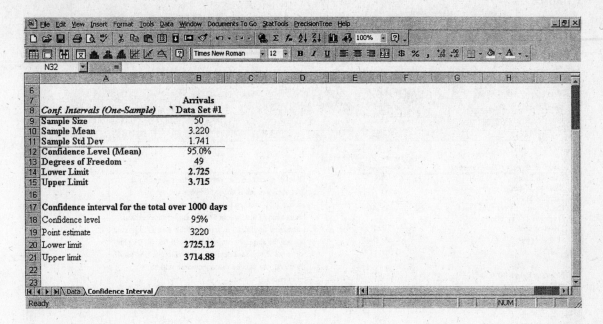

Problem 9_13

The random sample generated is not shown. For an example of how to generate a random sample see Chapter 8. The exact solution depends on the random sample generated. Your solution may differ.

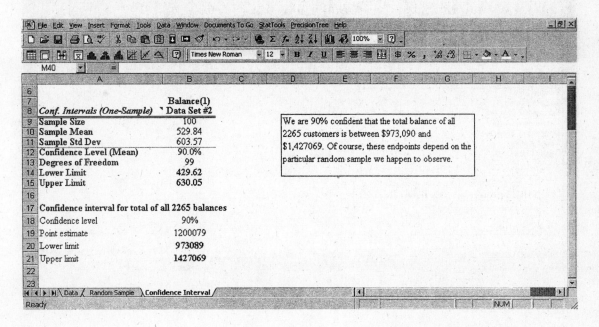

Problem 9_21

Part a: Is not shown. For an example of how to generate a random sample see Chapter 8.

Part b: The exact solution depends on the random sample generated. Your solution may differ.

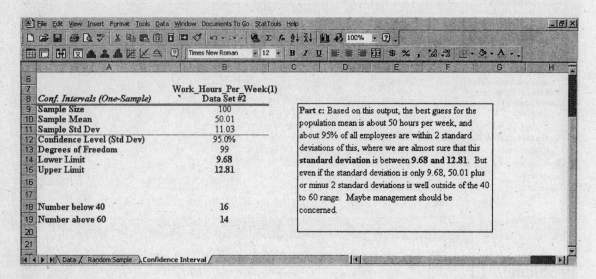

Problem 9_23

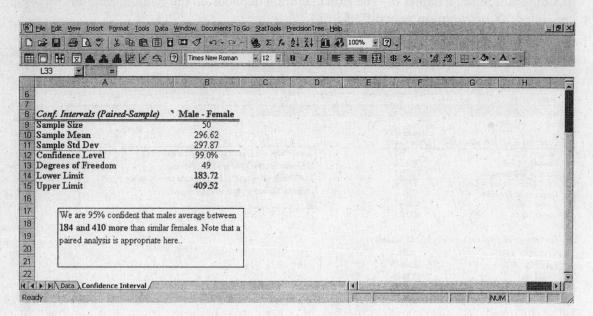

Problem 9_25

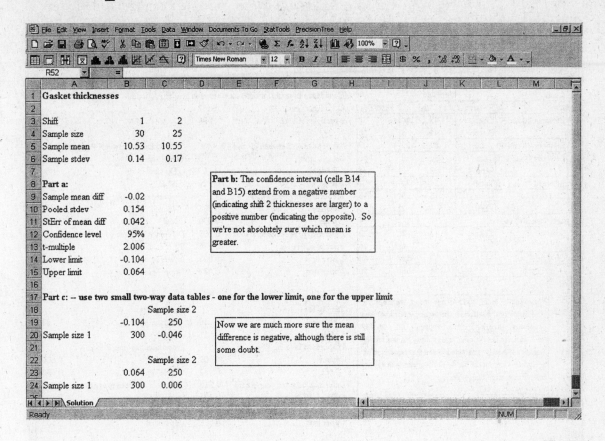

R52 =

	A	B	C
1	**Gasket thicknesses**		
2			
3	Shift	1	2
4	Sample size	30	25
5	Sample mean	10.53	10.55
6	Sample stdev	0.14	0.17
7			
8	**Part a:**		
9	Sample mean diff	-0.02	
10	Pooled stdev	0.154	
11	StErr of mean diff	0.042	
12	Confidence level	95%	
13	t-multiple	2.006	
14	Lower limit	-0.104	
15	Upper limit	0.064	
16			

Part b: The confidence interval (cells B14 and B15) extend from a negative number (indicating shift 2 thicknesses are larger) to a positive number (indicating the opposite). So we're not absolutely sure which mean is greater.

	A	B	C
17	**Part c: -- use two small two-way data tables - one for the lower limit, one for the upper limit**		
18			Sample size 2
19		-0.104	250
20	Sample size 1	300	-0.046
21			
22			Sample size 2
23		0.064	250
24	Sample size 1	300	0.006

Now we are much more sure the mean difference is negative, although there is still some doubt.

Solution

Ready

NUM

Problem 9_29

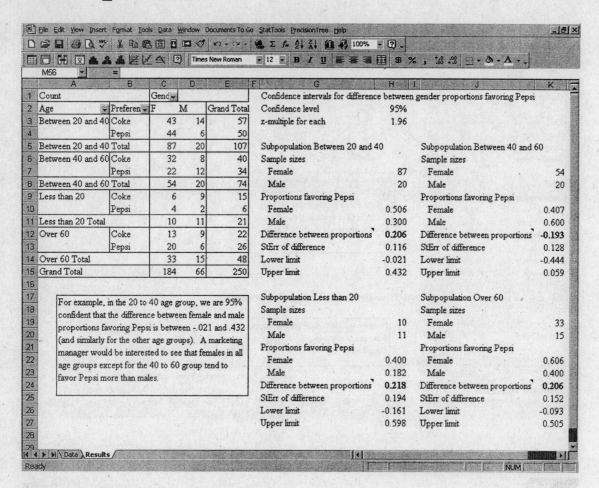

The spreadsheet contains:

Count		Gender				Confidence intervals for difference between gender proportions favoring Pepsi
Age	Preference	F	M	Grand Total		

Cells A1–E15:

	A	B	C	D	E
1	Count		Gender		
2	Age	Preference	F	M	Grand Total
3	Between 20 and 40	Coke	43	14	57
4		Pepsi	44	6	50
5	Between 20 and 40 Total		87	20	107
6	Between 40 and 60	Coke	32	8	40
7		Pepsi	22	12	34
8	Between 40 and 60 Total		54	20	74
9	Less than 20	Coke	6	9	15
10		Pepsi	4	2	6
11	Less than 20 Total		10	11	21
12	Over 60	Coke	13	9	22
13		Pepsi	20	6	26
14	Over 60 Total		33	15	48
15	Grand Total		184	66	250

Confidence intervals for difference between gender proportions favoring Pepsi

Confidence level	95%			
z-multiple for each	1.96			

Subpopulation Between 20 and 40		Subpopulation Between 40 and 60	
Sample sizes		Sample sizes	
Female	87	Female	54
Male	20	Male	20
Proportions favoring Pepsi		Proportions favoring Pepsi	
Female	0.506	Female	0.407
Male	0.300	Male	0.600
Difference between proportions	0.206	Difference between proportions	-0.193
StErr of difference	0.116	StErr of difference	0.128
Lower limit	-0.021	Lower limit	-0.444
Upper limit	0.432	Upper limit	0.059

Subpopulation Less than 20		Subpopulation Over 60	
Sample sizes		Sample sizes	
Female	10	Female	33
Male	11	Male	15
Proportions favoring Pepsi		Proportions favoring Pepsi	
Female	0.400	Female	0.606
Male	0.182	Male	0.400
Difference between proportions	0.218	Difference between proportions	0.206
StErr of difference	0.194	StErr of difference	0.152
Lower limit	-0.161	Lower limit	-0.093
Upper limit	0.598	Upper limit	0.505

For example, in the 20 to 40 age group, we are 95% confident that the difference between female and male proportions favoring Pepsi is between -.021 and .432 (and similarly for the other age groups). A marketing manager would be interested to see that females in all age groups except for the 40 to 60 group tend to favor Pepsi more than males.

Problem 9_33

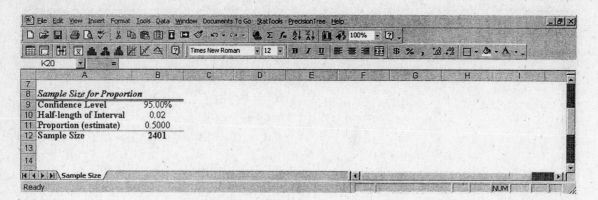

	A	B
8	Sample Size for Proportion	
9	Confidence Level	95.00%
10	Half-length of Interval	0.02
11	Proportion (estimate)	0.5000
12	Sample Size	2401

Problem 9_35

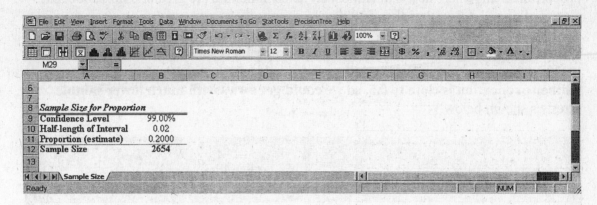

Sample Size for Proportion

Confidence Level	99.00%
Half-length of Interval	0.02
Proportion (estimate)	0.2000
Sample Size	2654

Problem 9_37

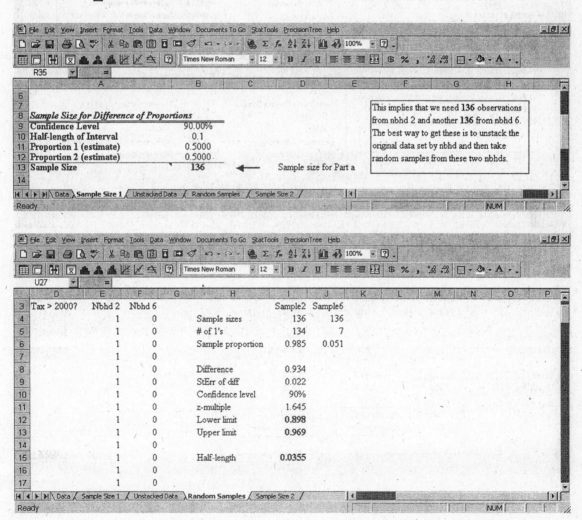

Sample Size for Difference of Proportions

Confidence Level	90.00%
Half-length of Interval	0.1
Proportion 1 (estimate)	0.5000
Proportion 2 (estimate)	0.5000
Sample Size	136

← Sample size for Part a

This implies that we need **136** observations from nbhd 2 and another **136** from nbhd 6. The best way to get these is to unstack the original data set by nbhd and then take random samples from these two nbhds.

Tax > 2000?	Nbhd 2	Nbhd 6			Sample2	Sample6
	1	0	Sample sizes		136	136
	1	0	# of 1's		134	7
	1	0	Sample proportion		0.985	0.051
	1	0				
	1	0	Difference		0.934	
	1	0	StErr of diff		0.022	
	1	0	Confidence level		90%	
	1	0	z-multiple		1.645	
	1	0	Lower limit		**0.898**	
	1	0	Upper limit		**0.969**	
	1	0				
	1	0	Half-length		**0.0355**	
	1	0				
	1	0				

To get a random sample from the Unstacked Data sheet, make sure to check the Sample Multiple Variables Independently option in StatTools's Random Sample dialog box.

Next, form the 0-1 variables in columns E and F with IF functions. Clearly, neither proportion is anywhere near 0.5. Almost all taxes in nbhd 2 are greater than $2000 and almost all in nbhd 6 are less than $2000.

The confidence interval based on these random samples is shown, with half-length 0.0355. This is much shorter than the requested half-length of 0.10. This is because **neither proportion is close to 0.5**, so **we could get away with much lower sample sizes**, as shown below.

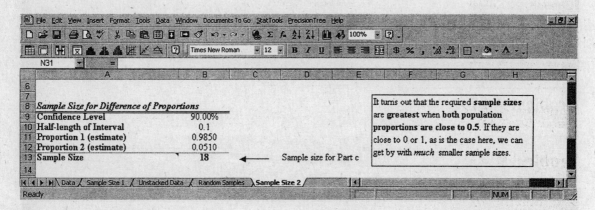

Problem 9_39

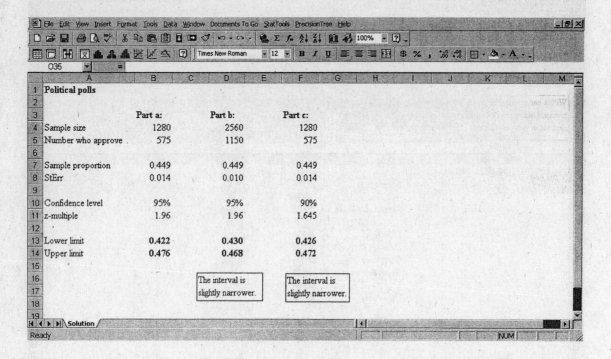

Problem 9_41

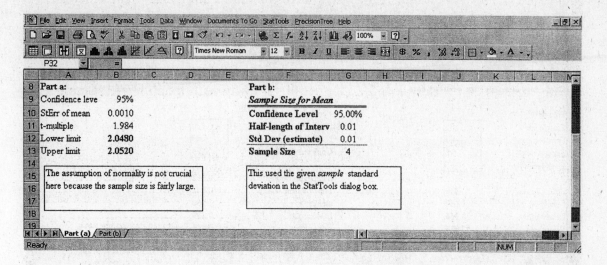

	A	B	C	D	E	F	G
8	Part a:					Part b:	
9	Confidence leve	95%				*Sample Size for Mean*	
10	StErr of mean	0.0010				Confidence Level	95.00%
11	t-multiple	1.984				Half-length of Interv	0.01
12	Lower limit	**2.0480**				Std Dev (estimate)	0.01
13	Upper limit	**2.0520**				Sample Size	4
14							
15	The assumption of normality is not crucial					This used the given *sample* standard	
16	here because the sample size is fairly large.					deviation in the StatTools dialog box.	

Problem 9_43

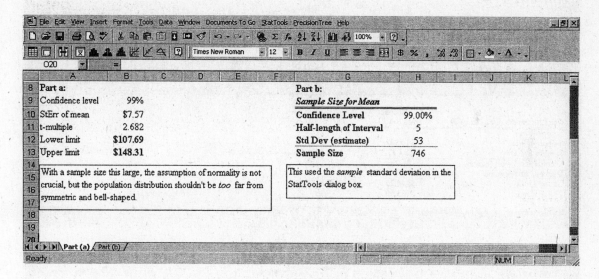

	A	B	C	D	E	F	G	H
8	Part a:						Part b:	
9	Confidence level	99%					*Sample Size for Mean*	
10	StErr of mean	$7.57					Confidence Level	99.00%
11	t-multiple	2.682					Half-length of Interval	5
12	Lower limit	**$107.69**					Std Dev (estimate)	53
13	Upper limit	**$148.31**					Sample Size	746
14								
15	With a sample size this large, the assumption of normality is not						This used the *sample* standard deviation in the	
16	crucial, but the population distribution shouldn't be *too* far from						StatTools dialog box.	
17	symmetric and bell-shaped.							

Problem 9_45

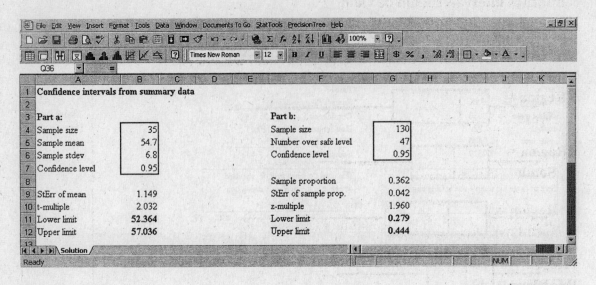

Problem 9_49

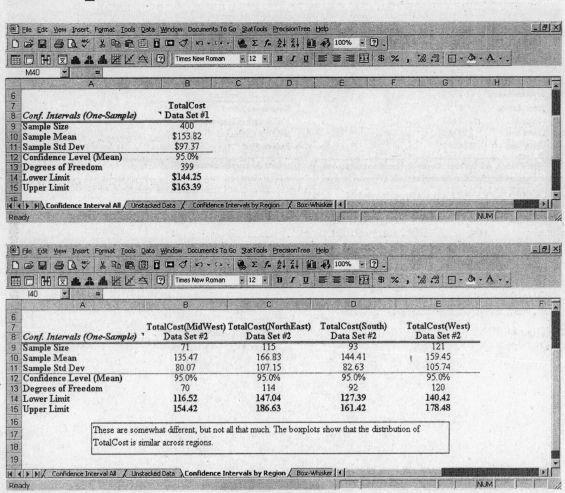

There is some skewness to the right, but the sample sizes are sufficiently large, so the **confidence intervals should be valid.**

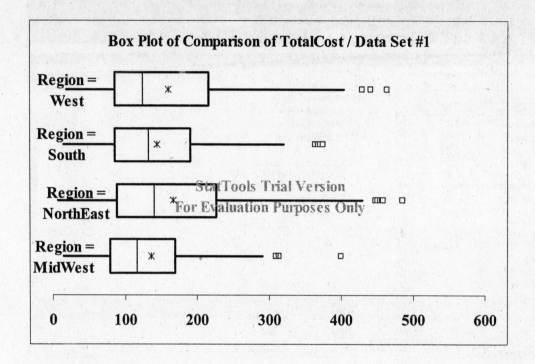

Problem 9_51

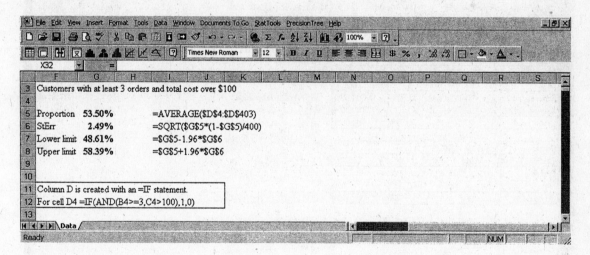

Problem 9_53

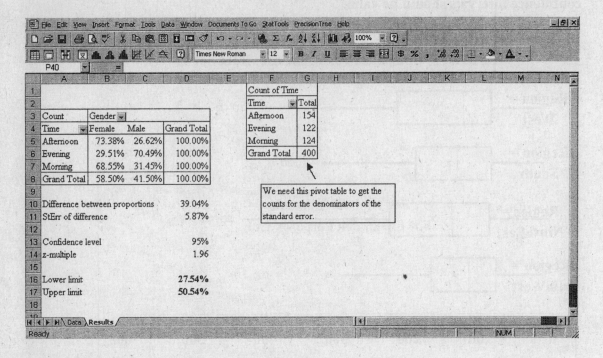

Problem 9_57

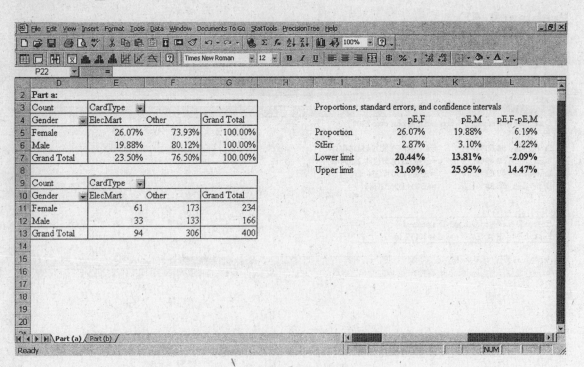

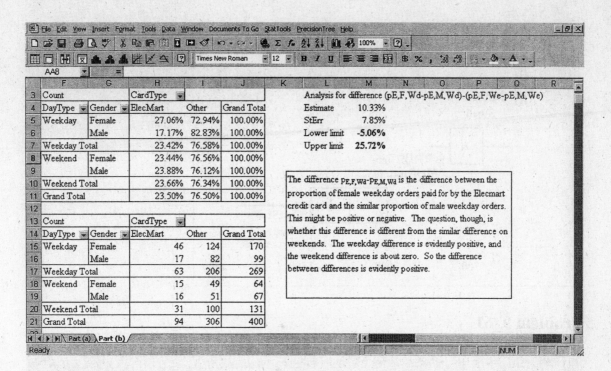

The difference $p_{E,F,Wd}-p_{E,M,Wd}$ is the difference between the proportion of female weekday orders paid for by the Elecmart credit card and the similar proportion of male weekday orders. This might be positive or negative. The question, though, is whether this difference is different from the similar difference on weekends. The weekday difference is evidently positive, and the weekend difference is about zero. So the difference between differences is evidently positive.

Problem 9_59

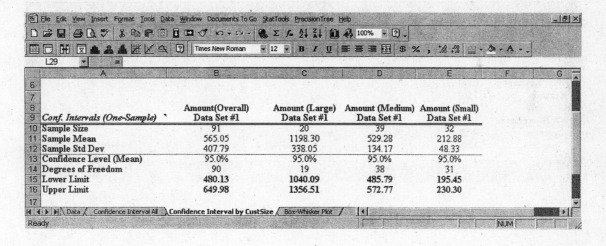

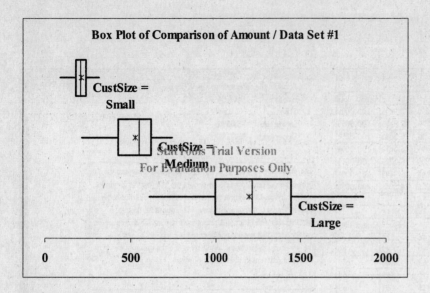

Box Plot of Comparison of Amount / Data Set #1

Problem 9_61

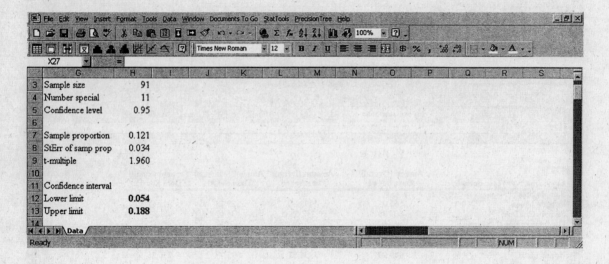

	G	H
3	Sample size	91
4	Number special	11
5	Confidence level	0.95
6		
7	Sample proportion	0.121
8	StErr of samp prop	0.034
9	t-multiple	1.960
10		
11	Confidence interval	
12	Lower limit	**0.054**
13	Upper limit	**0.188**

Problem 9_63

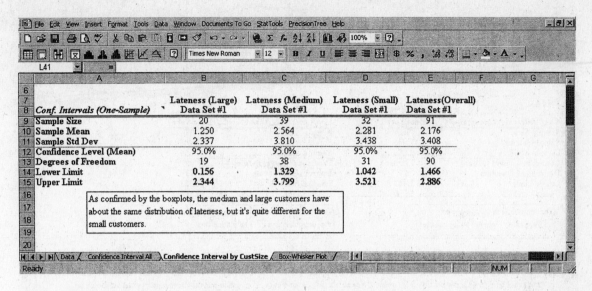

Conf. Intervals (One-Sample)	Lateness (Large) Data Set #1	Lateness (Medium) Data Set #1	Lateness (Small) Data Set #1	Lateness(Overall) Data Set #1
Sample Size	20	39	32	91
Sample Mean	1.250	2.564	2.281	2.176
Sample Std Dev	2.337	3.810	3.438	3.408
Confidence Level (Mean)	95.0%	95.0%	95.0%	95.0%
Degrees of Freedom	19	38	31	90
Lower Limit	0.156	1.329	1.042	1.466
Upper Limit	2.344	3.799	3.521	2.886

As confirmed by the boxplots, the medium and large customers have about the same distribution of lateness, but it's quite different for the small customers.

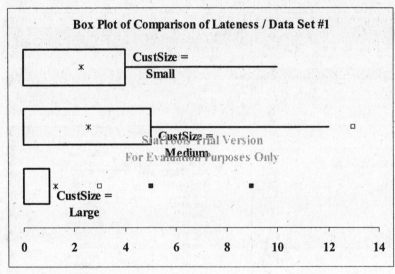

Box Plot of Comparison of Lateness / Data Set #1

Problem 9_65

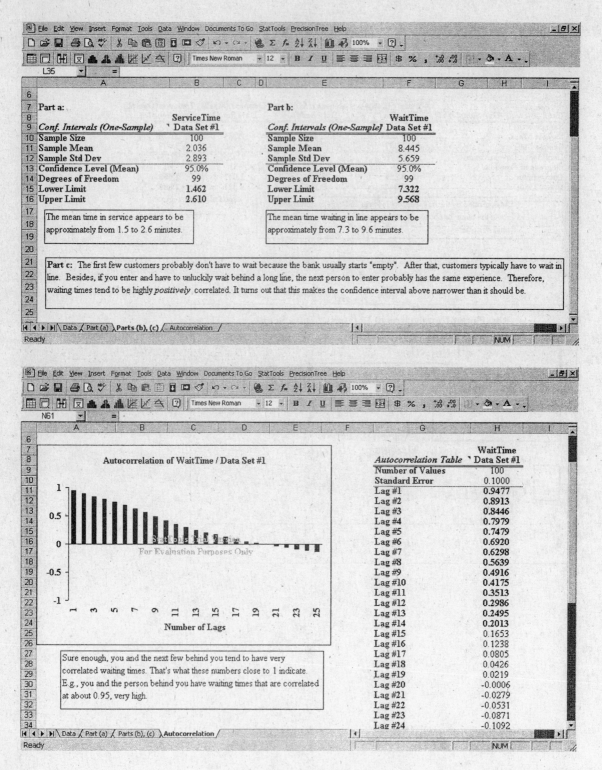

Part a:

Conf. Intervals (One-Sample)	ServiceTime Data Set #1
Sample Size	100
Sample Mean	2.036
Sample Std Dev	2.893
Confidence Level (Mean)	95.0%
Degrees of Freedom	99
Lower Limit	1.462
Upper Limit	2.610

The mean time in service appears to be approximately from 1.5 to 2.6 minutes.

Part b:

Conf. Intervals (One-Sample)	WaitTime Data Set #1
Sample Size	100
Sample Mean	8.445
Sample Std Dev	5.659
Confidence Level (Mean)	95.0%
Degrees of Freedom	99
Lower Limit	7.322
Upper Limit	9.568

The mean time waiting in line appears to be approximately from 7.3 to 9.6 minutes.

Part c: The first few customers probably don't have to wait because the bank usually starts "empty". After that, customers typically have to wait in line. Besides, if you enter and have to unluckily wait behind a long line, the next person to enter probably has the same experience. Therefore, waiting times tend to be highly *positively* correlated. It turns out that this makes the confidence interval above narrower than it should be.

Autocorrelation of WaitTime / Data Set #1

Autocorrelation Table	WaitTime Data Set #1
Number of Values	100
Standard Error	0.1000
Lag #1	0.9477
Lag #2	0.8913
Lag #3	0.8446
Lag #4	0.7979
Lag #5	0.7479
Lag #6	0.6920
Lag #7	0.6298
Lag #8	0.5639
Lag #9	0.4916
Lag #10	0.4175
Lag #11	0.3513
Lag #12	0.2986
Lag #13	0.2495
Lag #14	0.2013
Lag #15	0.1653
Lag #16	0.1238
Lag #17	0.0805
Lag #18	0.0426
Lag #19	0.0219
Lag #20	-0.0006
Lag #21	-0.0279
Lag #22	-0.0531
Lag #23	-0.0871
Lag #24	-0.1092

Sure enough, you and the next few behind you tend to have very correlated waiting times. That's what these numbers close to 1 indicate. E.g., you and the person behind you have waiting times that are correlated at about 0.95, very high.

Problem 9_69

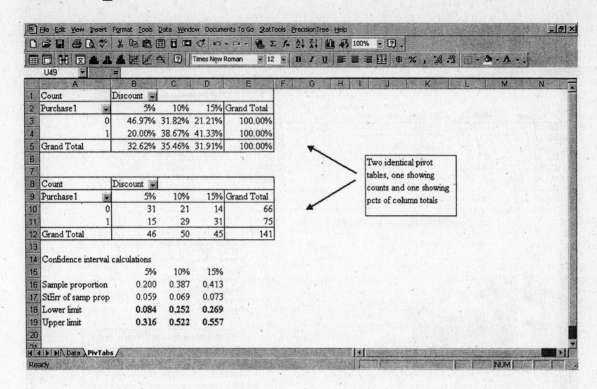

Problem 9_73

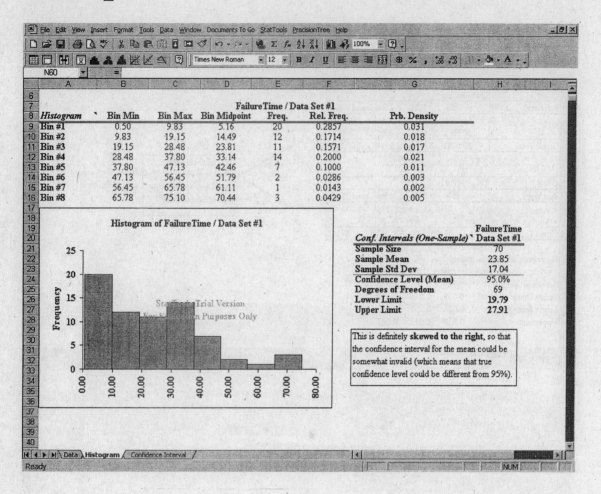

CHAPTER 10

Problem 10_1

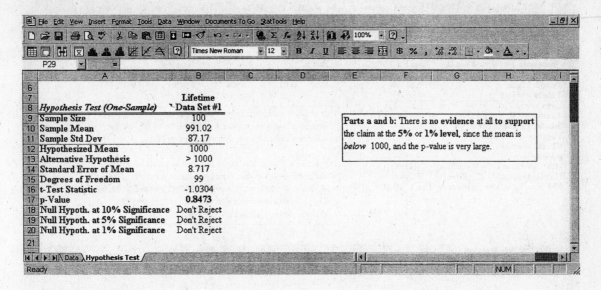

Parts a and b: There is no evidence at all to support the claim at the 5% or 1% level, since the mean is *below* 1000, and the p-value is very large.

Hypothesis Test (One-Sample)	Lifetime Data Set #1
Sample Size	100
Sample Mean	991.02
Sample Std Dev	87.17
Hypothesized Mean	1000
Alternative Hypothesis	> 1000
Standard Error of Mean	8.717
Degrees of Freedom	99
t-Test Statistic	-1.0304
p-Value	**0.8473**
Null Hypoth. at 10% Significance	Don't Reject
Null Hypoth. at 5% Significance	Don't Reject
Null Hypoth. at 1% Significance	Don't Reject

Problem 10_3

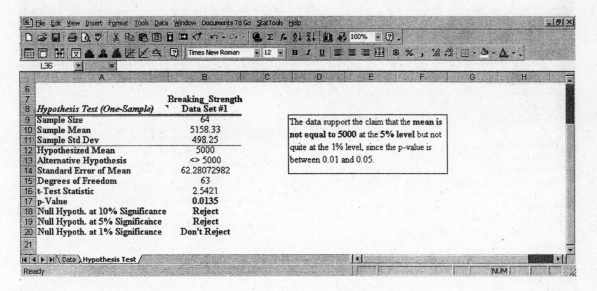

The data support the claim that the **mean is not equal to 5000** at the **5% level** but not quite at the 1% level, since the p-value is between 0.01 and 0.05.

Hypothesis Test (One-Sample)	Breaking_Strength Data Set #1
Sample Size	64
Sample Mean	5158.33
Sample Std Dev	498.25
Hypothesized Mean	5000
Alternative Hypothesis	<> 5000
Standard Error of Mean	62.28072982
Degrees of Freedom	63
t-Test Statistic	2.5421
p-Value	**0.0135**
Null Hypoth. at 10% Significance	Reject
Null Hypoth. at 5% Significance	Reject
Null Hypoth. at 1% Significance	Don't Reject

Problem 10_5

This is certainly possible. The main reason is that when n is larger, the standard error of the sample mean decreases, so the sample mean is a more precise estimate of the true mean. Therefore, any sample mean over 10 is more likely to lead to rejection of the null hypothesis when n increases.

Problem 10_7

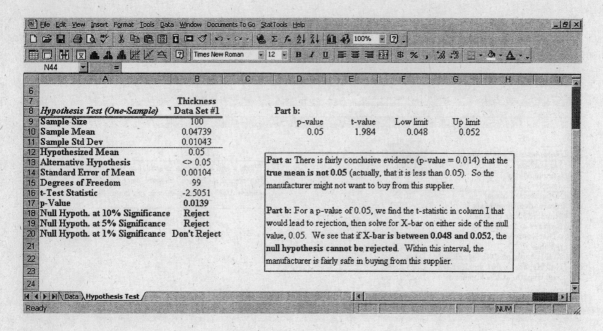

Problem 10_9

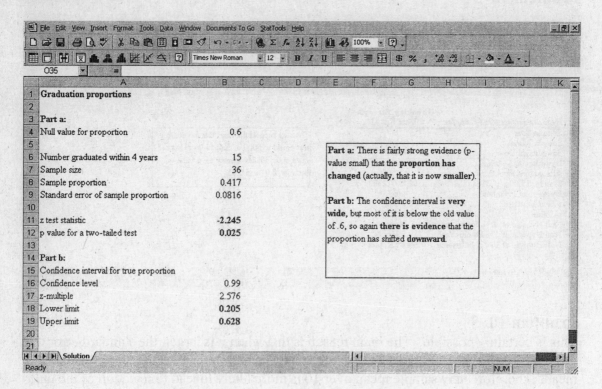

Problem 10_11

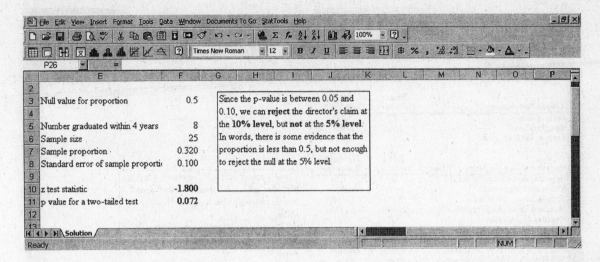

	E	F	G H I J K L M N O P
2			
3	Null value for proportion	0.5	Since the p-value is between 0.05 and
4			0.10, we can **reject** the director's claim at
5	Number graduated within 4 years	8	the **10% level**, but **not** at the **5% level**.
6	Sample size	25	In words, there is some evidence that the
7	Sample proportion	0.320	proportion is less than 0.5, but not enough
8	Standard error of sample proportic	0.100	to reject the null at the 5% level.
9			
10	z test statistic	**-1.800**	
11	p value for a two-tailed test	**0.072**	
12			

Problem 10_15

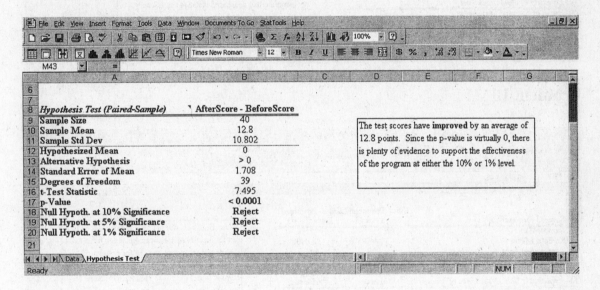

	A	B
8	*Hypothesis Test (Paired-Sample)*	AfterScore - BeforeScore
9	Sample Size	40
10	Sample Mean	12.8
11	Sample Std Dev	10.802
12	Hypothesized Mean	0
13	Alternative Hypothesis	> 0
14	Standard Error of Mean	1.708
15	Degrees of Freedom	39
16	t-Test Statistic	7.495
17	p-Value	< 0.0001
18	Null Hypoth. at 10% Significance	Reject
19	Null Hypoth. at 5% Significance	Reject
20	Null Hypoth. at 1% Significance	Reject
21		

The test scores have **improved** by an average of 12.8 points. Since the p-value is virtually 0, there is plenty of evidence to support the effectiveness of the program at either the 10% or 1% level.

Problem 10_17

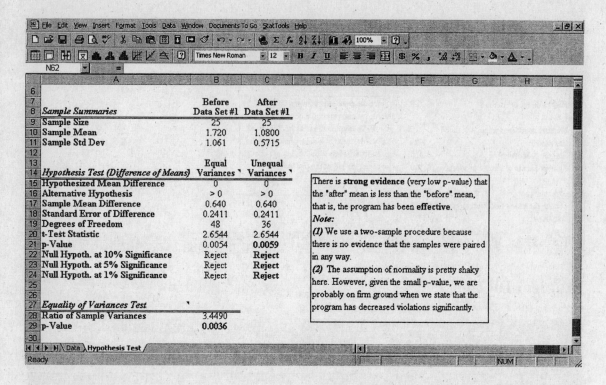

	A	B	C
6			
7		Before	After
8	*Sample Summaries*	Data Set #1	Data Set #1
9	Sample Size	25	25
10	Sample Mean	1.720	1.0800
11	Sample Std Dev	1.061	0.5715
12			
13		Equal	Unequal
14	*Hypothesis Test (Difference of Means)*	Variances	Variances
15	Hypothesized Mean Difference	0	0
16	Alternative Hypothesis	> 0	> 0
17	Sample Mean Difference	0.640	0.640
18	Standard Error of Difference	0.2411	0.2411
19	Degrees of Freedom	48	36
20	t-Test Statistic	2.6544	2.6544
21	p-Value	0.0054	0.0059
22	Null Hypoth. at 10% Significance	Reject	Reject
23	Null Hypoth. at 5% Significance	Reject	Reject
24	Null Hypoth. at 1% Significance	Reject	Reject
25			
26			
27	*Equality of Variances Test*		
28	Ratio of Sample Variances	3.4490	
29	p-Value	0.0036	
30			

There is **strong evidence** (very low p-value) that the "after" mean is less than the "before" mean, that is, the program has been **effective**.

Note:

(1) We use a two-sample procedure because there is no evidence that the samples were paired in any way.

(2) The assumption of normality is pretty shaky here. However, given the small p-value, we are probably on firm ground when we state that the program has decreased violations significantly.

Problem 10_21

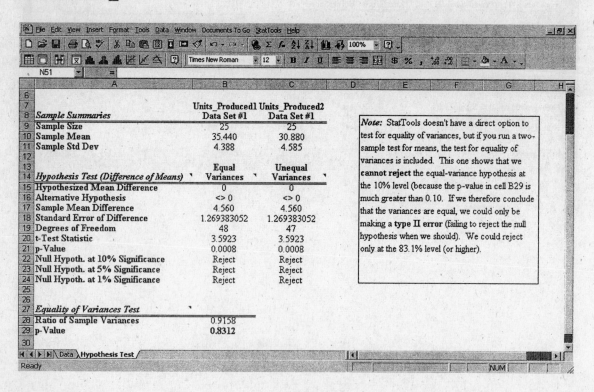

	A	B	C
6			
7		Units_Produced1	Units_Produced2
8	*Sample Summaries*	Data Set #1	Data Set #1
9	Sample Size	25	25
10	Sample Mean	35.440	30.880
11	Sample Std Dev	4.388	4.585
12			
13		Equal	Unequal
14	*Hypothesis Test (Difference of Means)*	Variances	Variances
15	Hypothesized Mean Difference	0	0
16	Alternative Hypothesis	<> 0	<> 0
17	Sample Mean Difference	4.560	4.560
18	Standard Error of Difference	1.269383052	1.269383052
19	Degrees of Freedom	48	47
20	t-Test Statistic	3.5923	3.5923
21	p-Value	0.0008	0.0008
22	Null Hypoth. at 10% Significance	Reject	Reject
23	Null Hypoth. at 5% Significance	Reject	Reject
24	Null Hypoth. at 1% Significance	Reject	Reject
25			
26			
27	*Equality of Variances Test*		
28	Ratio of Sample Variances	0.9158	
29	p-Value	0.8312	
30			

Note: StatTools doesn't have a direct option to test for equality of variances, but if you run a two-sample test for means, the test for equality of variances is included. This one shows that we **cannot reject** the equal-variance hypothesis at the 10% level (because the p-value in cell B29 is much greater than 0.10. If we therefore conclude that the variances are equal, we could only be making a **type II error** (failing to reject the null hypothesis when we should). We could reject only at the 83.1% level (or higher).

Problem 10_25

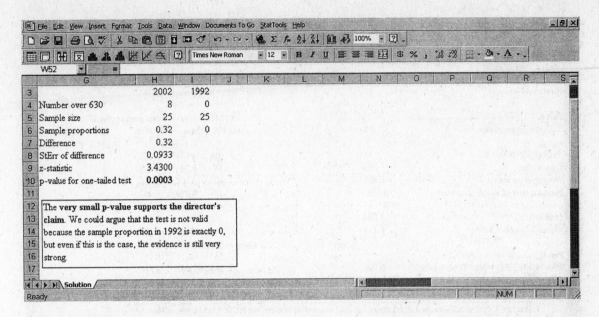

	G	H	I
3		2002	1992
4	Number over 630	8	0
5	Sample size	25	25
6	Sample proportions	0.32	0
7	Difference	0.32	
8	StErr of difference	0.0933	
9	z-statistic	3.4300	
10	p-value for one-tailed test	**0.0003**	
11			
12	**The very small p-value supports the director's**		
13	**claim.** We could argue that the test is not valid		
14	because the sample proportion in 1992 is exactly 0,		
15	but even if this is the case, the evidence is still very		
16	strong.		
17			

Problem 10_27

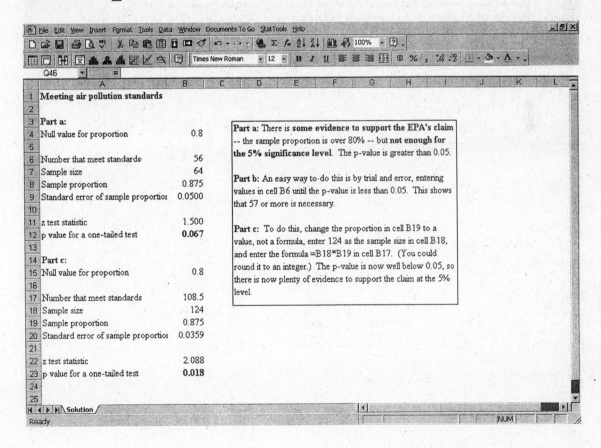

	A	B
1	**Meeting air pollution standards**	
2		
3	**Part a:**	
4	Null value for proportion	0.8
5		
6	Number that meet standards	56
7	Sample size	64
8	Sample proportion	0.875
9	Standard error of sample proportion	0.0500
10		
11	z test statistic	1.500
12	p value for a one-tailed test	**0.067**
13		
14	**Part c:**	
15	Null value for proportion	0.8
16		
17	Number that meet standards	108.5
18	Sample size	124
19	Sample proportion	0.875
20	Standard error of sample proportion	0.0359
21		
22	z test statistic	2.088
23	p value for a one-tailed test	**0.018**
24		
25		

Part a: There is **some evidence to support the EPA's claim** -- the sample proportion is over 80% -- but **not enough for the 5% significance level.** The p-value is greater than 0.05.

Part b: An easy way to do this is by trial and error, entering values in cell B6 until the p-value is less than 0.05. This shows that 57 or more is necessary.

Part c: To do this, change the proportion in cell B19 to a value, not a formula, enter 124 as the sample size in cell B18, and enter the formula =B18*B19 in cell B17. (You could round it to an integer.) The p-value is now well below 0.05, so there is now plenty of evidence to support the claim at the 5% level.

Problem 10_29

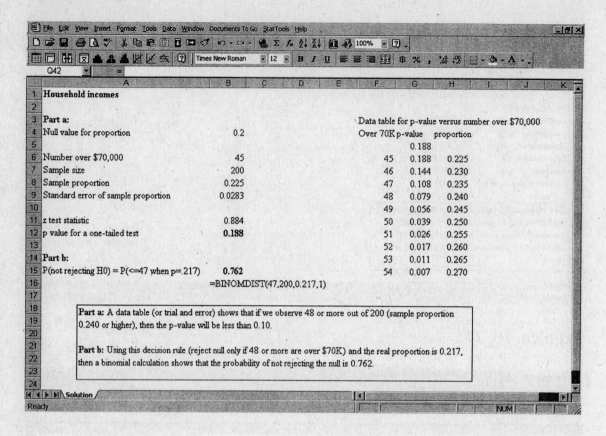

	A	B	C	D	E	F	G	H	I	J	K
1	Household incomes										
2											
3	Part a:						Data table for p-value versus number over $70,000				
4	Null value for proportion	0.2					Over 70K	p-value	proportion		
5								0.188			
6	Number over $70,000	45					45	0.188	0.225		
7	Sample size	200					46	0.144	0.230		
8	Sample proportion	0.225					47	0.108	0.235		
9	Standard error of sample proportion	0.0283					48	0.079	0.240		
10							49	0.056	0.245		
11	z test statistic	0.884					50	0.039	0.250		
12	p value for a one-tailed test	**0.188**					51	0.026	0.255		
13							52	0.017	0.260		
14	Part b:						53	0.011	0.265		
15	P(not rejecting H0) = P(<=47 when p=.217)	**0.762**					54	0.007	0.270		
16		=BINOMDIST(47,200,0.217,1)									

Part a: A data table (or trial and error) shows that if we observe 48 or more out of 200 (sample proportion 0.240 or higher), then the p-value will be less than 0.10.

Part b: Using this decision rule (reject null only if 48 or more are over $70K) and the real proportion is 0.217, then a binomial calculation shows that the probability of not rejecting the null is 0.762.

Problem 10_35

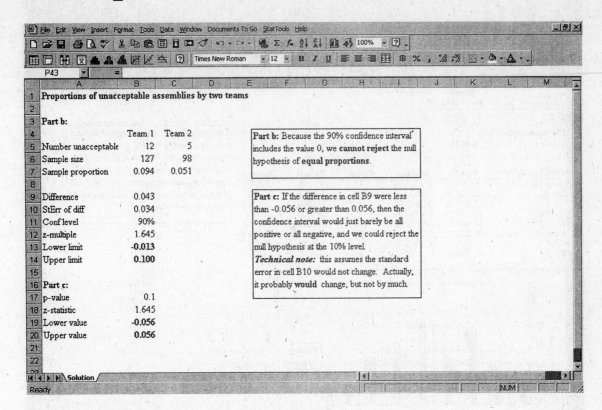

		Team 1	Team 2
1	Proportions of unacceptable assemblies by two teams		
2			
3	Part b:		
4		Team 1	Team 2
5	Number unacceptable	12	5
6	Sample size	127	98
7	Sample proportion	0.094	0.051
8			
9	Difference	0.043	
10	StErr of diff	0.034	
11	Conf level	90%	
12	z-multiple	1.645	
13	Lower limit	-0.013	
14	Upper limit	0.100	
15			
16	Part c:		
17	p-value	0.1	
18	z-statistic	1.645	
19	Lower value	-0.056	
20	Upper value	0.056	

Part b: Because the 90% confidence interval includes the value 0, we **cannot reject** the null hypothesis of **equal proportions.**

Part c: If the difference in cell B9 were less than -0.056 or greater than 0.056, then the confidence interval would just barely be all positive or all negative, and we could reject the null hypothesis at the 10% level.
Technical note: this assumes the standard error in cell B10 would not change. Actually, it probably **would** change, but not by much.

Problem 10_39

Under the null hypothesis that the **two proportions are equal** (but we don't know either of them), it makes sense to **pool all of the observations into one sample** and replace each unknown p in the standard error formula by the combined proportion in the pooled sample. But this **wouldn't make sense** if the **null hypothesis** were, say, that **p1-p2=0.5**. Then about the best we could do is to use the individual sample proportions for p1 and p2 in the standard error formula.

Problem 10_41

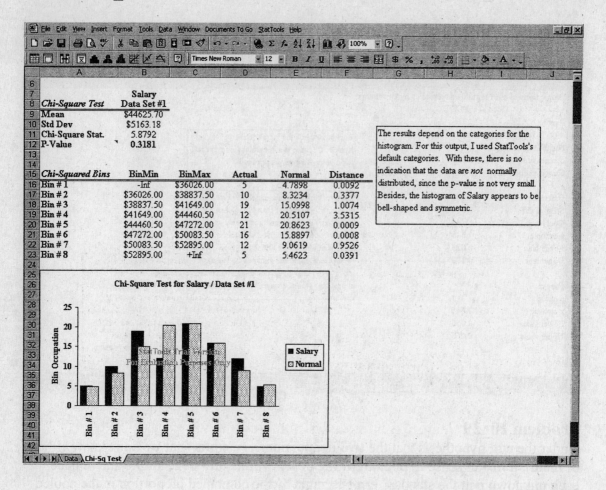

Problem 10_45

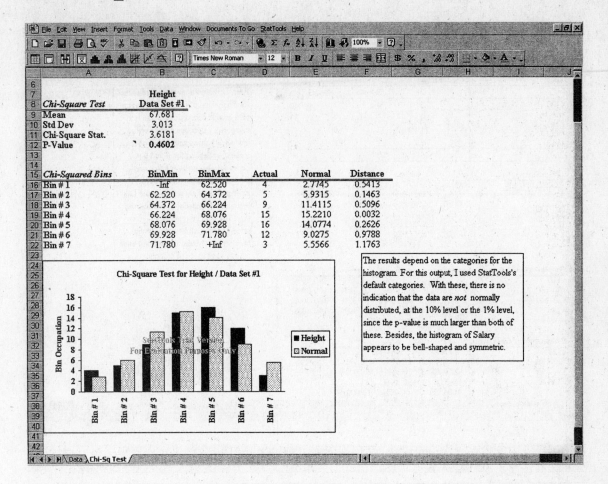

Chi-Square Test	Height Data Set #1
Mean	67.681
Std Dev	3.013
Chi-Square Stat.	3.6181
P-Value	0.4602

Chi-Squared Bins	BinMin	BinMax	Actual	Normal	Distance
Bin # 1	-Inf	62.520	4	2.7745	0.5413
Bin # 2	62.520	64.372	5	5.9315	0.1463
Bin # 3	64.372	66.224	9	11.4115	0.5096
Bin # 4	66.224	68.076	15	15.2210	0.0032
Bin # 5	68.076	69.928	16	14.0774	0.2626
Bin # 6	69.928	71.780	12	9.0275	0.9788
Bin # 7	71.780	+Inf	3	5.5566	1.1763

The results depend on the categories for the histogram. For this output, I used StatTools's default categories. With these, there is no indication that the data are *not* normally distributed, at the 10% level or the 1% level, since the p-value is much larger than both of these. Besides, the histogram of Salary appears to be bell-shaped and symmetric.

Problem 10_49

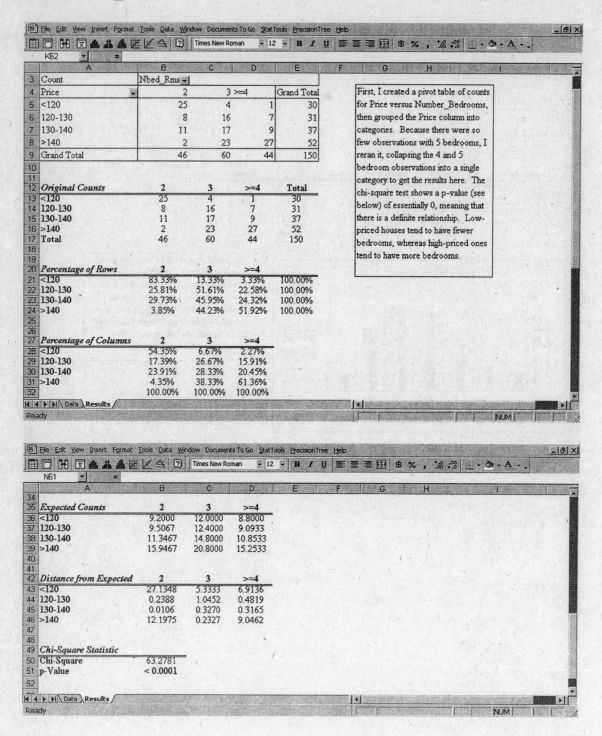

First, I created a pivot table of counts for Price versus Number_Bedrooms, then grouped the Price column into categories. Because there were so few observations with 5 bedrooms, I reran it, collapsing the 4 and 5 bedroom observations into a single category to get the results here. The chi-square test shows a p-value (see below) of essentially 0, meaning that there is a definite relationship. Low-priced houses tend to have fewer bedrooms, whereas high-priced ones tend to have more bedrooms.

Count	Nbed_Rms			
Price	2	3	>=4	Grand Total
<120	25	4	1	30
120-130	8	16	7	31
130-140	11	17	9	37
>140	2	23	27	52
Grand Total	46	60	44	150

Original Counts	2	3	>=4	Total
<120	25	4	1	30
120-130	8	16	7	31
130-140	11	17	9	37
>140	2	23	27	52
Total	46	60	44	150

Percentage of Rows	2	3	>=4	
<120	83.33%	13.33%	3.33%	100.00%
120-130	25.81%	51.61%	22.58%	100.00%
130-140	29.73%	45.95%	24.32%	100.00%
>140	3.85%	44.23%	51.92%	100.00%

Percentage of Columns	2	3	>=4
<120	54.35%	6.67%	2.27%
120-130	17.39%	26.67%	15.91%
130-140	23.91%	28.33%	20.45%
>140	4.35%	38.33%	61.36%
	100.00%	100.00%	100.00%

Expected Counts	2	3	>=4
<120	9.2000	12.0000	8.8000
120-130	9.5067	12.4000	9.0933
130-140	11.3467	14.8000	10.8533
>140	15.9467	20.8000	15.2533

Distance from Expected	2	3	>=4
<120	27.1348	5.3333	6.9136
120-130	0.2388	1.0452	0.4819
130-140	0.0106	0.3270	0.3165
>140	12.1975	0.2327	9.0462

Chi-Square Statistic	
Chi-Square	63.2781
p-Value	< 0.0001

Problem 10_53

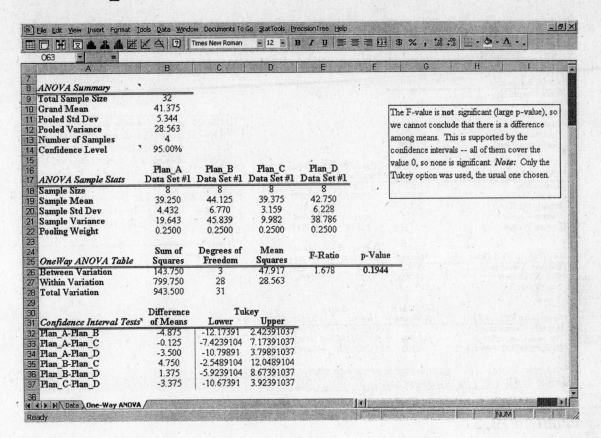

File Edit View Insert Format Tools Data Window Documents To Go StatTools PrecisionTree Help

Times New Roman 12 B I U

O63

	A	B	C	D	E	F	G	H	I
7									
8	*ANOVA Summary*								
9	Total Sample Size	32							
10	Grand Mean	41.375							
11	Pooled Std Dev	5.344							
12	Pooled Variance	28.563							
13	Number of Samples	4							
14	Confidence Level	95.00%							
15									
16		Plan_A	Plan_B	Plan_C	Plan_D				
17	*ANOVA Sample Stats*	Data Set #1	Data Set #1	Data Set #1	Data Set #1				
18	Sample Size	8	8	8	8				
19	Sample Mean	39.250	44.125	39.375	42.750				
20	Sample Std Dev	4.432	6.770	3.159	6.228				
21	Sample Variance	19.643	45.839	9.982	38.786				
22	Pooling Weight	0.2500	0.2500	0.2500	0.2500				
23									
24		Sum of	Degrees of	Mean					
25	*OneWay ANOVA Table*	Squares	Freedom	Squares	F-Ratio	p-Value			
26	Between Variation	143.750	3	47.917	1.678	0.1944			
27	Within Variation	799.750	28	28.563					
28	Total Variation	943.500	31						
29									
30		Difference		Tukey					
31	*Confidence Interval Tests*	of Means	Lower	Upper					
32	Plan_A-Plan_B	-4.875	-12.17391	2.42391037					
33	Plan_A-Plan_C	-0.125	-7.4239104	7.17391037					
34	Plan_A-Plan_D	-3.500	-10.79891	3.79891037					
35	Plan_B-Plan_C	4.750	-2.5489104	12.0489104					
36	Plan_B-Plan_D	1.375	-5.9239104	8.67391037					
37	Plan_C-Plan_D	-3.375	-10.67391	3.92391037					
38									

The F-value is **not** significant (large p-value), so we cannot conclude that there is a difference among means. This is supported by the confidence intervals -- all of them cover the value 0, so none is significant. *Note:* Only the Tukey option was used, the usual one chosen.

Data \ One-Way ANOVA

Ready

NUM

Problem 10_55

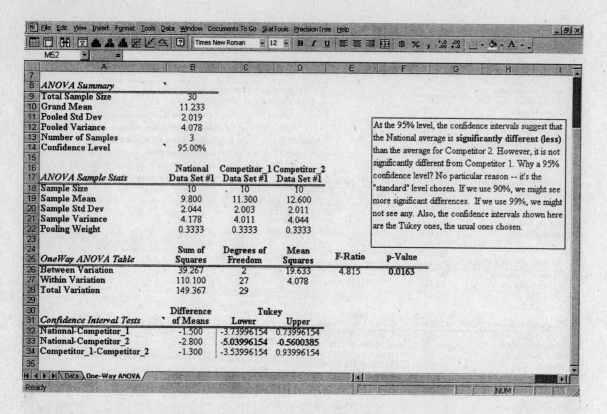

Spreadsheet content:

	A	B	C	D	E	F
8	*ANOVA Summary*					
9	Total Sample Size	30				
10	Grand Mean	11.233				
11	Pooled Std Dev	2.019				
12	Pooled Variance	4.078				
13	Number of Samples	3				
14	Confidence Level	95.00%				
15						
16		National	Competitor_1	Competitor_2		
17	*ANOVA Sample Stats*	Data Set #1	Data Set #1	Data Set #1		
18	Sample Size	10	10	10		
19	Sample Mean	9.800	11.300	12.600		
20	Sample Std Dev	2.044	2.003	2.011		
21	Sample Variance	4.178	4.011	4.044		
22	Pooling Weight	0.3333	0.3333	0.3333		
23						
24		Sum of	Degrees of	Mean		
25	*OneWay ANOVA Table*	Squares	Freedom	Squares	F-Ratio	p-Value
26	Between Variation	39.267	2	19.633	4.815	0.0163
27	Within Variation	110.100	27	4.078		
28	Total Variation	149.367	29			
29						
30		Difference	Tukey			
31	*Confidence Interval Tests*	of Means	Lower	Upper		
32	National-Competitor_1	-1.500	-3.73996154	0.73996154		
33	National-Competitor_2	-2.800	-5.03996154	-0.5600385		
34	Competitor_1-Competitor_2	-1.300	-3.53996154	0.93996154		

Text box:

At the 95% level, the confidence intervals suggest that the National average is **significantly different (less)** than the average for Competitor 2. However, it is not significantly different from Competitor 1. Why a 95% confidence level? No particular reason -- it's the "standard" level chosen. If we use 90%, we might see more significant differences. If we use 99%, we might not see any. Also, the confidence intervals shown here are the Tukey ones, the usual ones chosen.

Problem 10_57

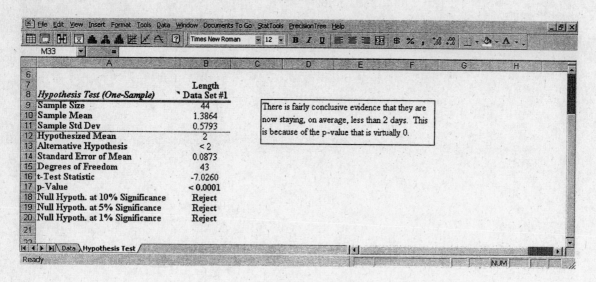

	A	B
7		Length
8	*Hypothesis Test (One-Sample)*	Data Set #1
9	Sample Size	44
10	Sample Mean	1.3864
11	Sample Std Dev	0.5793
12	Hypothesized Mean	2
13	Alternative Hypothesis	< 2
14	Standard Error of Mean	0.0873
15	Degrees of Freedom	43
16	t-Test Statistic	-7.0260
17	p-Value	< 0.0001
18	Null Hypoth. at 10% Significance	Reject
19	Null Hypoth. at 5% Significance	Reject
20	Null Hypoth. at 1% Significance	Reject

Text box:

There is fairly conclusive evidence that they are now staying, on average, less than 2 days. This is because of the p-value that is virtually 0.

Problem 10_59

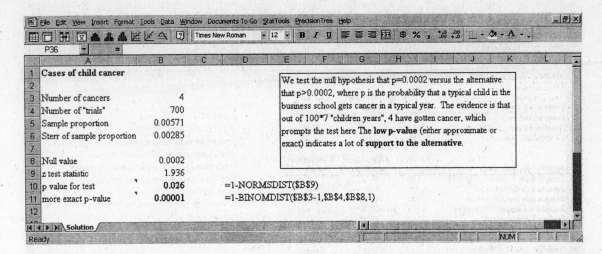

	A	B				
1	**Cases of child cancer**					
2						
3	Number of cancers	4				
4	Number of "trials"	700				
5	Sample proportion	0.00571				
6	Sterr of sample proportion	0.00285				
7						
8	Null value	0.0002				
9	z test statistic	1.936				
10	p value for test	**0.026**	=1-NORMSDIST($B$9)			
11	more exact p-value	**0.00001**	=1-BINOMDIST($B$3-1,$B$4,$B$8,1)			
12						

We test the null hypothesis that p=0.0002 versus the alternative that p>0.0002, where p is the probability that a typical child in the business school gets cancer in a typical year. The evidence is that out of 100*7 "children years", 4 have gotten cancer, which prompts the test here The **low p-value** (either approximate or exact) indicates a lot of **support to the alternative**.

Problem 10_61

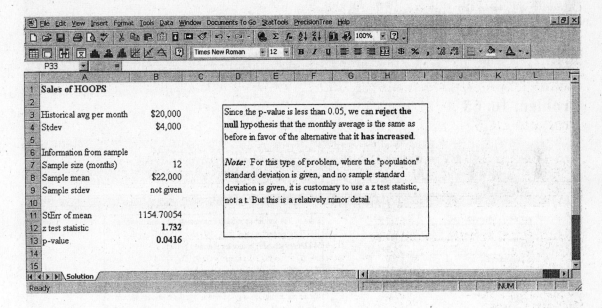

	A	B				
1	**Sales of HOOPS**					
2						
3	Historical avg per month	$20,000				
4	Stdev	$4,000				
5						
6	Information from sample					
7	Sample size (months)	12				
8	Sample mean	$22,000				
9	Sample stdev	not given				
10						
11	StErr of mean	1154.70054				
12	z test statistic	**1.732**				
13	p-value	**0.0416**				
14						
15						

Since the p-value is less than 0.05, we can **reject the null** hypothesis that the monthly average is the same as before in favor of the alternative that **it has increased**.

Note: For this type of problem, where the "population" standard deviation is given, and no sample standard deviation is given, it is customary to use a z test statistic, not a t. But this is a relatively minor detail.

Problem 10_63

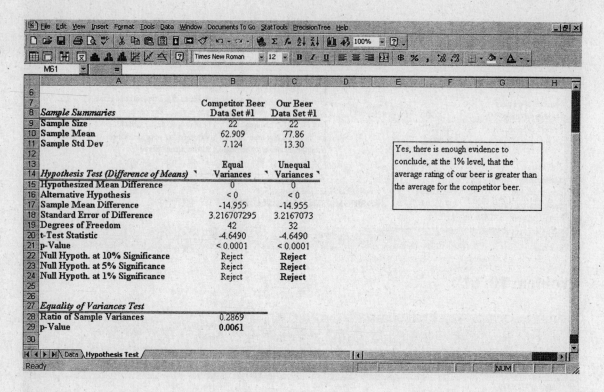

The spreadsheet for Problem 10_63 shows:

Sample Summaries

	Competitor Beer Data Set #1	Our Beer Data Set #1
Sample Size	22	22
Sample Mean	62.909	77.86
Sample Std Dev	7.124	13.30

Hypothesis Test (Difference of Means)

	Equal Variances	Unequal Variances
Hypothesized Mean Difference	0	0
Alternative Hypothesis	< 0	< 0
Sample Mean Difference	-14.955	-14.955
Standard Error of Difference	3.216707295	3.2167073
Degrees of Freedom	42	32
t-Test Statistic	-4.6490	-4.6490
p-Value	< 0.0001	< 0.0001
Null Hypoth. at 10% Significance	Reject	Reject
Null Hypoth. at 5% Significance	Reject	Reject
Null Hypoth. at 1% Significance	Reject	Reject

Equality of Variances Test

Ratio of Sample Variances	0.2869
p-Value	0.0061

Yes, there is enough evidence to conclude, at the 1% level, that the average rating of our beer is greater than the average for the competitor beer.

Problem 10_65

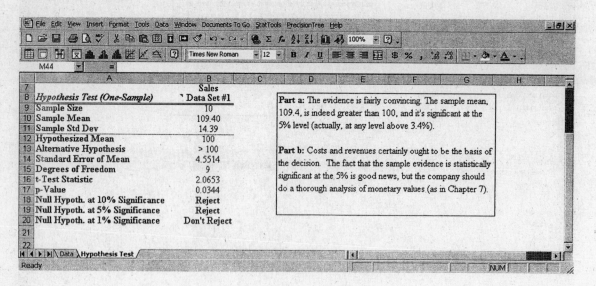

The spreadsheet for Problem 10_65 shows:

Hypothesis Test (One-Sample)

	Sales Data Set #1
Sample Size	10
Sample Mean	109.40
Sample Std Dev	14.39
Hypothesized Mean	100
Alternative Hypothesis	> 100
Standard Error of Mean	4.5514
Degrees of Freedom	9
t-Test Statistic	2.0653
p-Value	0.0344
Null Hypoth. at 10% Significance	Reject
Null Hypoth. at 5% Significance	Reject
Null Hypoth. at 1% Significance	Don't Reject

Part a: The evidence is fairly convincing. The sample mean, 109.4, is indeed greater than 100, and it's significant at the 5% level (actually, at any level above 3.4%).

Part b: Costs and revenues certainly ought to be the basis of the decision. The fact that the sample evidence is statistically significant at the 5% is good news, but the company should do a thorough analysis of monetary values (as in Chapter 7).

Problem 10_67

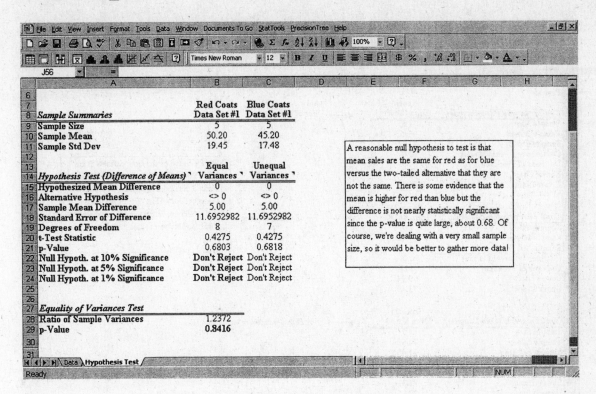

Problem 10_69

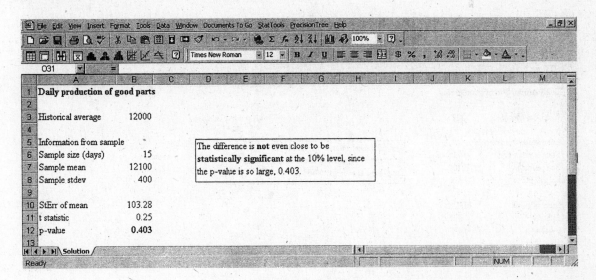

Problem 10_81

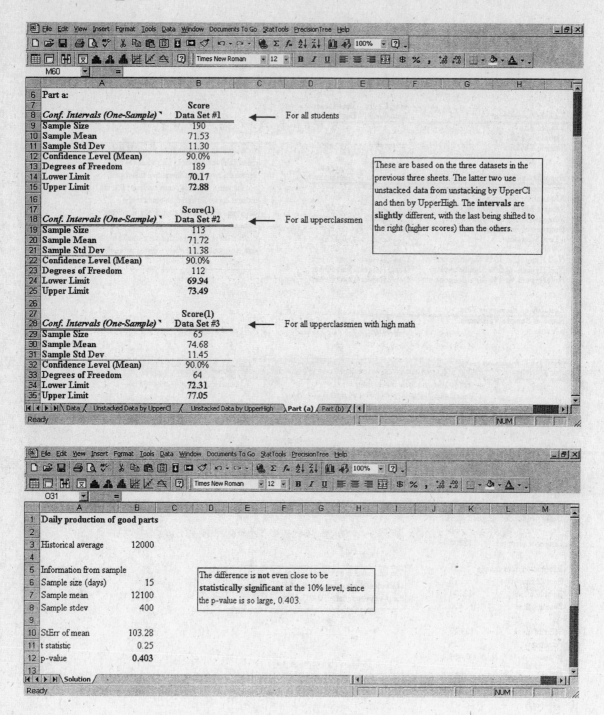

File Edit View Insert Format Tools Data Window Documents To Go StatTools PrecisionTree Help

Times New Roman ▾ 12 ▾

M60

	A	B
6	**Part a:**	
7		**Score**
8	*Conf. Intervals (One-Sample)* `	**Data Set #1** ← For all students
9	Sample Size	190
10	Sample Mean	71.53
11	Sample Std Dev	11.30
12	Confidence Level (Mean)	90.0%
13	Degrees of Freedom	189
14	Lower Limit	**70.17**
15	Upper Limit	**72.88**
16		
17		**Score(1)**
18	*Conf. Intervals (One-Sample)* `	**Data Set #2** ← For all upperclassmen
19	Sample Size	113
20	Sample Mean	71.72
21	Sample Std Dev	11.38
22	Confidence Level (Mean)	90.0%
23	Degrees of Freedom	112
24	Lower Limit	**69.94**
25	Upper Limit	**73.49**
26		
27		**Score(1)**
28	*Conf. Intervals (One-Sample)* `	**Data Set #3** ← For all upperclassmen with high math
29	Sample Size	65
30	Sample Mean	74.68
31	Sample Std Dev	11.45
32	Confidence Level (Mean)	90.0%
33	Degrees of Freedom	64
34	Lower Limit	**72.31**
35	Upper Limit	**77.05**

> These are based on the three datasets in the previous three sheets. The latter two use unstacked data from unstacking by UpperCl and then by UpperHigh. The **intervals** are **slightly** different, with the last being shifted to the right (higher scores) than the others.

Data ⟍ Unstacked Data by UpperCl ⟍ Unstacked Data by UpperHigh ⟍ **Part (a)** ⟍ Part (b) ⟍

Ready NUM

File Edit View Insert Format Tools Data Window Documents To Go StatTools PrecisionTree Help

Times New Roman ▾ 12 ▾

O31

	A	B
1	**Daily production of good parts**	
2		
3	Historical average	12000
4		
5	Information from sample	
6	Sample size (days)	15
7	Sample mean	12100
8	Sample stdev	400
9		
10	StErr of mean	103.28
11	t statistic	0.25
12	p-value	**0.403**
13		

> The difference is **not** even close to be **statistically significant** at the 10% level, since the p-value is so large, 0.403.

Solution

Ready NUM

CHAPTER 11

Problem 11_5

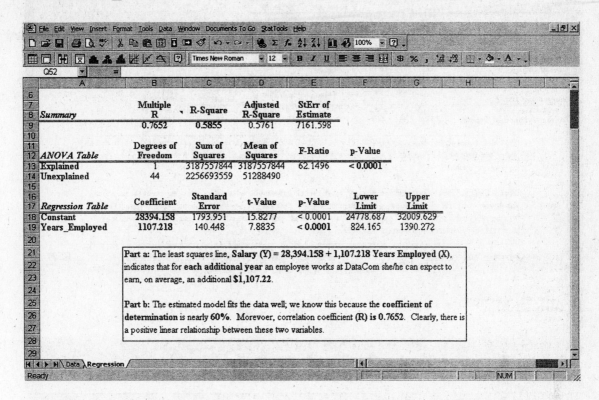

The spreadsheet contains the following:

Summary	Multiple R	R-Square	Adjusted R-Square	StErr of Estimate		
	0.7652	0.5855	0.5761	7161.598		

ANOVA Table	Degrees of Freedom	Sum of Squares	Mean of Squares	F-Ratio	p-Value	
Explained	1	3187557844	3187557844	62.1496	< 0.0001	
Unexplained	44	2256693559	51288490			

Regression Table	Coefficient	Standard Error	t-Value	p-Value	Lower Limit	Upper Limit
Constant	28394.158	1793.951	15.8277	< 0.0001	24778.687	32009.629
Years_Employed	1107.218	140.448	7.8835	< 0.0001	824.165	1390.272

Part a: The least squares line, **Salary (Y) = 28,394.158 + 1,107.218 Years Employed (X)**, indicates that for **each additional year** an employee works at DataCom she/he can expect to earn, on average, an additional **$1,107.22**.

Part b: The estimated model fits the data well; we know this because the **coefficient of determination** is nearly **60%**. Morevoer, correlation coefficient (R) is 0.7652. Clearly, there is a positive linear relationship between these two variables.

Problem 11_7

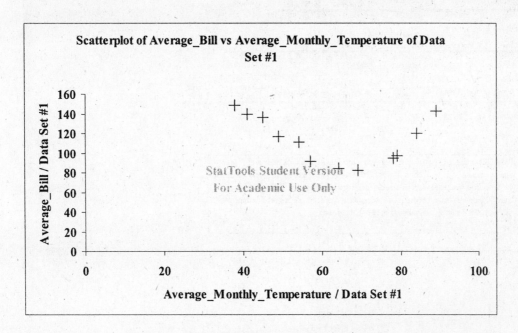

Scatterplot of Average_Bill vs Average_Monthly_Temperature of Data Set #1

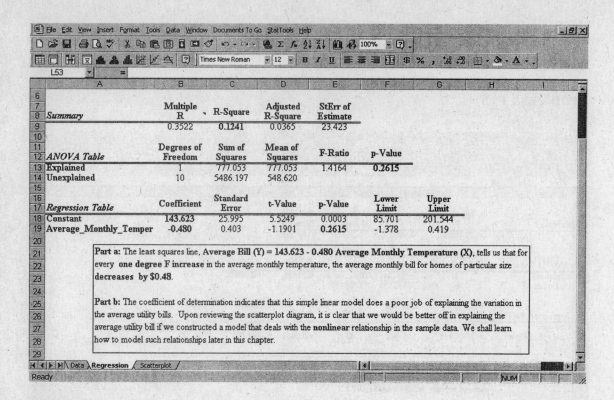

L53

	A	B	C	D	E	F	G	H	I
7		Multiple R	R-Square	Adjusted R-Square	StErr of Estimate				
8	*Summary*								
9		0.3522	0.1241	0.0365	23.423				
10									
11		Degrees of Freedom	Sum of Squares	Mean of Squares	F-Ratio	p-Value			
12	*ANOVA Table*								
13	Explained	1	777.053	777.053	1.4164	0.2615			
14	Unexplained	10	5486.197	548.620					
15									
16		Coefficient	Standard Error	t-Value	p-Value	Lower Limit	Upper Limit		
17	*Regression Table*								
18	Constant	143.623	25.995	5.5249	0.0003	85.701	201.544		
19	Average_Monthly_Temper	-0.480	0.403	-1.1901	0.2615	-1.378	0.419		

Part a: The least squares line, Average Bill (Y) = 143.623 - 0.480 Average Monthly Temperature (X), tells us that for every **one degree F increase** in the average monthly temperature, the average monthly bill for homes of particular size **decreases by $0.48.**

Part b: The coefficient of determination indicates that this simple linear model does a poor job of explaining the variation in the average utility bills. Upon reviewing the scatterplot diagram, it is clear that we would be better off in explaining the average utility bill if we constructed a model that deals with the **nonlinear** relationship in the sample data. We shall learn how to model such relationships later in this chapter.

Data / **Regression** / Scatterplot /

Ready   NUM

Problem 11_9

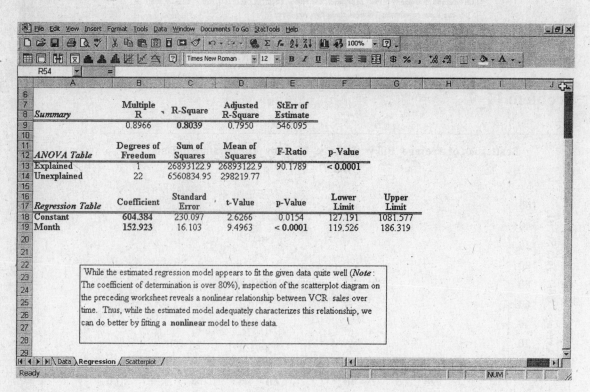

R54

	A	B	C	D	E	F	G	H	I
7		Multiple R	R-Square	Adjusted R-Square	StErr of Estimate				
8	*Summary*								
9		0.8966	0.8039	0.7950	546.095				
10									
11		Degrees of Freedom	Sum of Squares	Mean of Squares	F-Ratio	p-Value			
12	*ANOVA Table*								
13	Explained	1	26893122.9	26893122.9	90.1789	< 0.0001			
14	Unexplained	22	6560834.95	298219.77					
15									
16		Coefficient	Standard Error	t-Value	p-Value	Lower Limit	Upper Limit		
17	*Regression Table*								
18	Constant	604.384	230.097	2.6266	0.0154	127.191	1081.577		
19	Month	152.923	16.103	9.4963	< 0.0001	119.526	186.319		

While the estimated regression model appears to fit the given data quite well (*Note*: The coefficient of determination is over 80%), inspection of the scatterplot diagram on the preceding worksheet reveals a nonlinear relationship between VCR sales over time. Thus, while the estimated model adequately characterizes this relationship, we can do better by fitting a **nonlinear** model to these data.

Data / **Regression** / Scatterplot /

Ready   NUM

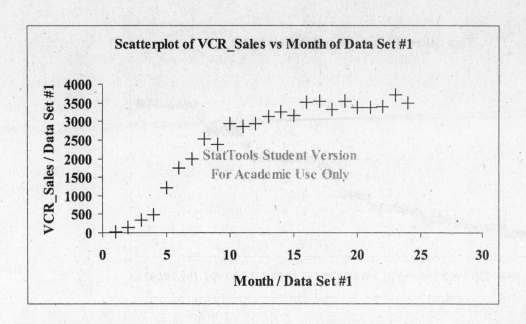

Scatterplot of VCR_Sales vs Month of Data Set #1

Problem 11_11

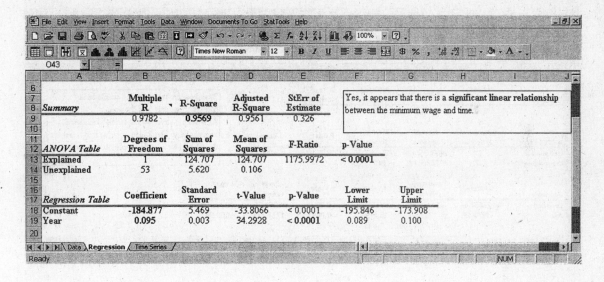

	Multiple R	R-Square	Adjusted R-Square	StErr of Estimate		
Summary	0.9782	**0.9569**	0.9561	0.326		
ANOVA Table	Degrees of Freedom	Sum of Squares	Mean of Squares	F-Ratio	p-Value	
Explained	1	124.707	124.707	1175.9972	**< 0.0001**	
Unexplained	53	5.620	0.106			
Regression Table	Coefficient	Standard Error	t-Value	p-Value	Lower Limit	Upper Limit
Constant	**-184.877**	5.469	-33.8066	**< 0.0001**	-195.846	-173.908
Year	**0.095**	0.003	34.2928	**< 0.0001**	0.089	0.100

Yes, it appears that there is a **significant linear relationship** between the minimum wage and time.

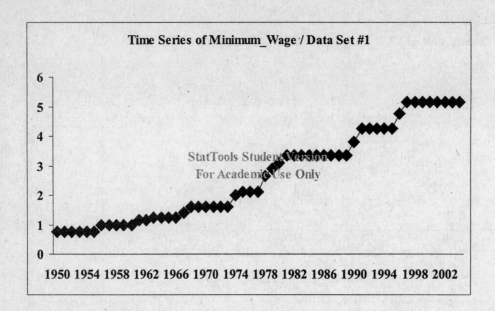

Time Series of Minimum_Wage / Data Set #1

StatTools Student Version
For Academic Use Only

Problem 11_15

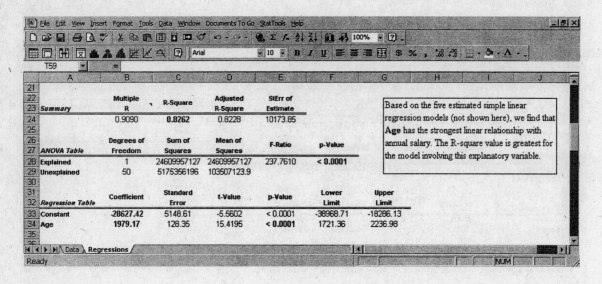

	Multiple R	R-Square	Adjusted R-Square	StErr of Estimate		
Summary						
	0.9090	**0.8262**	0.8228	10173.85		
	Degrees of Freedom	Sum of Squares	Mean of Squares	F-Ratio	p-Value	
ANOVA Table						
Explained	1	24609957127	24609957127	237.7610	**< 0.0001**	
Unexplained	50	5175356196	103507123.9			
	Coefficient	Standard Error	t-Value	p-Value	Lower Limit	Upper Limit
Regression Table						
Constant	-28627.42	5148.61	-5.5602	< 0.0001	-38968.71	-18286.13
Age	1979.17	128.35	15.4195	**< 0.0001**	1721.36	2236.98

Based on the five estimated simple linear regression models (not shown here), we find that **Age** has the strongest linear relationship with annual salary. The R-square value is greatest for the model involving this explanatory variable.

Problem 11_17

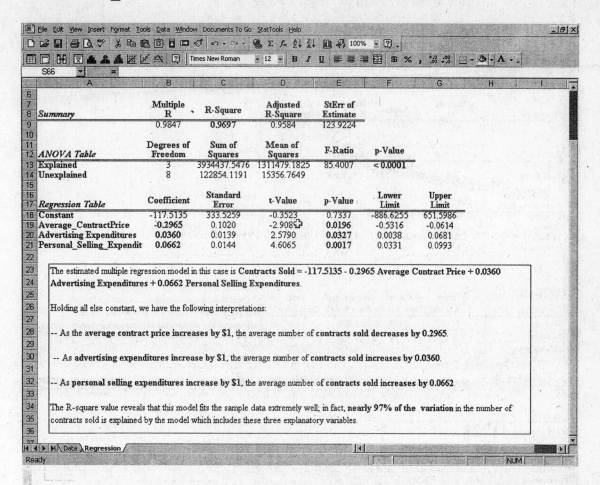

Summary	Multiple R	R-Square	Adjusted R-Square	StErr of Estimate		
	0.9847	0.9697	0.9584	123.9224		

ANOVA Table	Degrees of Freedom	Sum of Squares	Mean of Squares	F-Ratio	p-Value	
Explained	3	3934437.5476	1311479.1825	85.4007	< 0.0001	
Unexplained	8	122854.1191	15356.7649			

Regression Table	Coefficient	Standard Error	t-Value	p-Value	Lower Limit	Upper Limit
Constant	-117.5135	333.5259	-0.3523	0.7337	-886.6255	651.5986
Average_ContractPrice	-0.2965	0.1020	-2.908	0.0196	-0.5316	-0.0614
Advertising Expenditures	0.0360	0.0139	2.5790	0.0327	0.0038	0.0681
Personal_Selling_Expendit	0.0662	0.0144	4.6065	0.0017	0.0331	0.0993

The estimated multiple regression model in this case is **Contracts Sold = -117.5135 - 0.2965 Average Contract Price + 0.0360 Advertising Expenditures + 0.0662 Personal Selling Expenditures.**

Holding all else constant, we have the following interpretations:

-- As the **average contract price increases by $1,** the average number of **contracts sold decreases by 0.2965.**

-- As **advertising expenditures increase by $1,** the average number of **contracts sold increases by 0.0360.**

-- As **personal selling expenditures increase by $1,** the average number of **contracts sold increases by 0.0662.**

The R-square value reveals that this model fits the sample data extremely well; in fact, **nearly 97% of the variation** in the number of contracts sold is explained by the model which includes these three explanatory variables.

Problem 11_21

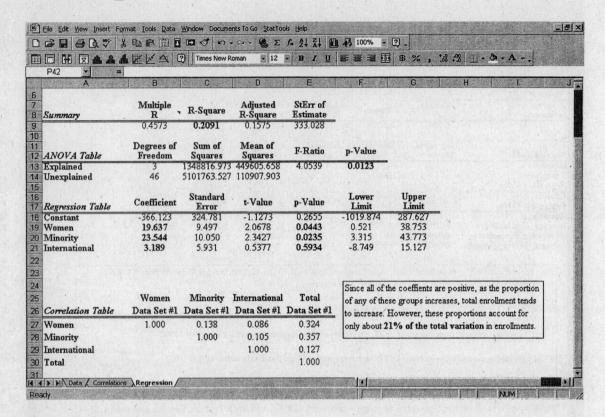

File Edit View Insert Format Tools Data Window Documents To Go StatTools Help

P42

	A	B	C	D	E	F	G	H	I	J

	Multiple R	R-Square	Adjusted R-Square	StErr of Estimate
Summary				
	0.4573	0.2091	0.1575	333.028

ANOVA Table	Degrees of Freedom	Sum of Squares	Mean of Squares	F-Ratio	p-Value
Explained	3	1348816.973	449605.658	4.0539	0.0123
Unexplained	46	5101763.527	110907.903		

Regression Table	Coefficient	Standard Error	t-Value	p-Value	Lower Limit	Upper Limit
Constant	-366.123	324.781	-1.1273	0.2655	-1019.874	287.627
Women	19.637	9.497	2.0678	0.0443	0.521	38.753
Minority	23.544	10.050	2.3427	0.0235	3.315	43.773
International	3.189	5.931	0.5377	0.5934	-8.749	15.127

Correlation Table	Women Data Set #1	Minority Data Set #1	International Data Set #1	Total Data Set #1
Women	1.000	0.138	0.086	0.324
Minority		1.000	0.105	0.357
International			1.000	0.127
Total				1.000

> Since all of the coeffients are positive, as the proportion of any of these groups increases, total enrollment tends to increase. However, these proportions account for only about **21% of the total variation** in enrollments.

Data / Correlations / **Regression**

Ready — NUM

Problem 11_23

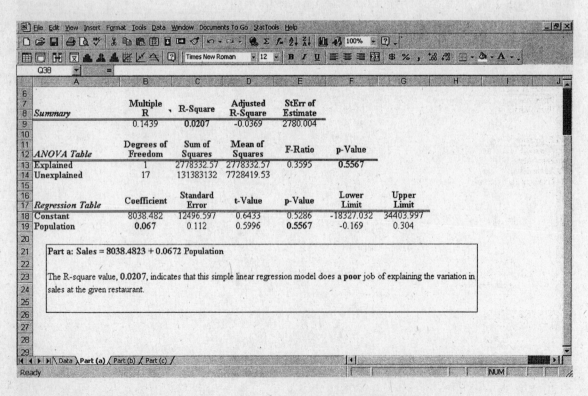

File Edit View Insert Format Tools Data Window Documents To Go StatTools Help

Q38

	A	B	C	D	E	F	G	H	I	J

	Multiple R	R-Square	Adjusted R-Square	StErr of Estimate
Summary				
	0.1439	0.0207	-0.0369	2780.004

ANOVA Table	Degrees of Freedom	Sum of Squares	Mean of Squares	F-Ratio	p-Value
Explained	1	2778332.57	2778332.57	0.3595	0.5567
Unexplained	17	131383132	7728419.53		

Regression Table	Coefficient	Standard Error	t-Value	p-Value	Lower Limit	Upper Limit
Constant	8038.482	12496.597	0.6433	0.5286	-18327.032	34403.997
Population	0.067	0.112	0.5996	0.5567	-0.169	0.304

> Part a: Sales = 8038.4823 + 0.0672 Population
>
> The R-square value, 0.0207, indicates that this simple linear regression model does a **poor** job of explaining the variation in sales at the given restaurant.

Data / **Part (a)** / Part (b) / Part (c)

Ready — NUM

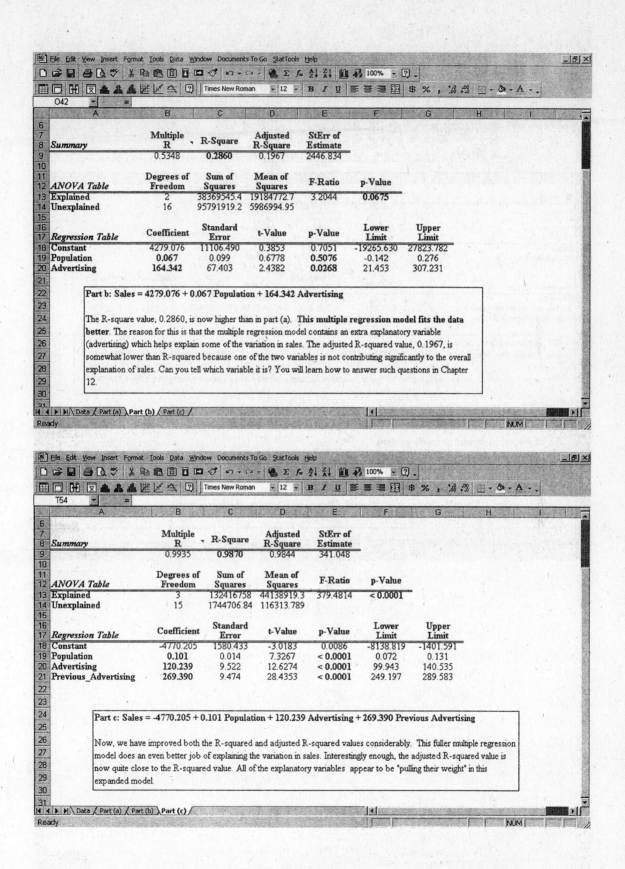

Part b: Sales = 4279.076 + 0.067 Population + 164.342 Advertising

The R-square value, 0.2860, is now higher than in part (a). **This multiple regression model fits the data better.** The reason for this is that the multiple regression model contains an extra explanatory variable (advertising) which helps explain some of the variation in sales. The adjusted R-squared value, 0.1967, is somewhat lower than R-squared because one of the two variables is not contributing significantly to the overall explanation of sales. Can you tell which variable it is? You will learn how to answer such questions in Chapter 12.

Part c: Sales = -4770.205 + 0.101 Population + 120.239 Advertising + 269.390 Previous Advertising

Now, we have improved both the R-squared and adjusted R-squared values considerably. This fuller multiple regression model does an even better job of explaining the variation in sales. Interestingly enough, the adjusted R-squared value is now quite close to the R-squared value. All of the explanatory variables appear to be "pulling their weight" in this expanded model.

Problem 11_31

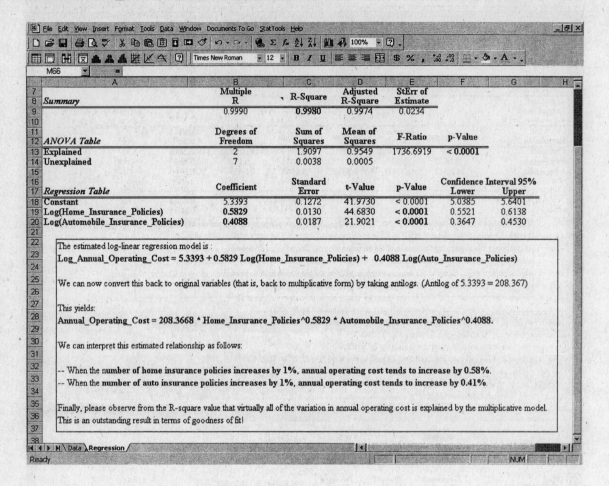

	A	B	C	D	E	F	G	H
7		Multiple R	R-Square	Adjusted R-Square	StErr of Estimate			
8	*Summary*							
9		0.9990	0.9980	0.9974	0.0234			
10								
11		Degrees of Freedom	Sum of Squares	Mean of Squares	F-Ratio	p-Value		
12	*ANOVA Table*							
13	Explained	2	1.9097	0.9549	1736.6919	< 0.0001		
14	Unexplained	7	0.0038	0.0005				
15								
16		Coefficient	Standard Error	t-Value	p-Value	Confidence Interval 95%		
17	*Regression Table*					Lower	Upper	
18	Constant	5.3393	0.1272	41.9730	< 0.0001	5.0385	5.6401	
19	Log(Home_Insurance_Policies)	0.5829	0.0130	44.6830	< 0.0001	0.5521	0.6138	
20	Log(Automobile_Insurance_Policies)	0.4088	0.0187	21.9021	< 0.0001	0.3647	0.4530	

The estimated log-linear regression model is :

Log_Annual_Operating_Cost = 5.3393 + 0.5829 Log(Home_Insurance_Policies) + 0.4088 Log(Auto_Insurance_Policies)

We can now convert this back to original variables (that is, back to multiplicative form) by taking antilogs. (Antilog of 5.3393 = 208.367)

This yields:

Annual_Operating_Cost = 208.3668 * Home_Insurance_Policies^0.5829 * Automobile_Insurance_Policies^0.4088.

We can interpret this estimated relationship as follows:

-- When the number of **home insurance policies increases by 1%**, annual operating cost tends to increase by **0.58%**.
-- When the number of **auto insurance policies increases by 1%**, annual operating cost tends to increase by **0.41%**.

Finally, please observe from the R-square value that virtually all of the variation in annual operating cost is explained by the multiplicative model. This is an outstanding result in terms of goodness of fit!

Problem 11_35

	B Multiple R	C R-Square	D Adjusted R-Square	E StErr of Estimate	F	G
Summary						
	0.8246	0.6799	0.4830	981.90		
ANOVA Table	Degrees of Freedom	Sum of Squares	Mean of Squares	F-Ratio	p-Value	
Explained	8	26627914.3	3328489.29	3.4523	0.0233	
Unexplained	13	12533747.2	964134.398			
Regression Table	Coefficient	Standard Error	t-Value	p-Value	Confidence Interval 95% Lower	Upper
Constant	2129.61	1551.59	1.3725	0.1931	-1222.40	5481.62
Speed	-59.22	44.62	-1.3272	0.2073	-155.63	37.18
Charge	6.78	5.83	1.1623	0.2660	-5.82	19.38
RAM	-17.32	34.47	-0.5025	0.6237	-91.79	57.14
Chip_Type_DX	2826.13	1525.52	1.8526	0.0868	-469.56	6121.82
Chip_Type_SL	213.35	749.45	0.2847	0.7804	-1405.74	1832.44
Monitor_Type_COLOR	1993.31	714.14	2.7912	0.0153	450.51	3536.11
Pointing_Device_MOUSE	387.35	697.24	0.5555	0.5880	-1118.94	1893.64
Help_Line_NO	434.91	809.98	0.5369	0.6004	-1314.94	2184.76

Part a: Upon creating dummy variables for each of the original categorical variables in the given data set, we formulated the above multiple regression model and estimated it using the available data.

Note: One dummy variable associated with each of the original categorical variables was ommitted.

Part b: We now interpret each of the estimated model coefficients (assuming all else remains constant):

As the speed of the laptop increases by **one megahertz, the price decreases by $59.22.**

As the time the battery maintains its charge **increases by one minute, price increases by $6.78.**

As the size of RAM increases by **one megabyte, the price decreases by $17.32.**

If the **chip type is DX,** the price increases by **$2,826.13.** If the **chip type is SL,** the price increases by **$213.35.**

If the monitor type is **color, the price increases by $1,993.31.**

If the pointing device is a **mouse, the price increases by $387.35.**

If the manufacturer **does not provide a toll-free help line, the price increases by $434.91.**

Part c: Yes, the estimated regression model fits the given data reasonably well. The R-square value indicates that nearly 68% of the variation in the sales price is explained by this model.

Part d:

Speed	60
Charge	240
RAM	32
Chip_Type_DX	1
Chip_Type_SL	0
Monitor_Type_COLOR	1
Pointing_Device_MOUSE	1
Help_Line_NO	0
Predicted price	$4,856

Problem 11_37

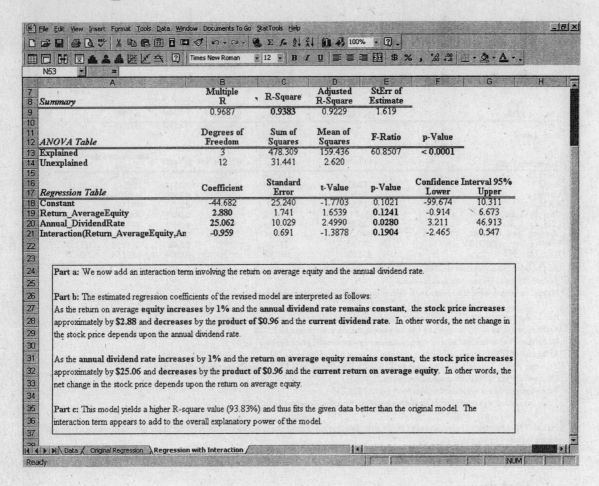

File Edit View Insert Format Tools Data Window Documents To Go StatTools Help

Times New Roman ▾ 12 ▾ **B** *I* U

N53

	A	B	C	D	E	F	G	H
7		**Multiple R**	**R-Square**	**Adjusted R-Square**	**StErr of Estimate**			
8	*Summary*							
9		0.9687	**0.9383**	0.9229	1.619			
10								
11		**Degrees of Freedom**	**Sum of Squares**	**Mean of Squares**	**F-Ratio**	**p-Value**		
12	*ANOVA Table*							
13	Explained	3	478.309	159.436	60.8507	< 0.0001		
14	Unexplained	12	31.441	2.620				
15								
16		**Coefficient**	**Standard Error**	**t-Value**	**p-Value**	**Confidence Interval 95%**		
17	*Regression Table*						**Lower**	**Upper**
18	Constant	-44.682	25.240	-1.7703	0.1021		-99.674	10.311
19	Return_AverageEquity	2.880	1.741	1.6539	**0.1241**		-0.914	6.673
20	Annual_DividendRate	25.062	10.029	2.4990	**0.0280**		3.211	46.913
21	Interaction(Return_AverageEquity,Ar	-0.959	0.691	-1.3878	**0.1904**		-2.465	0.547

Part a: We now add an interaction term involving the return on average equity and the annual dividend rate.

Part b: The estimated regression coefficients of the revised model are interpreted as follows:
As the return on average **equity increases** by **1%** and the **annual dividend rate remains constant**, the **stock price increases** approximately by **$2.88** and **decreases** by the **product of $0.96** and the **current dividend rate**. In other words, the net change in the stock price depends upon the annual dividend rate.

As the **annual dividend rate increases** by **1%** and the **return on average equity remains constant**, the **stock price increases** approximately by **$25.06** and **decreases** by the **product of $0.96** and the **current return on average equity**. In other words, the net change in the stock price depends upon the return on average equity.

Part c: This model yields a higher R-square value (93.83%) and thus fits the given data better than the original model. The interaction term appears to add to the overall explanatory power of the model.

Data / Original Regression / **Regression with Interaction** /

Ready   NUM

Problem 11_39

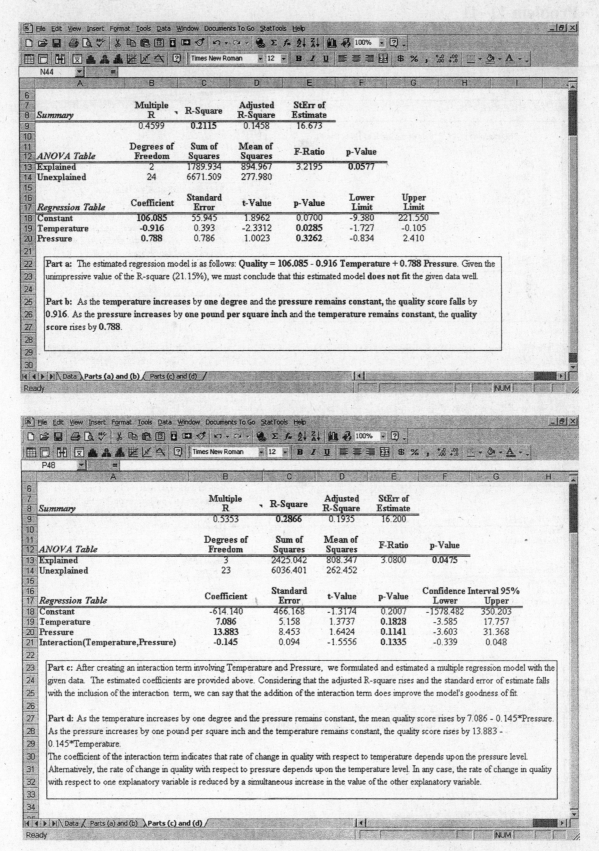

Times New Roman   12   B I U $ % ,

N44

	A	B	C	D	E	F	G	H	I
7	*Summary*	Multiple R	R-Square	Adjusted R-Square	StErr of Estimate				
9		0.4599	0.2115	0.1458	16.673				
11	*ANOVA Table*	Degrees of Freedom	Sum of Squares	Mean of Squares	F-Ratio	p-Value			
13	Explained	2	1789.934	894.967	3.2195	0.0577			
14	Unexplained	24	6671.509	277.980					
17	*Regression Table*	Coefficient	Standard Error	t-Value	p-Value	Lower Limit	Upper Limit		
18	Constant	106.085	55.945	1.8962	0.0700	-9.380	221.550		
19	Temperature	-0.916	0.393	-2.3312	0.0285	-1.727	-0.105		
20	Pressure	0.788	0.786	1.0023	0.3262	-0.834	2.410		

Part a: The estimated regression model is as follows: **Quality = 106.085 - 0.916 Temperature + 0.788 Pressure**. Given the unimpressive value of the R-square (21.15%), we must conclude that this estimated model **does not fit** the given data well.

Part b: As the **temperature increases** by **one degree** and the **pressure remains constant**, the **quality score falls by 0.916**. As the **pressure increases** by **one pound per square inch** and the **temperature remains constant**, the **quality score rises by 0.788**.

Data \ **Parts (a) and (b)** \ Parts (c) and (d)

Ready   NUM

Times New Roman   12   B I U $ % ,

P48

	A	B	C	D	E	F	G	H
7	*Summary*	Multiple R	R-Square	Adjusted R-Square	StErr of Estimate			
9		0.5353	0.2866	0.1935	16.200			
11	*ANOVA Table*	Degrees of Freedom	Sum of Squares	Mean of Squares	F-Ratio	p-Value		
13	Explained	3	2425.042	808.347	3.0800	0.0475		
14	Unexplained	23	6036.401	262.452				
17	*Regression Table*	Coefficient	Standard Error	t-Value	p-Value	Confidence Interval 95% Lower	Upper	
18	Constant	-614.140	466.168	-1.3174	0.2007	-1578.482	350.203	
19	Temperature	7.086	5.158	1.3737	0.1828	-3.585	17.757	
20	Pressure	13.883	8.453	1.6424	0.1141	-3.603	31.368	
21	Interaction(Temperature,Pressure)	-0.145	0.094	-1.5556	0.1335	-0.339	0.048	

Part c: After creating an interaction term involving Temperature and Pressure, we formulated and estimated a multiple regression model with the given data. The estimated coefficients are provided above. Considering that the adjusted R-square rises and the standard error of estimate falls with the inclusion of the interaction term, we can say that the addition of the interaction term does improve the model's goodness of fit.

Part d: As the temperature increases by one degree and the pressure remains constant, the mean quality score rises by 7.086 - 0.145*Pressure. As the pressure increases by one pound per square inch and the temperature remains constant, the quality score rises by 13.883 - 0.145*Temperature.

The coefficient of the interaction term indicates that rate of change in quality with respect to temperature depends upon the pressure level. Alternatively, the rate of change in quality with respect to pressure depends upon the temperature level. In any case, the rate of change in quality with respect to one explanatory variable is reduced by a simultaneous increase in the value of the other explanatory variable.

Data \ Parts (a) and (b) \ **Parts (c) and (d)**

Ready   NUM

Problem 11_41

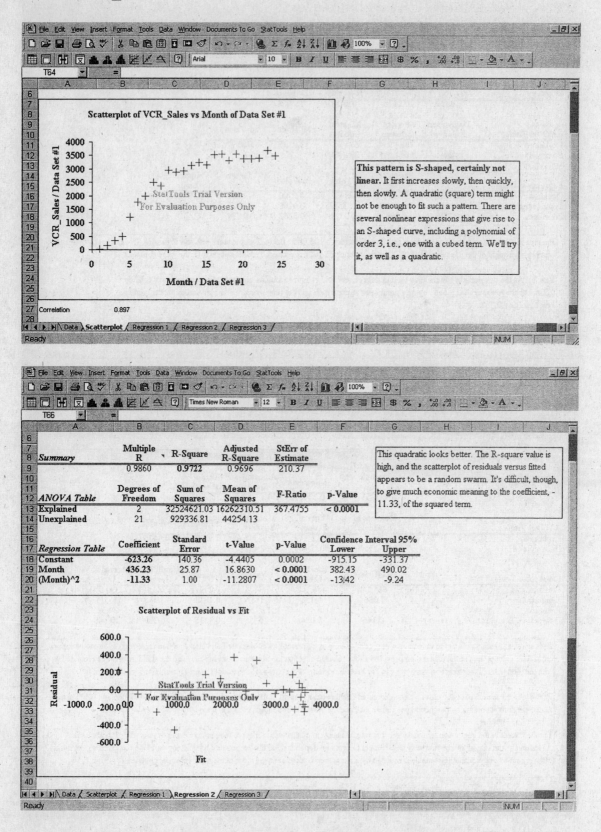

Problem 11_43

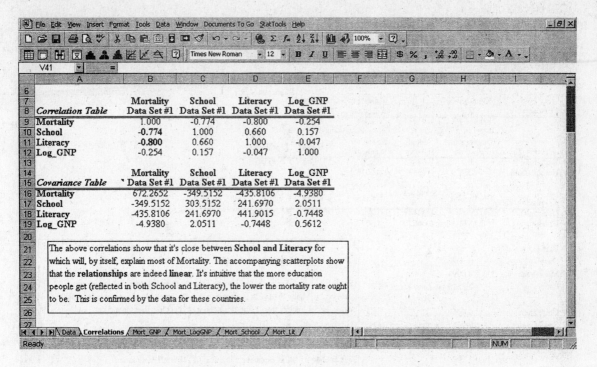

Correlation Table	Mortality Data Set #1	School Data Set #1	Literacy Data Set #1	Log_GNP Data Set #1
Mortality	1.000	-0.774	-0.800	-0.254
School	-0.774	1.000	0.660	0.157
Literacy	-0.800	0.660	1.000	-0.047
Log_GNP	-0.254	0.157	-0.047	1.000

Covariance Table	Mortality Data Set #1	School Data Set #1	Literacy Data Set #1	Log_GNP Data Set #1
Mortality	672.2652	-349.5152	-435.8106	-4.9380
School	-349.5152	303.5152	241.6970	2.0511
Literacy	-435.8106	241.6970	441.9015	-0.7448
Log_GNP	-4.9380	2.0511	-0.7448	0.5612

The above correlations show that it's close between **School and Literacy** for which will, by itself, explain most of Mortality. The accompanying scatterplots show that the **relationships** are indeed **linear**. It's intuitive that the more education people get (reflected in both School and Literacy), the lower the mortality rate ought to be. This is confirmed by the data for these countries.

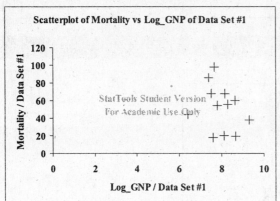

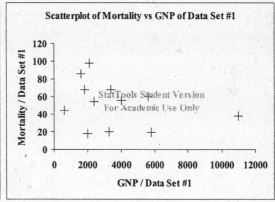

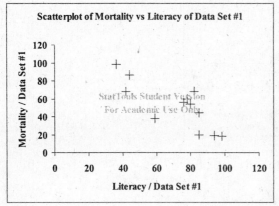

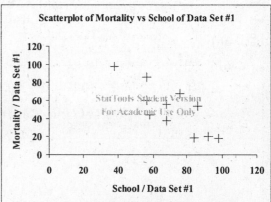

Problem 11_45

	A	B	C	D	E	F	G

Summary	Multiple R	R-Square	Adjusted R-Square	StErr of Estimate		
	0.4667	0.2178	0.2084	0.0406		

ANOVA Table	Degrees of Freedom	Sum of Squares	Mean of Squares	F-Ratio	p-Value	
Explained	1	0.0381	0.0381	23.1144	< 0.0001	
Unexplained	83	0.1367	0.0016			

Regression Tab	Coefficient	Standard Error	t-Value	p-Value	Lower Limit	Upper Limit
Constant	0.0099	0.0044	2.2374	0.0279	0.0011	0.0186
Market	0.2224	0.0463	4.8077	< 0.0001	0.1304	0.3144

Part e:

Covariance	0.0020	
Market variance	0.0091	
Ratio	0.2224	the same as cell C19
Correlation	0.4667	
Sqrt of R-square	0.4667	the same as cell B9

Part a: We would expect most stocks to be *positively* correlated with the market. This is true of Ford (see scatterplot), although the relationship isn't strong.

Part b: The beta is the expected change in the stock return when the market return increases by 1 unit. So if beta is greater than 1, the stock tends to react more than the market, and if it is less than 1, the stock tends to react less than the market.

Part c: The beta for Ford is 0.2224.

Part d: Only 21.8% is explained; the other 78.2% is left unexplained.

Data / Regression / Scatterplot

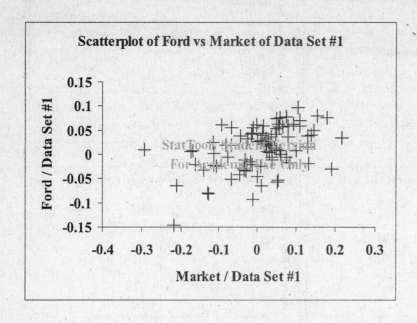

Scatterplot of Ford vs Market of Data Set #1

Problem 11_49

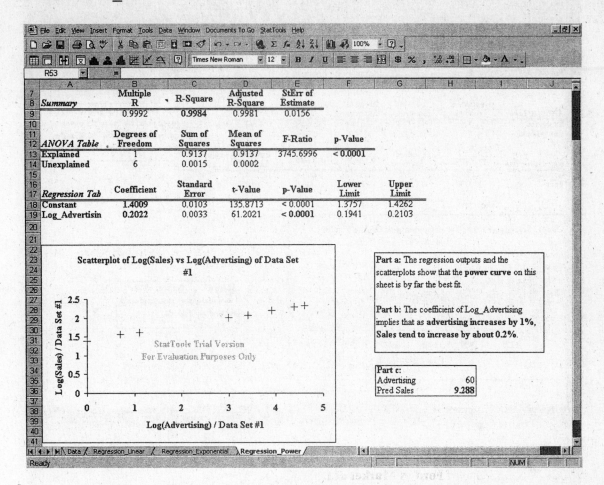

Summary	Multiple R	R-Square	Adjusted R-Square	StErr of Estimate		
	0.9992	0.9984	0.9981	0.0156		

ANOVA Table	Degrees of Freedom	Sum of Squares	Mean of Squares	F-Ratio	p-Value	
Explained	1	0.9137	0.9137	3745.6996	< 0.0001	
Unexplained	6	0.0015	0.0002			

Regression Tab	Coefficient	Standard Error	t-Value	p-Value	Lower Limit	Upper Limit
Constant	1.4009	0.0103	135.8713	< 0.0001	1.3757	1.4262
Log_Advertisin	0.2022	0.0033	61.2021	< 0.0001	0.1941	0.2103

Scatterplot of Log(Sales) vs Log(Advertising) of Data Set #1

Part a: The regression outputs and the scatterplots show that the **power curve** on this sheet is by far the best fit.

Part b: The coefficient of Log_Advertising implies that as **advertising increases by 1%, Sales tend to increase by about 0.2%.**

Part c:	
Advertising	60
Pred Sales	**9.288**

Problem 11_53

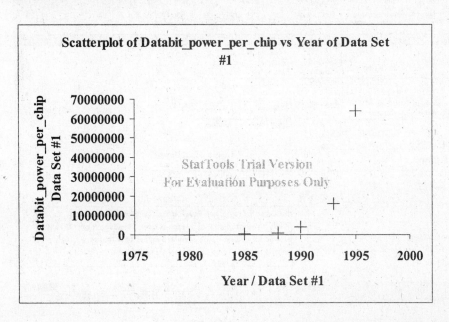

Scatterplot of Databit_power_per_chip vs Year of Data Set #1

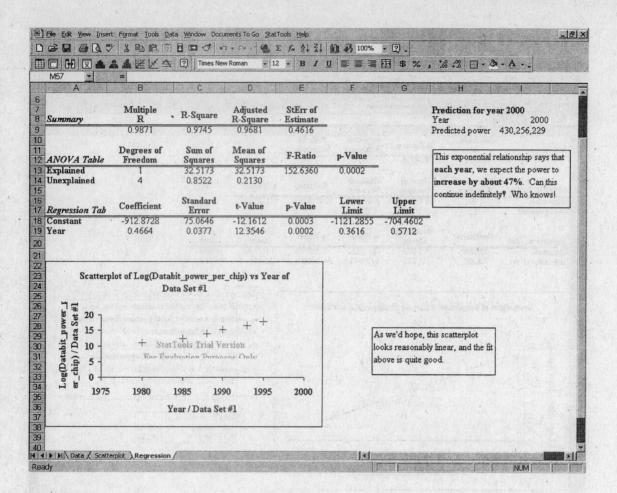

Summary	Multiple R	R-Square	Adjusted R-Square	StErr of Estimate
	0.9871	0.9745	0.9681	0.4616

Prediction for year 2000
Year 2000
Predicted power 430,256,229

ANOVA Table	Degrees of Freedom	Sum of Squares	Mean of Squares	F-Ratio	p-Value
Explained	1	32.5173	32.5173	152.6360	0.0002
Unexplained	4	0.8522	0.2130		

Regression Tab	Coefficient	Standard Error	t-Value	p-Value	Lower Limit	Upper Limit
Constant	-912.8728	75.0646	-12.1612	0.0003	-1121.2855	-704.4602
Year	0.4664	0.0377	12.3546	0.0002	0.3616	0.5712

This exponential relationship says that **each year**, we expect the power to **increase by about 47%.** Can this continue indefinitely? Who knows!

Scatterplot of Log(Databit_power_per_chip) vs Year of Data Set #1

As we'd hope, this scatterplot looks reasonably linear, and the fit above is quite good.

Problem 11_57

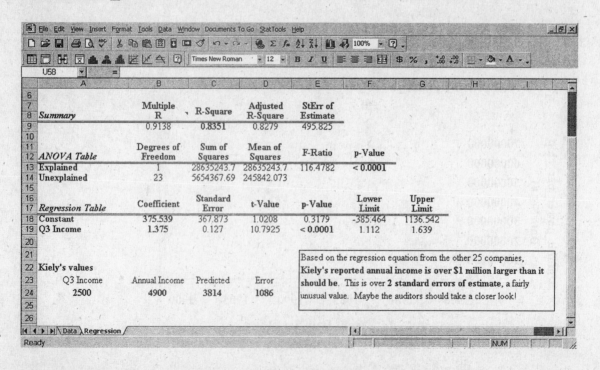

Summary	Multiple R	R-Square	Adjusted R-Square	StErr of Estimate
	0.9138	0.8351	0.8279	495.825

ANOVA Table	Degrees of Freedom	Sum of Squares	Mean of Squares	F-Ratio	p-Value
Explained	1	28635243.7	28635243.7	116.4782	< 0.0001
Unexplained	23	5654367.69	245842.073		

Regression Table	Coefficient	Standard Error	t-Value	p-Value	Lower Limit	Upper Limit
Constant	375.539	367.873	1.0208	0.3179	-385.464	1136.542
Q3 Income	1.375	0.127	10.7925	< 0.0001	1.112	1.639

Kiely's values

Q3 Income	Annual Income	Predicted	Error
2500	4900	3814	1086

Based on the regression equation from the other 25 companies, **Kiely's reported annual income is over $1 million larger than it should be.** This is over **2 standard errors of estimate,** a fairly unusual value. Maybe the auditors should take a closer look!

Problem 11_61

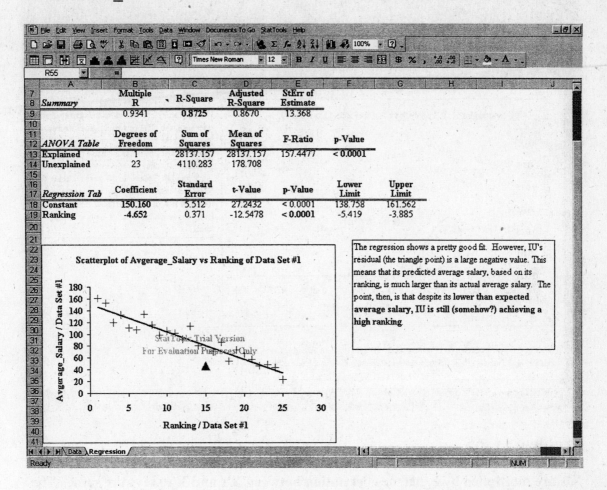

| File Edit View Insert Format Tools Data Window Documents To Go StatTools Help |

	A	B	C	D	E	F	G	H	I	J
7	*Summary*	Multiple R	R-Square	Adjusted R-Square	StErr of Estimate					
8										
9		0.9341	**0.8725**	0.8670	13.368					
10										
11	*ANOVA Table*	Degrees of Freedom	Sum of Squares	Mean of Squares	F-Ratio	p-Value				
12										
13	Explained	1	28137.157	28137.157	157.4477	< 0.0001				
14	Unexplained	23	4110.283	178.708						
15										
16	*Regression Tab*	Coefficient	Standard Error	t-Value	p-Value	Lower Limit	Upper Limit			
17										
18	Constant	**150.160**	5.512	27.2432	< 0.0001	138.758	161.562			
19	Ranking	**-4.652**	0.371	-12.5478	< 0.0001	-5.419	-3.885			

The regression shows a pretty good fit. However, IU's residual (the triangle point) is a large negative value. This means that its predicted average salary, based on its ranking, is much larger than its actual average salary. The point, then, is that despite its lower than expected average salary, IU is still (somehow?) achieving a high ranking.

Scatterplot of Avgerage_Salary vs Ranking of Data Set #1

StatTools Trial Version
For Evaluation Purposes Only

Problem 11_63

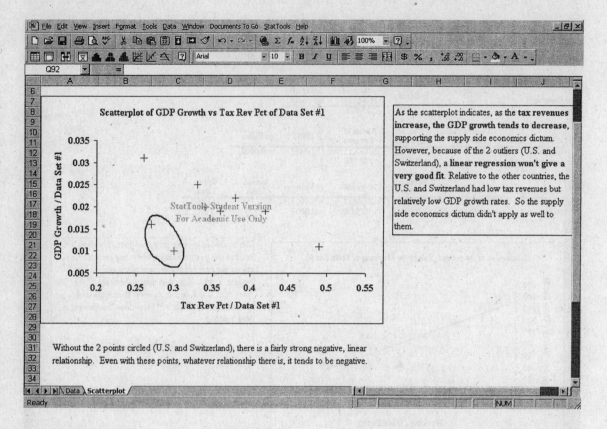

Problem 11_65

Part a: When each X is multiplied by a factor k, both the **mean and stdev of the X's are multiplied by k**, but the **correlation between X's and Y's stays the same**. The effect on the **slope** is that it is also **multiplied by k** (becomes -6 when k=2). We can't say what the new intercept will be exactly. It was Y-bar - slope*X-bar. We know that slope changes to k*slope, and X-bar changes to k*X-bar, but without more information, we can't say what the new numerical value of the intercept is.

Part b: When each Y is multiplied by a factor k, both the **mean and stdev of the Y's are multiplied by k**, but the **correlation between X's and Y's stays the same**. The effect on the **slope** is that it is **divided by k** (becomes -1 when k=3). We can't say what the new intercept will be exactly. It was Y-bar - slope*X-bar. We know that slope changes to slope/k, and Y-bar changes to k*Y-bar, but without more information, we can't say what the new numerical value of the intercept is.

Part c: When a constant c is added to each X, the **mean of the X's is the old mean plus c**, the **stdev of the X's does not change**, and the **correlation between X's and Y's stays the same**. The effect on the **slope** is that it **does not change**. The new intercept is the old intercept (12) minus the slope (-3) times c. With c=6, this is 12-(-3)(6)=30.

Part d: When a constant c is added to each Y, the mean of the **Y's is the old mean plus c**, the **stdev of the Y's does not change**, and the **correlation between X's and Y's stays the same**. The effect on the **slope** is that it **does not change**. The new intercept is the old intercept (12) plus c. With c=-4, this is 12+(-4)=8.

Problem 11_67

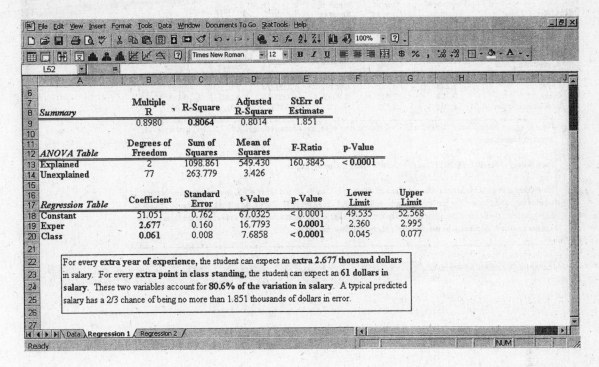

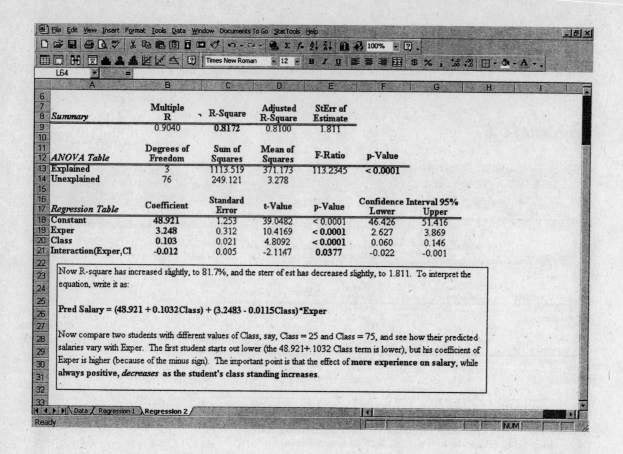

Now R-square has increased slightly, to 81.7%, and the sterr of est has decreased slightly, to 1.811. To interpret the equation, write it as:

Pred Salary = (48.921 + 0.1032Class) + (3.2483 - 0.0115Class)*Exper

Now compare two students with different values of Class, say, Class = 25 and Class = 75, and see how their predicted salaries vary with Exper. The first student starts out lower (the 48.921+.1032 Class term is lower), but his coefficient of Exper is higher (because of the minus sign). The important point is that the effect of **more experience on salary**, while **always positive**, *decreases* as the student's class standing increases.

CHAPTER 12

Problem 12_1

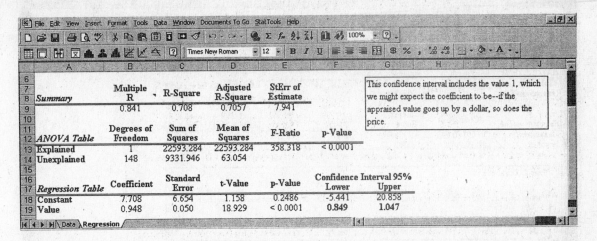

	Multiple R	R-Square	Adjusted R-Square	StErr of Estimate		
Summary						
	0.841	0.708	0.7057	7.941		
ANOVA Table	Degrees of Freedom	Sum of Squares	Mean of Squares	F-Ratio	p-Value	
Explained	1	22593.284	22593.284	358.318	< 0.0001	
Unexplained	148	9331.946	63.054			
Regression Table	Coefficient	Standard Error	t-Value	p-Value	Confidence Interval 95% Lower	Upper
Constant	7.708	6.654	1.158	0.2486	-5.441	20.858
Value	0.948	0.050	18.929	< 0.0001	0.849	1.047

This confidence interval includes the value 1, which we might expect the coefficient to be--if the appraised value goes up by a dollar, so does the price.

Problem 12_3

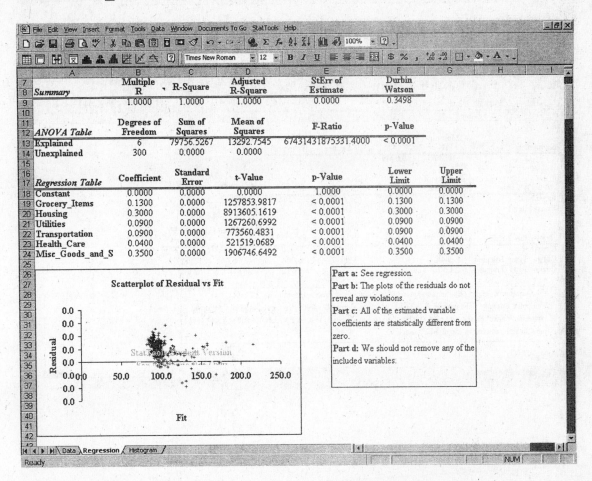

	Multiple R	R-Square	Adjusted R-Square	StErr of Estimate	Durbin Watson	
Summary						
	1.0000	1.0000	1.0000	0.0000	0.3498	
ANOVA Table	Degrees of Freedom	Sum of Squares	Mean of Squares	F-Ratio	p-Value	
Explained	6	79756.5267	13292.7545	67431431875331.4000	< 0.0001	
Unexplained	300	0.0000	0.0000			
Regression Table	Coefficient	Standard Error	t-Value	p-Value	Lower Limit	Upper Limit
Constant	0.0000	0.0000	0.0000	1.0000	0.0000	0.0000
Grocery_Items	0.1300	0.0000	1257853.9817	< 0.0001	0.1300	0.1300
Housing	0.3000	0.0000	8913605.1619	< 0.0001	0.3000	0.3000
Utilities	0.0900	0.0000	1267260.6992	< 0.0001	0.0900	0.0900
Transportation	0.0900	0.0000	773560.4831	< 0.0001	0.0900	0.0900
Health_Care	0.0400	0.0000	521519.0689	< 0.0001	0.0400	0.0400
Misc_Goods_and_S	0.3500	0.0000	1906746.6492	< 0.0001	0.3500	0.3500

Part a: See regression.
Part b: The plots of the residuals do not reveal any violations.
Part c: All of the estimated variable coefficients are statistically different from zero.
Part d: We should not remove any of the included variables.

Problem 12_5

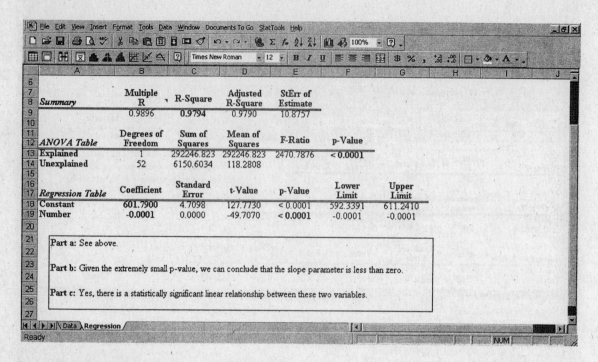

	A	B	C	D	E	F	G	H	I	J

Summary		Multiple R	R-Square	Adjusted R-Square	StErr of Estimate			
		0.9896	0.9794	0.9790	10.8757			

ANOVA Table	Degrees of Freedom	Sum of Squares	Mean of Squares	F-Ratio	p-Value		
Explained	1	292246.823	292246.823	2470.7876	< 0.0001		
Unexplained	52	6150.6034	118.2808				

Regression Table	Coefficient	Standard Error	t-Value	p-Value	Lower Limit	Upper Limit
Constant	601.7900	4.7098	127.7730	< 0.0001	592.3391	611.2410
Number	-0.0001	0.0000	-49.7070	< 0.0001	-0.0001	-0.0001

Part a: See above.

Part b: Given the extremely small p-value, we can conclude that the slope parameter is less than zero.

Part c: Yes, there is a statistically significant linear relationship between these two variables.

Problem 12_9

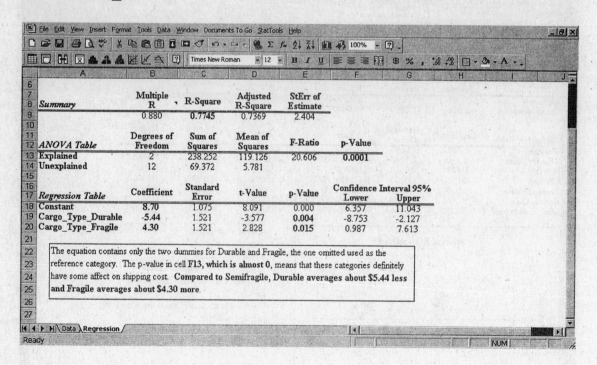

	A	B	C	D	E	F	G	H	I	J

Summary		Multiple R	R-Square	Adjusted R-Square	StErr of Estimate		
		0.880	0.7745	0.7369	2.404		

ANOVA Table	Degrees of Freedom	Sum of Squares	Mean of Squares	F-Ratio	p-Value	
Explained	2	238.252	119.126	20.606	0.0001	
Unexplained	12	69.372	5.781			

Regression Table	Coefficient	Standard Error	t-Value	p-Value	Confidence Interval 95%	
					Lower	Upper
Constant	8.70	1.075	8.091	0.000	6.357	11.043
Cargo_Type_Durable	-5.44	1.521	-3.577	0.004	-8.753	-2.127
Cargo_Type_Fragile	4.30	1.521	2.828	0.015	0.987	7.613

The equation contains only the two dummies for Durable and Fragile, the one omitted used as the reference category. The p-value in cell F13, which is almost 0, means that these categories definitely have some affect on shipping cost. Compared to Semifragile, Durable averages about $5.44 less and Fragile averages about $4.30 more.

Problem 12_15

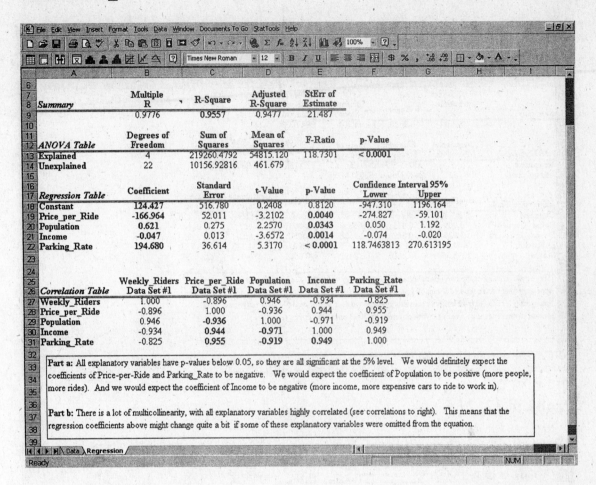

Summary	Multiple R	R-Square	Adjusted R-Square	StErr of Estimate			
	0.9776	0.9557	0.9477	21.487			

ANOVA Table	Degrees of Freedom	Sum of Squares	Mean of Squares	F-Ratio	p-Value		
Explained	4	219260.4792	54815.120	118.7301	< 0.0001		
Unexplained	22	10156.92816	461.679				

Regression Table	Coefficient	Standard Error	t-Value	p-Value	Confidence Interval 95% Lower	Upper
Constant	124.427	516.780	0.2408	0.8120	-947.310	1196.164
Price_per_Ride	-166.964	52.011	-3.2102	0.0040	-274.827	-59.101
Population	0.621	0.275	2.2570	0.0343	0.050	1.192
Income	-0.047	0.013	-3.6572	0.0014	-0.074	-0.020
Parking_Rate	194.680	36.614	5.3170	< 0.0001	118.7463813	270.613195

Correlation Table	Weekly_Riders Data Set #1	Price_per_Ride Data Set #1	Population Data Set #1	Income Data Set #1	Parking_Rate Data Set #1
Weekly_Riders	1.000	-0.896	0.946	-0.934	-0.825
Price_per_Ride	-0.896	1.000	-0.936	0.944	0.955
Population	0.946	-0.936	1.000	-0.971	-0.919
Income	-0.934	0.944	-0.971	1.000	0.949
Parking_Rate	-0.825	0.955	-0.919	0.949	1.000

Part a: All explanatory variables have p-values below 0.05, so they are all significant at the 5% level. We would definitely expect the coefficients of Price-per-Ride and Parking_Rate to be negative. We would expect the coefficient of Population to be positive (more people, more rides). And we would expect the coefficient of Income to be negative (more income, more expensive cars to ride to work in).

Part b: There is a lot of multicollinearity, with all explanatory variables highly correlated (see correlations to right). This means that the regression coefficients above might change quite a bit if some of these explanatory variables were omitted from the equation.

Problem 12_19

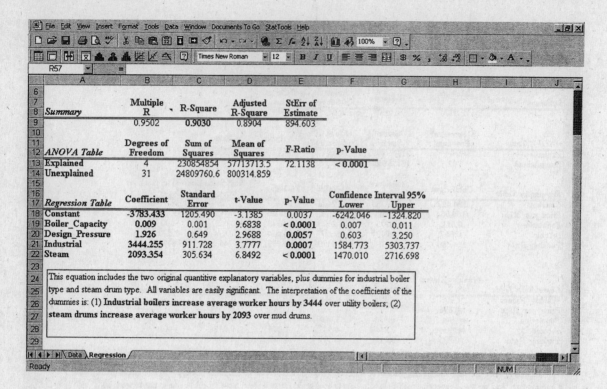

Summary	Multiple R	R-Square	Adjusted R-Square	StErr of Estimate			
	0.9502	0.9030	0.8904	894.603			

ANOVA Table	Degrees of Freedom	Sum of Squares	Mean of Squares	F-Ratio	p-Value		
Explained	4	230854854	57713713.5	72.1138	< 0.0001		
Unexplained	31	24809760.6	800314.859				

Regression Table	Coefficient	Standard Error	t-Value	p-Value	Confidence Interval 95% Lower	Upper
Constant	-3783.433	1205.490	-3.1385	0.0037	-6242.046	-1324.820
Boiler_Capacity	0.009	0.001	9.6838	< 0.0001	0.007	0.011
Design_Pressure	1.926	0.649	2.9688	0.0057	0.603	3.250
Industrial	3444.255	911.728	3.7777	0.0007	1584.773	5303.737
Steam	2093.354	305.634	6.8492	< 0.0001	1470.010	2716.698

This equation includes the two original quantitive explanatory variables, plus dummies for industrial boiler type and steam drum type. All variables are easily significant. The interpretation of the coefficients of the dummies is: (1) **Industrial boilers increase average worker hours by 3444** over utility boilers; (2) **steam drums increase average worker hours by 2093** over mud drums.

Problem 12_21

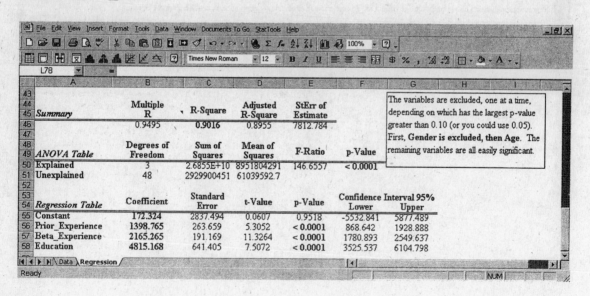

Summary	Multiple R	R-Square	Adjusted R-Square	StErr of Estimate		
	0.9495	0.9016	0.8955	7812.784		

ANOVA Table	Degrees of Freedom	Sum of Squares	Mean of Squares	F-Ratio	p-Value
Explained	3	2.6855E+10	8951804291	146.6557	< 0.0001
Unexplained	48	2929900451	61039592.7		

Regression Table	Coefficient	Standard Error	t-Value	p-Value	Confidence Interval 95% Lower	Upper
Constant	172.324	2837.494	0.0607	0.9518	-5532.841	5877.489
Prior_Experience	1398.765	263.659	5.3052	< 0.0001	868.642	1928.888
Beta_Experience	2165.265	191.169	11.3264	< 0.0001	1780.893	2549.637
Education	4815.168	641.405	7.5072	< 0.0001	3525.537	6104.798

The variables are excluded, one at a time, depending on which has the largest p-value greater than 0.10 (or you could use 0.05). First, **Gender** is excluded, then **Age**. The remaining variables are all easily significant.

Problem 12_23

Summary	Multiple R	R-Square	Adjusted R-Square	StErr of Estimate				
	0.7388	0.5459	0.5232	942.968				

ANOVA Table	Degrees of Freedom	Sum of Squares	Mean of Squares	F-Ratio	p-Value			
Explained	1	21377880.4	21377880.4	24.0420	< 0.0001			
Unexplained	20	17783781	889189.051					

Regression Table	Coefficient	Standard Error	t-Value	p-Value	Confidence Interval 95%			
					Lower	Upper		
Constant	2279.583	272.211	8.3743	< 0.0001	1711.760	2847.407		
Color	1979.717	403.755	4.9033	< 0.0001	1137.499	2821.935		

Correlation Table	Price Data Set #1
Price	1.000
Speed	0.518
Charge	-0.248
RAM	0.390
Chip_Type_DX	0.504
Chip_Type_SL	-0.336
Color	0.688
Mouse	0.555
Help	0.295

Using stepwise regression with the default parameters, only one variable, the dummy for color monitor, enters the equation. It simply tells us that there is a premium of about $1980 for having a color monitor as opposed to a monochrome monitor. None of the other variables appear to affect price significantly. Actually, the correlations below indicate that other variables are fairly highly correlated with price, but because of multicollinearity, they are evidently not needed (they don't pass the 5% significance level) once Color is in the equation.

Data / Regression

Problem 12_27

P62

Summary	Multiple R	R-Square	Adjusted R-Square	StErr of Estimate					
	0.9997	0.9993	0.9993	0.4220					

ANOVA Table	Degrees of Freedom	Sum of Squares	Mean of Squares	F-Ratio	p-Value				
Explained	5	79702.9109	15940.5822	89490.6554	< 0.0001				
Unexplained	301	53.6158	0.1781						

Regression Table	Coefficient	Standard Error	t-Value	p-Value	Lower Limit	Upper Limit			
Constant	-0.8037	0.4539	-1.7707	0.0776	-1.6969	0.0895			
Housing	0.3014	0.0010	298.7901	< 0.0001	0.2994	0.3034			
Misc_Goods_and_S	0.3789	0.0053	72.0129	< 0.0001	0.3685	0.3892			
Grocery_Items	0.1362	0.0031	44.1305	< 0.0001	0.1301	0.1423			
Utilities	0.0912	0.0021	42.7624	< 0.0001	0.0870	0.0954			
Transportation	0.1005	0.0034	29.1908	< 0.0001	0.0938	0.1073			

Step Information	Multiple R	R-Square	Adjusted R-Square	StErr of Estimate	Enter or Exit				
Housing	0.9767	0.9540	0.9538	3.4692	Enter				
Misc_Goods_and_S	0.9928	0.9856	0.9855	1.9416	Enter				
Grocery_Items	0.9967	0.9934	0.9934	1.3149	Enter				
Utilities	0.9987	0.9974	0.9974	0.8247	Enter				
Transportation	0.9997	0.9993	0.9993	0.4220	Enter				

Unlike the previous solution, this estimated model (which is found using StatTools stepwise regression procedure) omits the Health_Care expenditures variable. Of course, both models explain the variation in the Composite cost-of-living index extremely well.

Data / Regression

Ready

Problem 12_31

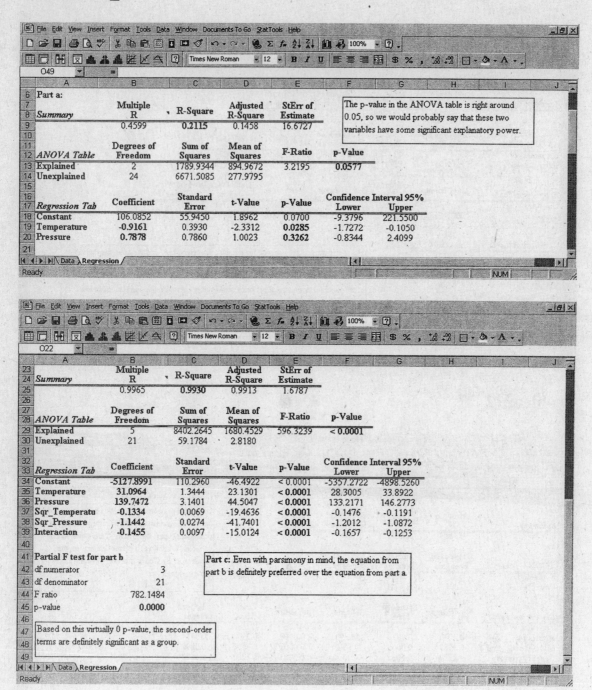

Part a:

Summary	Multiple R	R-Square	Adjusted R-Square	StErr of Estimate
	0.4599	0.2115	0.1458	16.6727

The p-value in the ANOVA table is right around 0.05, so we would probably say that these two variables have some significant explanatory power.

ANOVA Table	Degrees of Freedom	Sum of Squares	Mean of Squares	F-Ratio	p-Value
Explained	2	1789.9344	894.9672	3.2195	0.0577
Unexplained	24	6671.5085	277.9795		

Regression Tab	Coefficient	Standard Error	t-Value	p-Value	Confidence Interval 95% Lower	Upper
Constant	106.0852	55.9450	1.8962	0.0700	-9.3796	221.5500
Temperature	-0.9161	0.3930	-2.3312	0.0285	-1.7272	-0.1050
Pressure	0.7878	0.7860	1.0023	0.3262	-0.8344	2.4099

Summary	Multiple R	R-Square	Adjusted R-Square	StErr of Estimate
	0.9965	0.9930	0.9913	1.6787

ANOVA Table	Degrees of Freedom	Sum of Squares	Mean of Squares	F-Ratio	p-Value
Explained	5	8402.2645	1680.4529	596.3239	< 0.0001
Unexplained	21	59.1784	2.8180		

Regression Tab	Coefficient	Standard Error	t-Value	p-Value	Confidence Interval 95% Lower	Upper
Constant	-5127.8991	110.2960	-46.4922	< 0.0001	-5357.2722	-4898.5260
Temperature	31.0964	1.3444	23.1301	< 0.0001	28.3005	33.8922
Pressure	139.7472	3.1401	44.5047	< 0.0001	133.2171	146.2773
Sqr_Temperatu	-0.1334	0.0069	-19.4636	< 0.0001	-0.1476	-0.1191
Sqr_Pressure	-1.1442	0.0274	-41.7401	< 0.0001	-1.2012	-1.0872
Interaction	-0.1455	0.0097	-15.0124	< 0.0001	-0.1657	-0.1253

Partial F test for part b

df numerator	3
df denominator	21
F ratio	782.1484
p-value	0.0000

Part c: Even with parsimony in mind, the equation from part b is definitely preferred over the equation from part a.

Based on this virtually 0 p-value, the second-order terms are definitely significant as a group.

Problem 12_35
Part a:

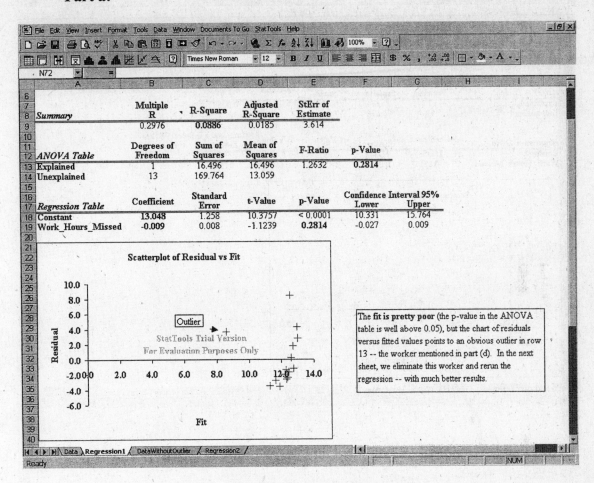

| | File Edit View Insert Format Tools Data Window Documents To Go StatTools Help |

	A	B	C	D	E	F	G	H	I
8	*Summary*	Multiple R	R-Square	Adjusted R-Square	StErr of Estimate				
9		0.2976	**0.0886**	0.0185	3.614				
12	*ANOVA Table*	Degrees of Freedom	Sum of Squares	Mean of Squares	F-Ratio	p-Value			
13	Explained	1	16.496	16.496	1.2632	**0.2814**			
14	Unexplained	13	169.764	13.059					
17	*Regression Table*	Coefficient	Standard Error	t-Value	p-Value	Confidence Interval 95% Lower	Upper		
18	Constant	13.048	1.258	10.3757	< 0.0001	10.331	15.764		
19	Work_Hours_Missed	-0.009	0.008	-1.1239	**0.2814**	-0.027	0.009		

Scatterplot of Residual vs Fit

The fit is pretty poor (the p-value in the ANOVA table is well above 0.05), but the chart of residuals versus fitted values points to an obvious outlier in row 13 -- the worker mentioned in part (d). In the next sheet, we eliminate this worker and rerun the regression -- with much better results.

Data / Regression1 / DataWithoutOutlier / Regression2

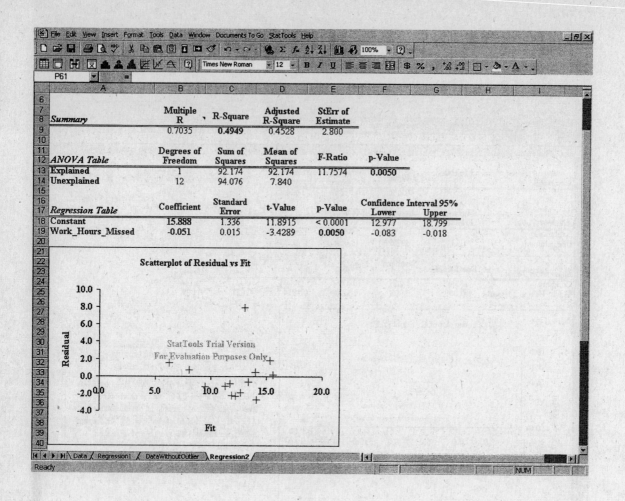

| P61 | | = | | | | | | |

	A	B	C	D	E	F	G	H	I
Summary		Multiple R	R-Square	Adjusted R-Square	StErr of Estimate				
		0.7035	0.4949	0.4528	2.800				
ANOVA Table		Degrees of Freedom	Sum of Squares	Mean of Squares	F-Ratio	p-Value			
Explained		1	92.174	92.174	11.7574	0.0050			
Unexplained		12	94.076	7.840					
Regression Table		Coefficient	Standard Error	t-Value	p-Value	Confidence Interval 95%			
						Lower	Upper		
Constant		15.888	1.336	11.8915	< 0.0001	12.977	18.799		
Work_Hours_Missed		-0.051	0.015	-3.4289	0.0050	-0.083	-0.018		

Scatterplot of Residual vs Fit

StatTools Trial Version
For Evaluation Purposes Only

Data / Regression1 / DataWithoutOutlier / **Regression2**

Problem 12_45

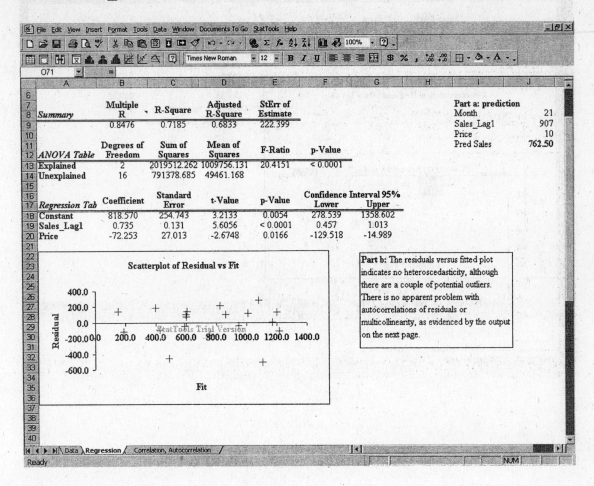

								Part a: prediction	
Summary	Multiple R	R-Square	Adjusted R-Square	StErr of Estimate				Month	21
	0.8476	0.7185	0.6833	222.399				Sales_Lag1	907
								Price	10
ANOVA Table	Degrees of Freedom	Sum of Squares	Mean of Squares	F-Ratio	p-Value			Pred Sales	762.50
Explained	2	2019512.262	1009756.131	20.4151	< 0.0001				
Unexplained	16	791378.685	49461.168						

Regression Tab	Coefficient	Standard Error	t-Value	p-Value	Confidence Interval 95% Lower	Upper
Constant	818.570	254.743	3.2133	0.0054	278.539	1358.602
Sales_Lag1	0.735	0.131	5.6056	< 0.0001	0.457	1.013
Price	-72.253	27.013	-2.6748	0.0166	-129.518	-14.989

Part b: The residuals versus fitted plot indicates no heteroscedasticity, although there are a couple of potential outliers. There is no apparent problem with autocorrelations of residuals or multicollinearity, as evidenced by the output on the next page.

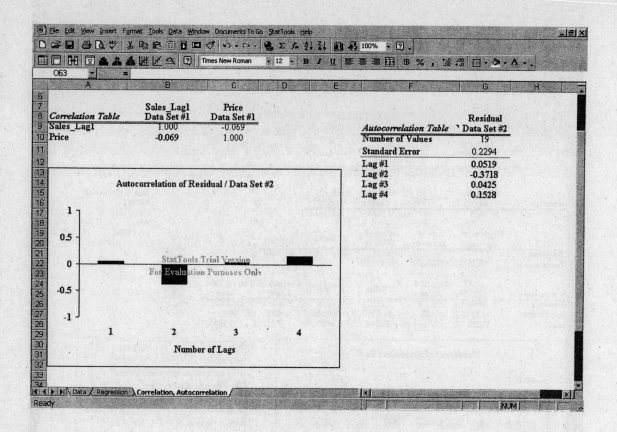

File Edit View Insert Format Tools Data Window Documents To Go StatTools Help

	A	B	C	D	E	F	G	H
6								
7		Sales_Lag1	Price				Residual	
8	*Correlation Table*	Data Set #1	Data Set #1			*Autocorrelation Table*	Data Set #2	
9	Sales_Lag1	1.000	-0.069			Number of Values	19	
10	Price	-0.069	1.000			Standard Error	0.2294	
11						Lag #1	0.0519	
12						Lag #2	-0.3718	
13						Lag #3	0.0425	
14						Lag #4	0.1528	

Autocorrelation of Residual / Data Set #2

StatTools Trial Version
For Evaluation Purposes Only

Number of Lags

Data / Regression / Correlation, Autocorrelation

Problem 12_49

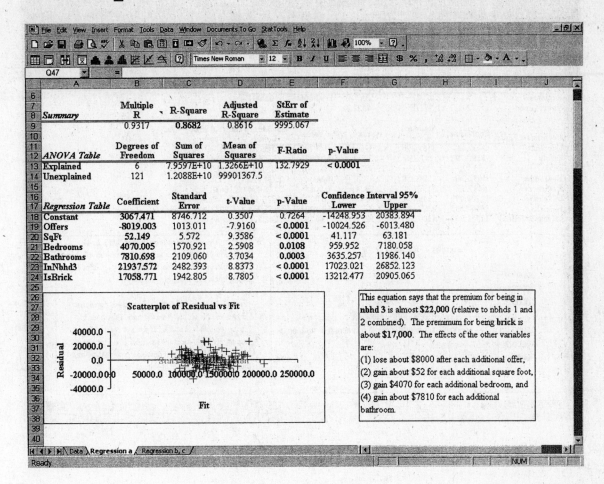

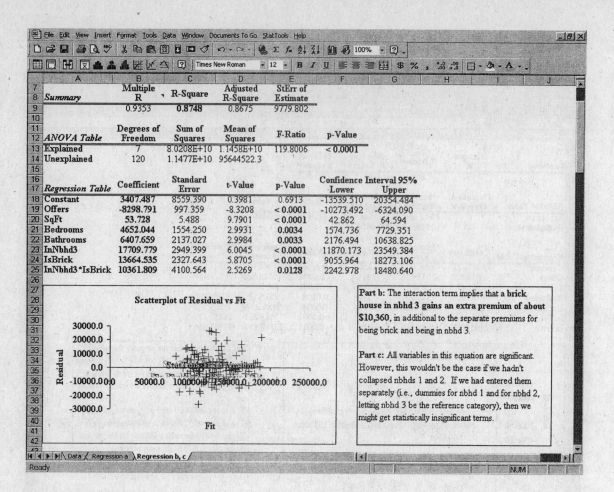

File Edit View Insert Format Tools Data Window Documents To Go StatTools Help									

	A	B	C	D	E	F	G	H	I	J
7		**Multiple R**	**R-Square**	**Adjusted R-Square**	**StErr of Estimate**					
8	*Summary*									
9		0.9353	**0.8748**	0.8675	9779.802					
10										
11		**Degrees of Freedom**	**Sum of Squares**	**Mean of Squares**	**F-Ratio**	**p-Value**				
12	*ANOVA Table*									
13	Explained	7	8.0208E+10	1.1458E+10	119.8006	< 0.0001				
14	Unexplained	120	1.1477E+10	95644522.3						
15										
16		**Coefficient**	**Standard Error**	**t-Value**	**p-Value**	**Confidence Interval 95%**				
17	*Regression Table*					**Lower**	**Upper**			
18	Constant	3407.487	8559.390	0.3981	0.6913	-13539.510	20354.484			
19	Offers	-8298.791	997.359	-8.3208	< 0.0001	-10273.492	-6324.090			
20	SqFt	53.728	5.488	9.7901	< 0.0001	42.862	64.594			
21	Bedrooms	4652.044	1554.250	2.9931	0.0034	1574.736	7729.351			
22	Bathrooms	6407.659	2137.027	2.9984	0.0033	2176.494	10638.825			
23	InNbhd3	17709.779	2949.399	6.0045	< 0.0001	11870.173	23549.384			
24	IsBrick	13664.535	2327.643	5.8705	< 0.0001	9055.964	18273.106			
25	InNbhd3*IsBrick	10361.809	4100.564	2.5269	0.0128	2242.978	18480.640			

Scatterplot of Residual vs Fit

Part b: The interaction term implies that a brick house in nbhd 3 gains an extra premium of about $10,360, in additional to the separate premiums for being brick and being in nbhd 3.

Part c: All variables in this equation are significant. However, this wouldn't be the case if we hadn't collapsed nbhds 1 and 2. If we had entered them separately (i.e., dummies for nbhd 1 and for nbhd 2, letting nbhd 3 be the reference category), then we might get statistically insignificant terms.

Problem 12_53

Correlation Table	**UnemployRate** Data Set #1	**PctGrUSEcon** Data Set #1	**PctGrPrices** Data Set #1
UnemployRate	1.000	-0.312	0.126
PctGrUSEcon	-0.312	1.000	-0.287
PctGrPrices	0.126	-0.287	1.000

The above correlations, plus the plots, indicate very weak relationships between these variables, although unemployment tends to decrease slightly with larger values of the other two variables. We could run a regression or two, but it's not clear what the response variable should be. An argument can be made that the cause and effect relationships go both ways between any of these variables.

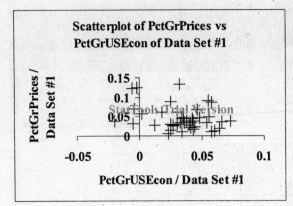

Scatterplot of PctGrPrices vs PctGrUSEcon of Data Set #1

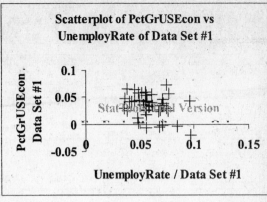

Scatterplot of PctGrUSEcon vs UnemployRate of Data Set #1

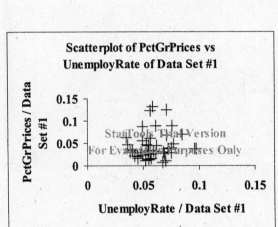

Scatterplot of PctGrPrices vs UnemployRate of Data Set #1

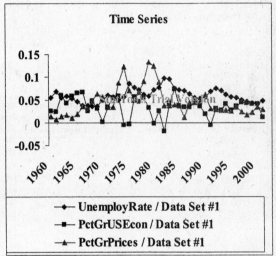

Time Series

Problem 12_57

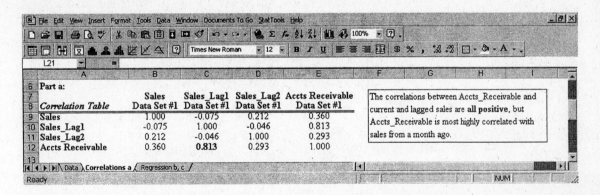

Correlation Table	Sales Data Set #1	Sales_Lag1 Data Set #1	Sales_Lag2 Data Set #1	Accts Receivable Data Set #1
Sales	1.000	-0.075	0.212	0.360
Sales_Lag1	-0.075	1.000	-0.046	0.813
Sales_Lag2	0.212	-0.046	1.000	0.293
Accts Receivable	0.360	0.813	0.293	1.000

The correlations between Accts_Receivable and current and lagged sales are all **positive**, but Accts_Receivable is most highly correlated with sales from a month ago.

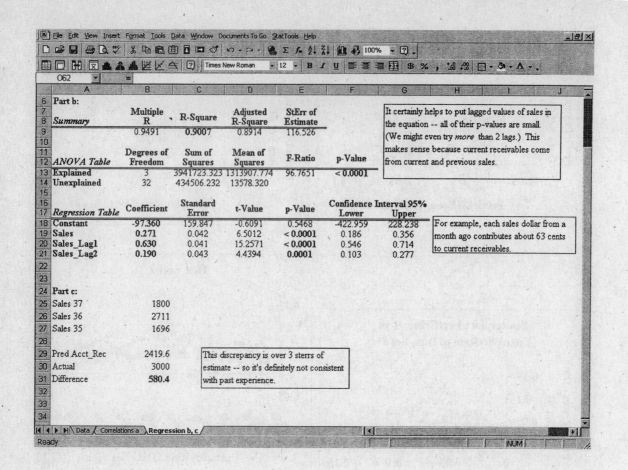

Part b:

Summary	Multiple R	R-Square	Adjusted R-Square	StErr of Estimate
	0.9491	0.9007	0.8914	116.526

It certainly helps to put lagged values of sales in the equation -- all of their p-values are small. (We might even try *more* than 2 lags.) This makes sense because current receivables come from current and previous sales.

ANOVA Table	Degrees of Freedom	Sum of Squares	Mean of Squares	F-Ratio	p-Value
Explained	3	3941723.323	1313907.774	96.7651	< 0.0001
Unexplained	32	434506.232	13578.320		

Regression Table	Coefficient	Standard Error	t-Value	p-Value	Confidence Interval 95% Lower	Upper
Constant	-97.360	159.847	-0.6091	0.5468	-422.959	228.238
Sales	0.271	0.042	6.5012	< 0.0001	0.186	0.356
Sales_Lag1	0.630	0.041	15.2571	< 0.0001	0.546	0.714
Sales_Lag2	0.190	0.043	4.4394	0.0001	0.103	0.277

For example, each sales dollar from a month ago contributes about 63 cents to current receivables.

Part c:

Sales 37	1800
Sales 36	2711
Sales 35	1696
Pred Acct_Rec	2419.6
Actual	3000
Difference	580.4

This discrepancy is over 3 sterrs of estimate -- so it's definitely not consistent with past experience.

Data / Correlations a / **Regression b, c**

Problem 12_59

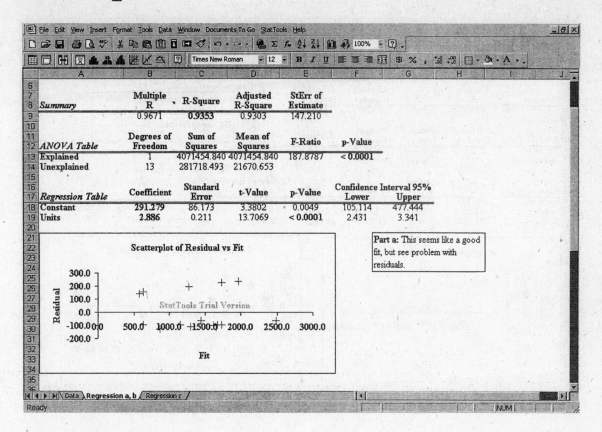

Summary	Multiple R	R-Square	Adjusted R-Square	StErr of Estimate		
	0.9671	0.9353	0.9303	147.210		

ANOVA Table	Degrees of Freedom	Sum of Squares	Mean of Squares	F-Ratio	p-Value	
Explained	1	4071454.840	4071454.840	187.8787	< 0.0001	
Unexplained	13	281718.493	21670.653			

Regression Table	Coefficient	Standard Error	t-Value	p-Value	Confidence Interval 95% Lower	Upper
Constant	291.279	86.173	3.3802	0.0049	105.114	477.444
Units	2.886	0.211	13.7069	< 0.0001	2.431	3.341

Scatterplot of Residual vs Fit

Part a: This seems like a good fit, but see problem with residuals.

Part b: The residuals are negative for the first 10 months, then positive for the last 5 months.

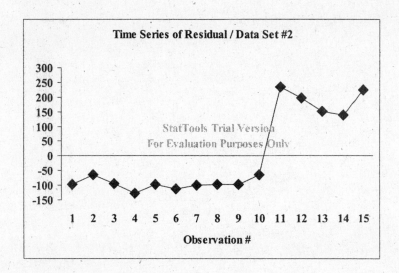

Time Series of Residual / Data Set #2

Part c:

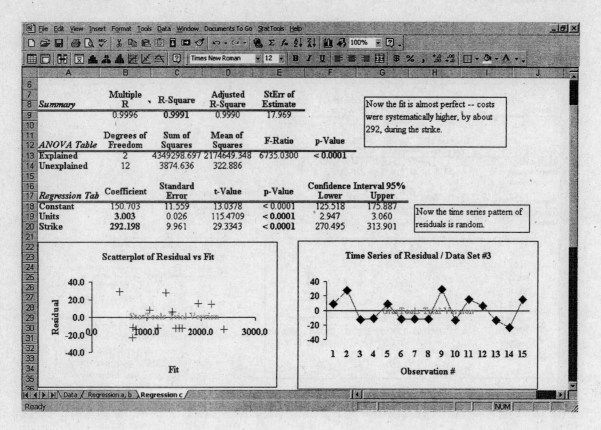

Summary	Multiple R	R-Square	Adjusted R-Square	StErr of Estimate
	0.9996	0.9991	0.9990	17.969

Now the fit is almost perfect -- costs were systematically higher, by about 292, during the strike.

ANOVA Table	Degrees of Freedom	Sum of Squares	Mean of Squares	F-Ratio	p-Value
Explained	2	4349298.697	2174649.348	6735.0300	< 0.0001
Unexplained	12	3874.636	322.886		

Regression Tab	Coefficient	Standard Error	t-Value	p-Value	Confidence Interval 95% Lower	Upper
Constant	150.703	11.559	13.0378	< 0.0001	125.518	175.887
Units	3.003	0.026	115.4709	< 0.0001	2.947	3.060
Strike	292.198	9.961	29.3343	< 0.0001	270.495	313.901

Now the time series pattern of residuals is random.

Problem 12_61

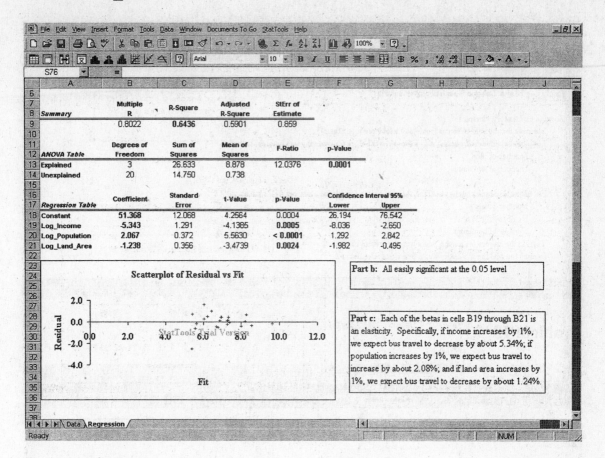

Problem 12_67

There is a **mild positive correlation** between GDP growth and govt. spending as a percentage of GDP. This is weak evidence in favor of the Keynsian theory. Of course, the GDP growth is in nominal (including inflation) terms. A better analysis would use real GDP growth after correcting for inflation.

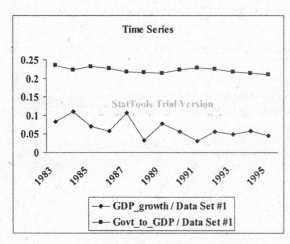

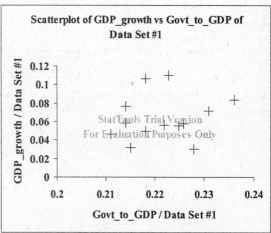

Problem 12_69

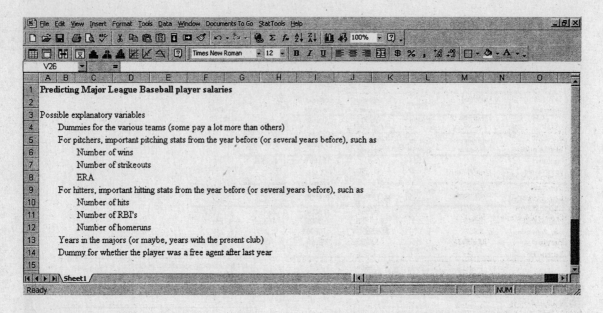

Problem 12_73

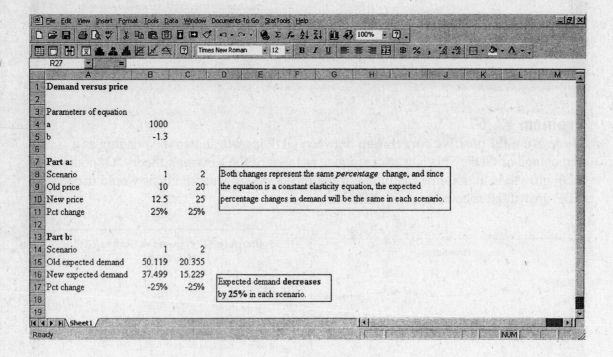

Problem 12_77

```
File  Edit  View  Insert  Format  Tools  Data  Window  Documents To Go  StatTools  Help
```

	A	B	C	D	E	F	G	H	I	J
6	Part a:	Multiple R	R-Square	Adjusted R-Square	StErr of Estimate		The R-square value isn't very high, the StErr of Est is quite high, and two of the explanatory variables are insignificant.			
7	Summary									
8		0.7103	0.5046	0.4581	2884.575					
9										
10		Degrees of Freedom	Sum of Squares	Mean of Squares	F-Ratio	p-Value				
11	ANOVA Table									
12	Explained	3	271202323	90400774.3	10.8645	< 0.0001				
13	Unexplained	32	266264649	8320770.29						
14										
15		Coefficient	Standard Error	t-Value	p-Value	Confidence Interval 95%				
16	Regression Table					Lower	Upper			
17	Constant	59279.264	3244.207	18.2723	< 0.0001	52671.030	65887.498			
18	Lots Produced	-1.799	2.495	-0.7210	0.4761	-6.881	3.283			
19	Labor Hours	6.961	5.208	1.3365	0.1908	-3.648	17.569			
20	Production Runs	906.435	254.596	3.5603	0.0012	387.840	1425.030			
21										
22	Part b:	Multiple R	R-Square	Adjusted R-Square	StErr of Estimate		Now the R-square value is much higher, the StErr of Est is considerably lower, all variables except for ChangeLP are significant, including the squared term.			
23	Summary									
24		0.8942	0.7995	0.7661	1895.222					
25										
26		Degrees of Freedom	Sum of Squares	Mean of Squares	F-Ratio	p-Value	We try this squared term here because of the statement that "the bigger the change in production, the greater the effect of the change in production on the increase in overhead."			
27	ANOVA Table									
28	Explained	5	429710996	85942199.2	23.9269	< 0.0001				
29	Unexplained	30	107755976	3591865.87						
30										
31		Coefficient	Standard Error	t-Value	p-Value	Confidence Interval 95%				
32	Regression Table					Lower	Upper			
33	Constant	49290.964	3046.756	16.1782	< 0.0001	43068.659	55513.269			
34	Lots Produced	-6.353	1.794	-3.5409	0.0013	-10.017	-2.689			
35	Labor Hours	18.127	3.813	4.7546	< 0.0001	10.341	25.914			
36	Production Runs	1060.659	168.920	6.2791	< 0.0001	715.678	1405.640			
37	ChangeLP	-0.427	0.272	-1.5674	0.1275	-0.983	0.129			
38	ChangeLP2	0.001	0.000	6.3586	< 0.0001	0.000	0.001			

```
Data  Regression a  Regression b
```

Problem 12_79
Part a:

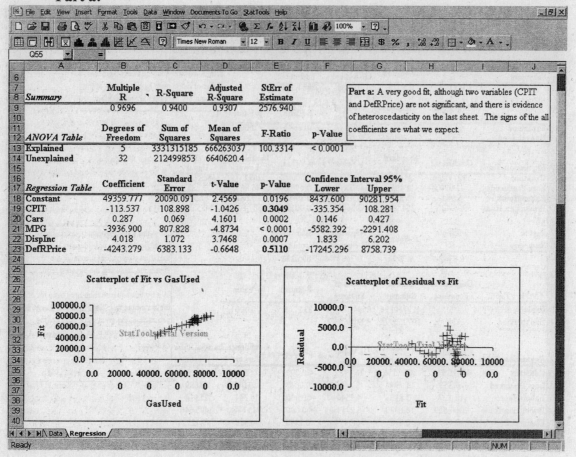

The spreadsheet shows:

Summary	Multiple R	R-Square	Adjusted R-Square	StErr of Estimate
	0.9696	0.9400	0.9307	2576.940

Part a: A very good fit, although two variables (CPIT and DefRPrice) are not significant, and there is evidence of heteroscedasticity on the last sheet. The signs of the all coefficients are what we expect.

ANOVA Table	Degrees of Freedom	Sum of Squares	Mean of Squares	F-Ratio	p-Value
Explained	5	3331315185	666263037	100.3314	< 0.0001
Unexplained	32	212499853	6640620.4		

Regression Table	Coefficient	Standard Error	t-Value	p-Value	Confidence Interval 95% Lower	Upper
Constant	49359.777	20090.091	2.4569	0.0196	8437.600	90281.954
CPIT	-113.537	108.898	-1.0426	0.3049	-335.354	108.281
Cars	0.287	0.069	4.1601	0.0002	0.146	0.427
MPG	-3936.900	807.828	-4.8734	< 0.0001	-5582.392	-2291.408
DispInc	4.018	1.072	3.7468	0.0007	1.833	6.202
DefRPrice	-4243.279	6383.133	-0.6648	0.5110	-17245.296	8758.739

Part b: For the government's claim (which I'll assume was made in 1999), suppose it raised the retail price in 1999 by one cent, from 1.165 to 1.175. Then the real price, DefRPrice, would increase from 100*RPrice/CPI to 100*(RPrice+1)/CPI, i.e., it would increase by 100(1)/166.6, or .6002. According to the regression equation, demand would decrease by 4243(.6002), or 2547.

So what's the net effect? Before the price increase, total revenue from gasoline sales was demand*price = 73372(1.165), or $85,478 million (since demand is expressed in millions of gallons). After the penny increase, total revenue becomes (73372-2547)*(1.175), or $83,219 million. This is a decrease in revenue, not at all what the government predicted. However, note that an important part of this calculation depends on the regression coefficient of DefRPrice, which has a very large standard error. So predictions based upon it shouldn't be trusted.

Problem 12_81

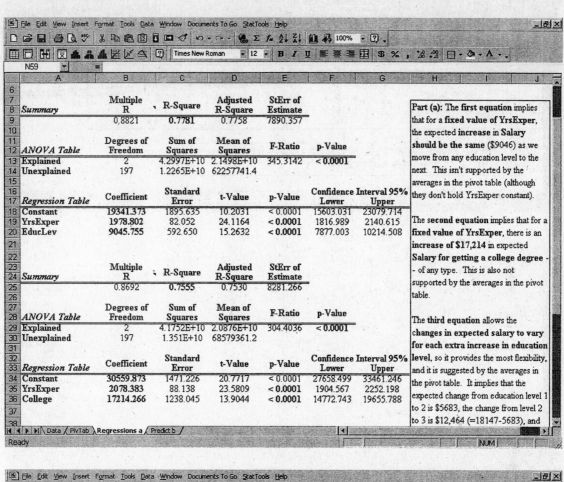

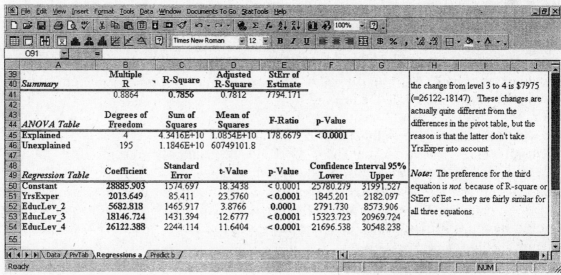

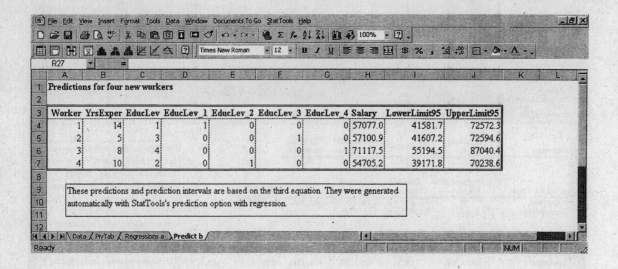

	Worker	YrsExper	EducLev	EducLev_1	EducLev_2	EducLev_3	EducLev_4	Salary	LowerLimit95	UpperLimit95
4	1	14	1	1	0	0	0	57077.0	41581.7	72572.3
5	2	5	3	0	0	1	0	57100.9	41607.2	72594.6
6	3	8	4	0	0	0	1	71117.5	55194.5	87040.4
7	4	10	2	0	1	0	0	54705.2	39171.8	70238.6

These predictions and prediction intervals are based on the third equation. They were generated automatically with StatTools's prediction option with regression.

CHAPTER 13

Problem 13_1

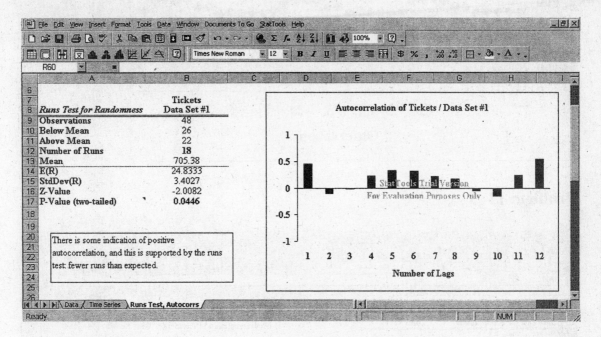

Problem 13_3

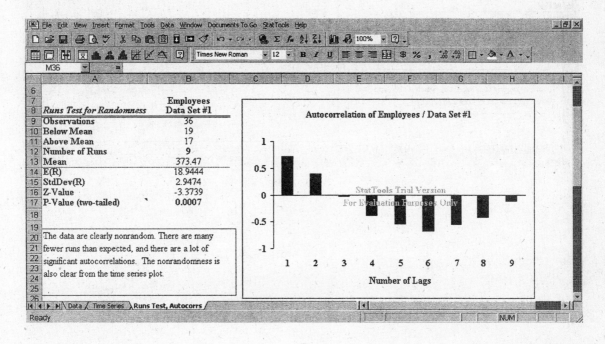

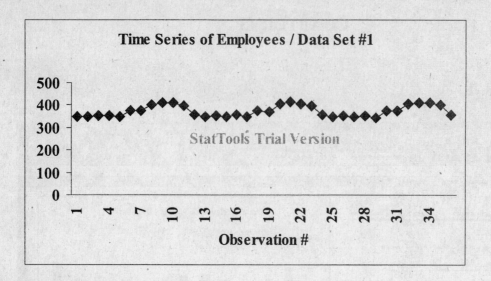

Time Series of Employees / Data Set #1

Problem 13_5

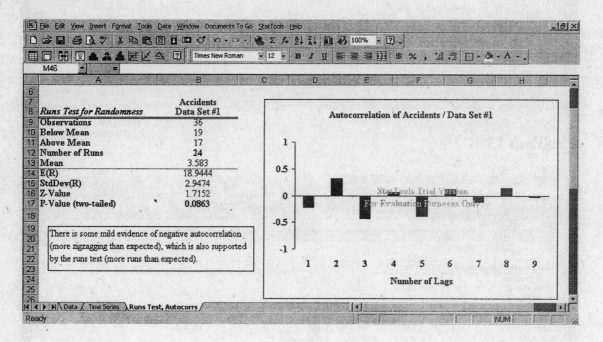

Runs Test for Randomness	Accidents Data Set #1
Observations	36
Below Mean	19
Above Mean	17
Number of Runs	24
Mean	3.583
E(R)	18.9444
StdDev(R)	2.9474
Z-Value	1.7152
P-Value (two-tailed)	0.0863

There is some mild evidence of negative autocorrelation (more zigzagging than expected), which is also supported by the runs test (more runs than expected).

Autocorrelation of Accidents / Data Set #1

Problem 13_11

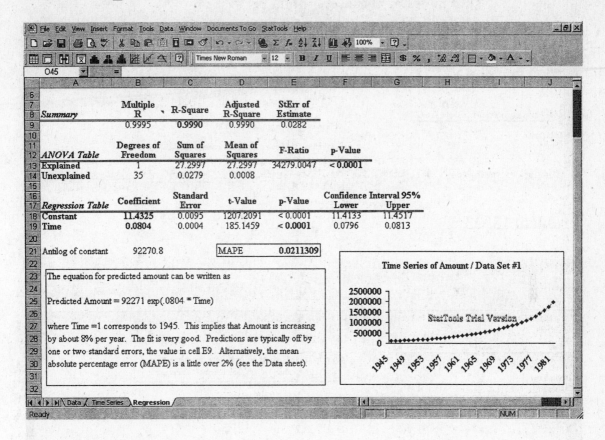

Problem 13_17

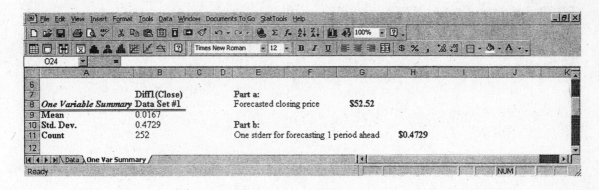

Problem 13_21

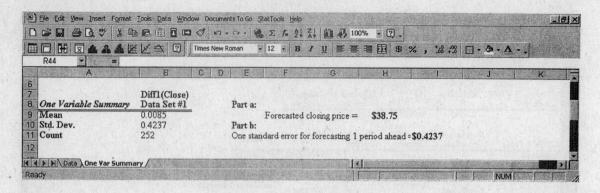

Problem 13_23

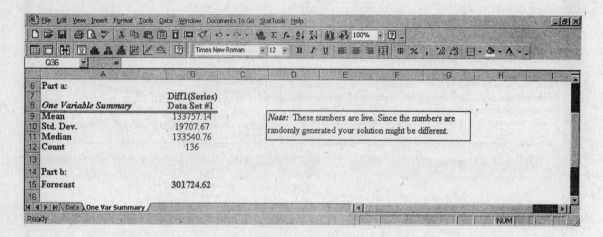

Problem 13_25

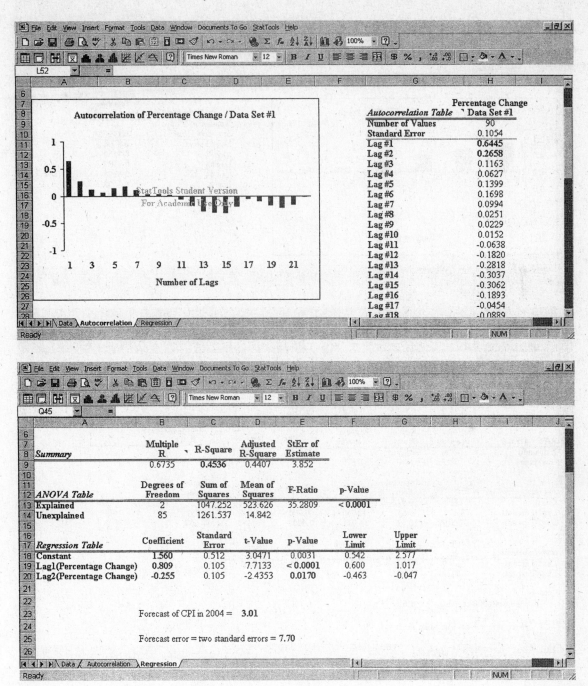

Problem 13_27

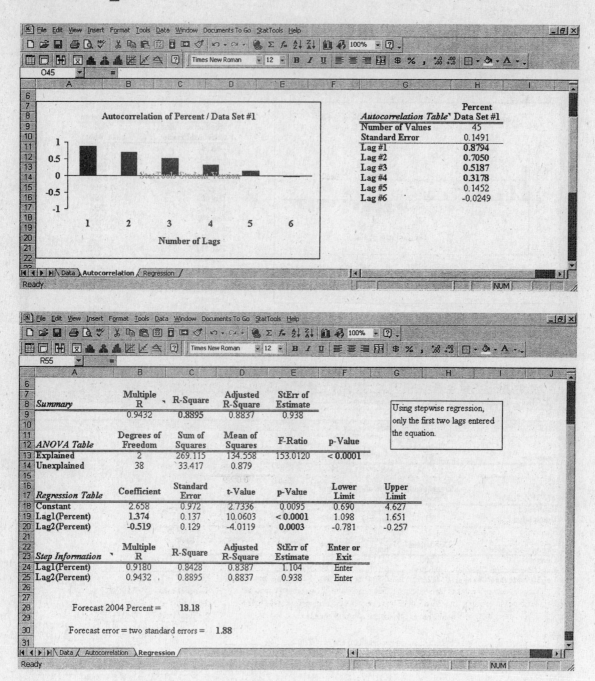

Problem 13_33
Part a:

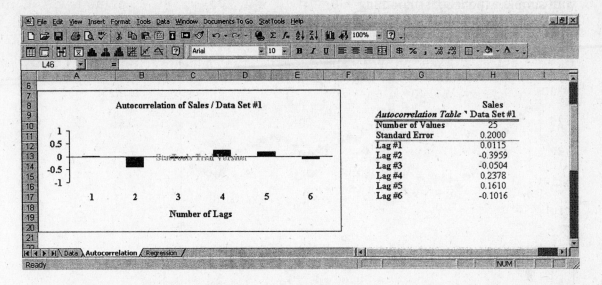

Part b:

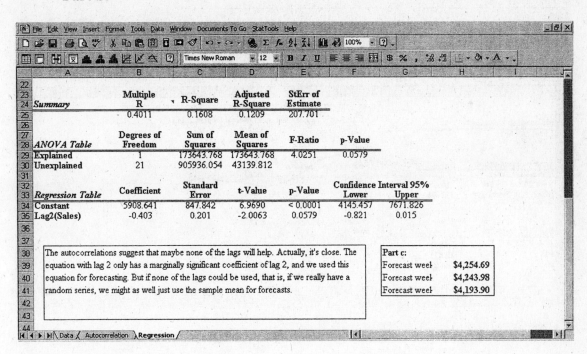

Summary	Multiple R	R-Square	Adjusted R-Square	StErr of Estimate			
	0.4011	0.1608	0.1209	207.701			

ANOVA Table	Degrees of Freedom	Sum of Squares	Mean of Squares	F-Ratio	p-Value		
Explained	1	173643.768	173643.768	4.0251	0.0579		
Unexplained	21	905936.054	43139.812				

Regression Table	Coefficient	Standard Error	t-Value	p-Value	Confidence Interval 95% Lower	Upper
Constant	5908.641	847.842	6.9690	< 0.0001	4145.457	7671.826
Lag2(Sales)	-0.403	0.201	-2.0063	0.0579	-0.821	0.015

The autocorrelations suggest that maybe none of the lags will help. Actually, it's close. The equation with lag 2 only has a marginally significant coefficient of lag 2, and we used this equation for forecasting. But if none of the lags could be used, that is, if we really have a random series, we might as well just use the sample mean for forecasts.

Part c:

Forecast week	$4,254.69
Forecast week	$4,243.98
Forecast week	$4,193.90

Problem 13_45

Part a: Given the lack of a clear trend or seasonaility, it is probably best to start with simple exponential smoothing.

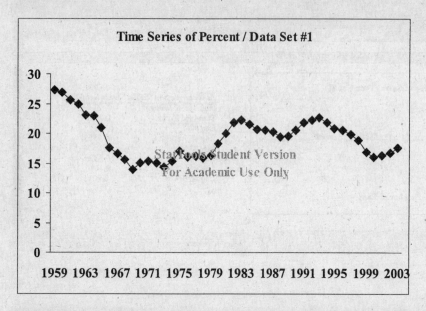

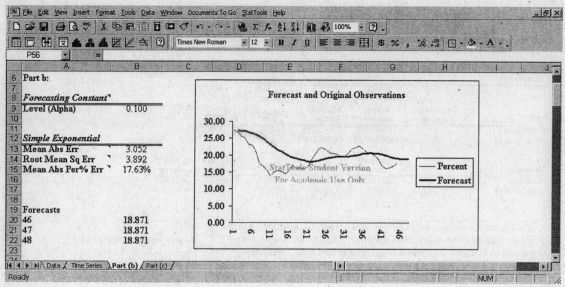

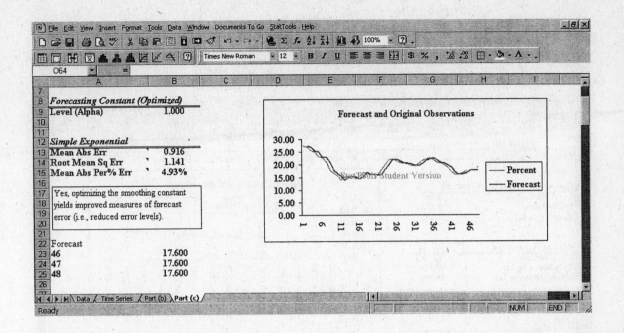

Problem 13_47

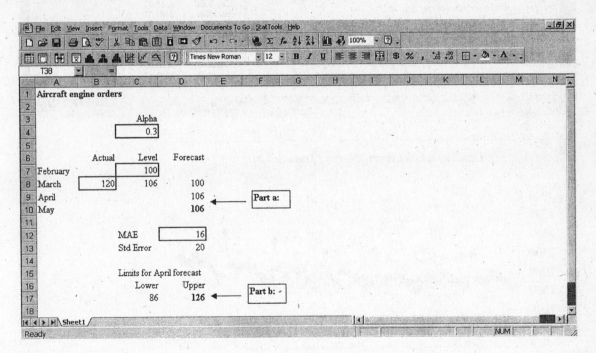

Problem 13_55

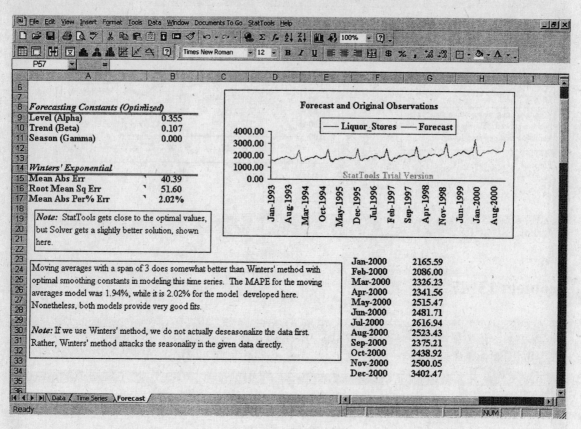

Jan-2000	2165.59
Feb-2000	2086.00
Mar-2000	2326.23
Apr-2000	2341.56
May-2000	2515.47
Jun-2000	2481.71
Jul-2000	2616.94
Aug-2000	2523.43
Sep-2000	2375.21
Oct-2000	2438.92
Nov-2000	2500.05
Dec-2000	3402.47

Moving averages with a span of 3 does somewhat better than Winters' method with optimal smoothing constants in modeling this time series. The MAPE for the moving averages model was 1.94%, while it is 2.02% for the model developed here. Nonetheless, both models provide very good fits.

Note: If we use Winters' method, we do not actually deseasonalize the data first. Rather, Winters' method attacks the seasonality in the given data directly.

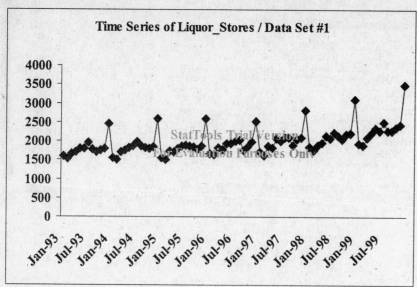

Problem 13_57

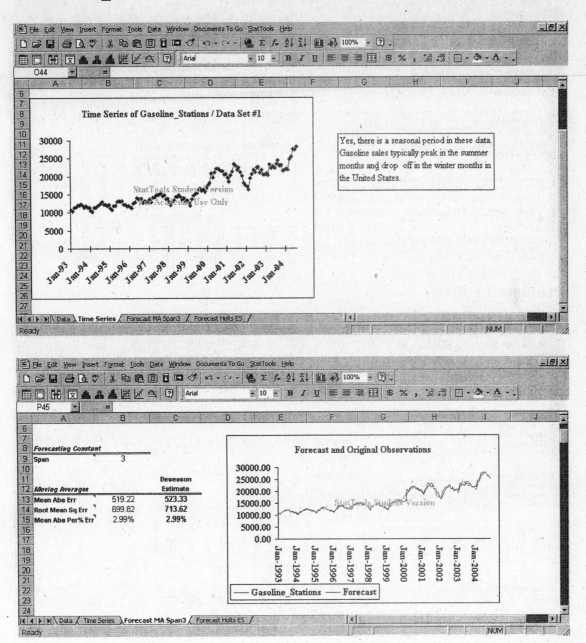

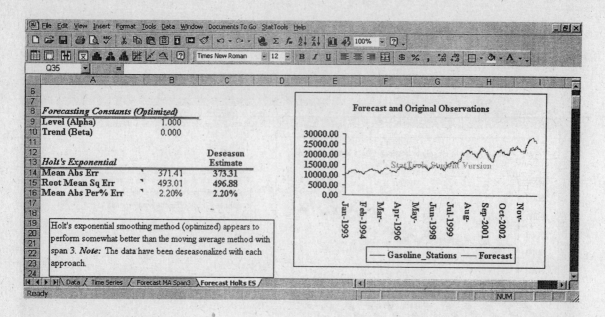

Problem 13_59

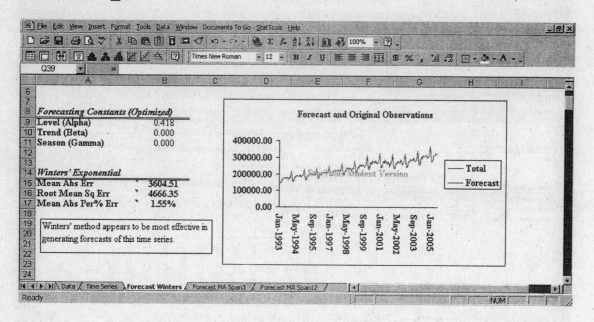

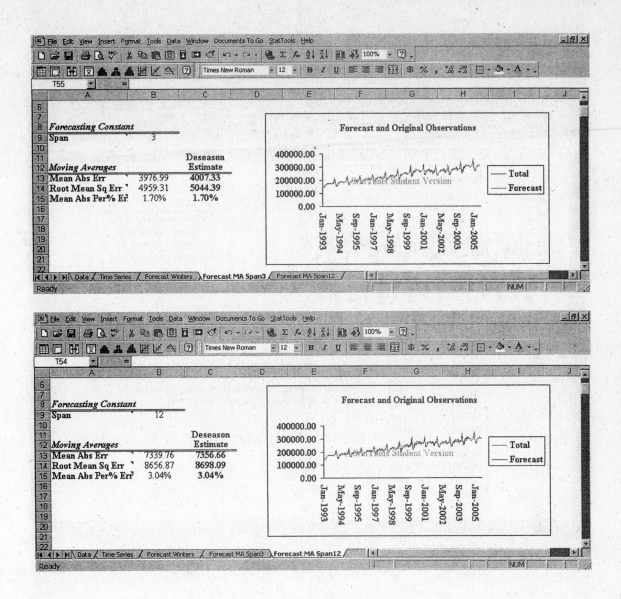

Problem 13_61

Part a:

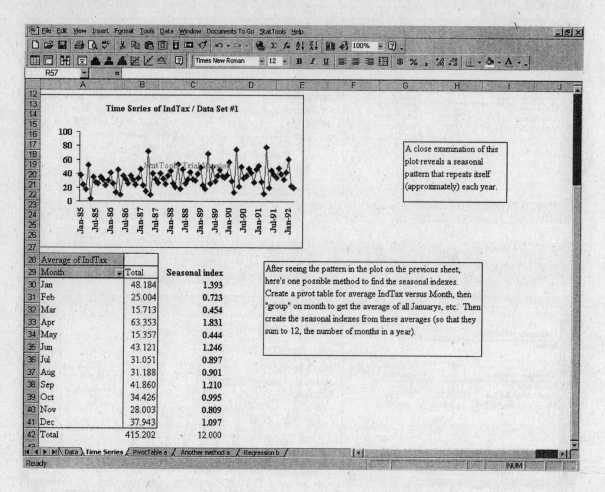

Time Series of IndTax / Data Set #1

A close examination of this plot reveals a seasonal pattern that repeats itself (approximately) each year.

Average of IndTax

Month	Total	Seasonal index
Jan	48.184	1.393
Feb	25.004	0.723
Mar	15.713	0.454
Apr	63.353	1.831
May	15.357	0.444
Jun	43.121	1.246
Jul	31.051	0.897
Aug	31.188	0.901
Sep	41.860	1.210
Oct	34.426	0.995
Nov	28.003	0.809
Dec	37.943	1.097
Total	415.202	12.000

After seeing the pattern in the plot on the previous sheet, here's one possible method to find the seasonal indexes. Create a pivot table for average IndTax versus Month, then "group" on month to get the average of all Januarys, etc. Then create the seasonal indexes from these averages (so that they sum to 12, the number of months in a year).

Here is another method:

Use StatTools's Forecasting procedure, using any forecasting method (we used the default, Moving Averages with Span 3) and making sure to check the box to deseasonalize. Then the seasonal indexes are part of the output. They are very close to the seasonal indexes from the pivot table method. (The parts of the output not needed here were deleted.) We used these for part b, since the required deseasonalized values are in column D.

Part b:

O53

	A	B	C	D	E	F	G	H	I	J
7		Multiple	R-Square	Adjusted	StErr of					
8	*Summary*	R		R-Square	Estimate					
9		0.6171	0.3808	0.3735	5.200					
10										
11		Degrees of	Sum of	Mean of		F-Ratio	p-Value			
12	*ANOVA Table*	Freedom	Squares	Squares						
13	Explained	1	1413.389	1413.389	52.2636	< 0.0001				
14	Unexplained	85	2298.694	27.043						
15										
16			Standard				Confidence Interval 95%			
17	*Regression Table*	Coefficient	Error	t-Value	p-Value	Lower	Upper			
18	Constant	27.530	1.125	24.4764	< 0.0001	25.294	29.766			
19	Month	0.160	0.022	7.2294	< 0.0001	0.116	0.205			
20										
21	Forecasts for next 12 months									
22	Month	Deseason FCast	Forecast							
23	88	41.654	57.517							
24	89	41.814	31.016							
25	90	41.975	18.058		Calculations for RMSE, MAPE					
26	91	42.135	77.658		Month	Ind Tax	Deseason FCast	Forecast	Error	AbsPctErro
27	92	42.296	20.334		1	37.852	27.690	38.236	-0.384	1.0%
28	93	42.456	53.400		2	23.769	27.851	20.658	3.111	13.1%
29	94	42.617	38.459		3	17.031	28.011	12.051	4.980	29.2%
30	95	42.777	38.278		4	52.476	28.172	51.923	0.553	1.1%
31	96	42.938	51.764		5	3.618	28.332	13.621	-10.003	276.5%
32	97	43.098	42.630		6	34.77	28.493	35.837	-1.067	3.1%
33	98	43.259	34.413		7	27.148	28.653	25.858	1.290	4.8%
34	99	43.419	46.811		8	25.776	28.814	25.783	-0.007	0.0%
35					9	34.65	28.974	34.930	-0.280	0.8%
36					10	30.596	29.135	28.818	1.778	5.8%

Method: Use regression with DeseasObs as the dependent variable, Month as the only explanatory variable. Then use this equation, along with the seasonal factors in the previous sheet, to forecast the series (current and future) back in original, "reseasonalized" units. Finally, use the usual method to calculate RMSE and MAPE based on the original 87 observations.

RMSE	3.718
MAPE	12.4%

Data / Time Series / PivotTable a / Another method a \ **Regression b** /

Ready   NUM

Problem 13_63

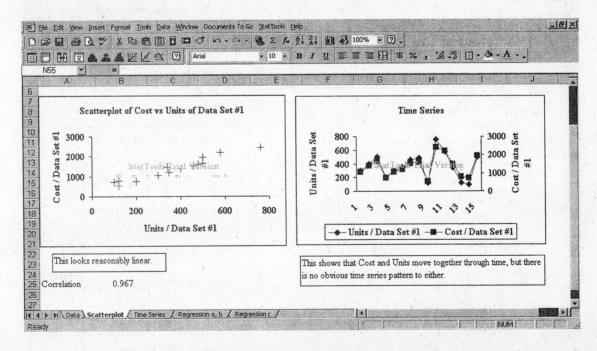

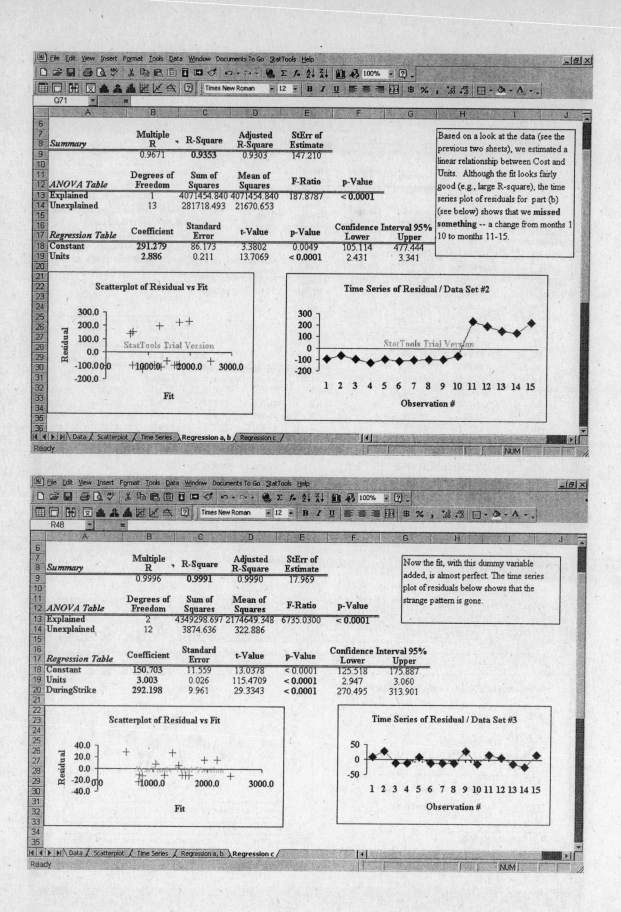

Problem 13_71

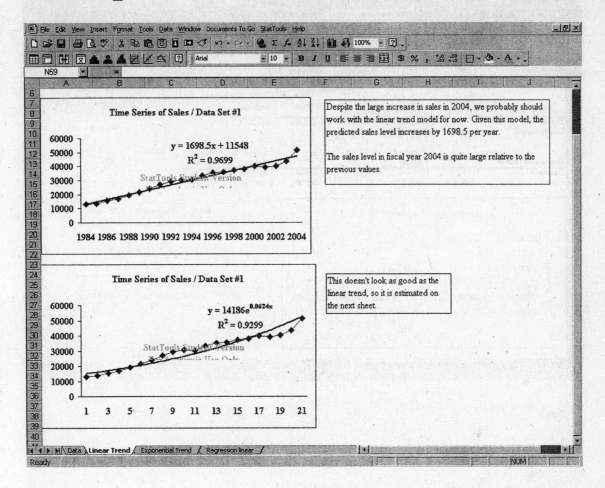

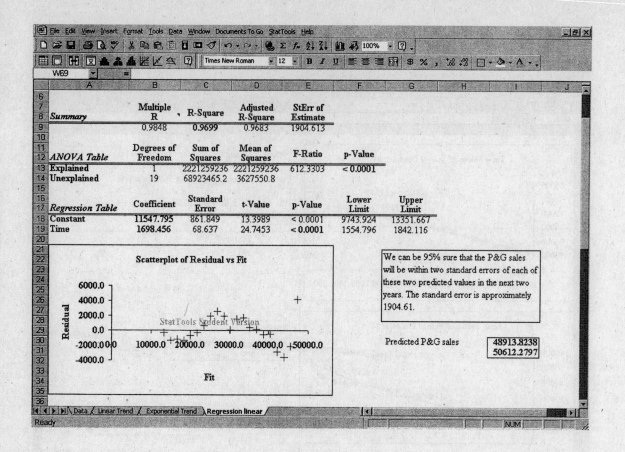

| File | Edit | View | Insert | Format | Tools | Data | Window | Documents To Go | StatTools | Help |

| W69 | = |

	A	B	C	D	E	F	G	H	I	J
6										
7		Multiple R	R-Square	Adjusted R-Square	StErr of Estimate					
8	*Summary*									
9		0.9848	0.9699	0.9683	1904.613					
10										
11		Degrees of Freedom	Sum of Squares	Mean of Squares	F-Ratio	p-Value				
12	*ANOVA Table*									
13	Explained	1	2221259236	2221259236	612.3303	< 0.0001				
14	Unexplained	19	68923465.2	3627550.8						
15										
16		Coefficient	Standard Error	t-Value	p-Value	Lower Limit	Upper Limit			
17	*Regression Table*									
18	Constant	11547.795	861.849	13.3989	< 0.0001	9743.924	13351.667			
19	Time	1698.456	68.637	24.7453	< 0.0001	1554.796	1842.116			

We can be 95% sure that the P&G sales will be within two standard errors of each of these two predicted values in the next two years. The standard error is approximately 1904.61.

Predicted P&G sales

| 48913.8238 |
| 50612.2797 |

Scatterplot of Residual vs Fit

StatTools Student Version

| Data | Linear Trend | Exponential Trend | **Regression linear** |

Ready | NUM

Problem 13_75

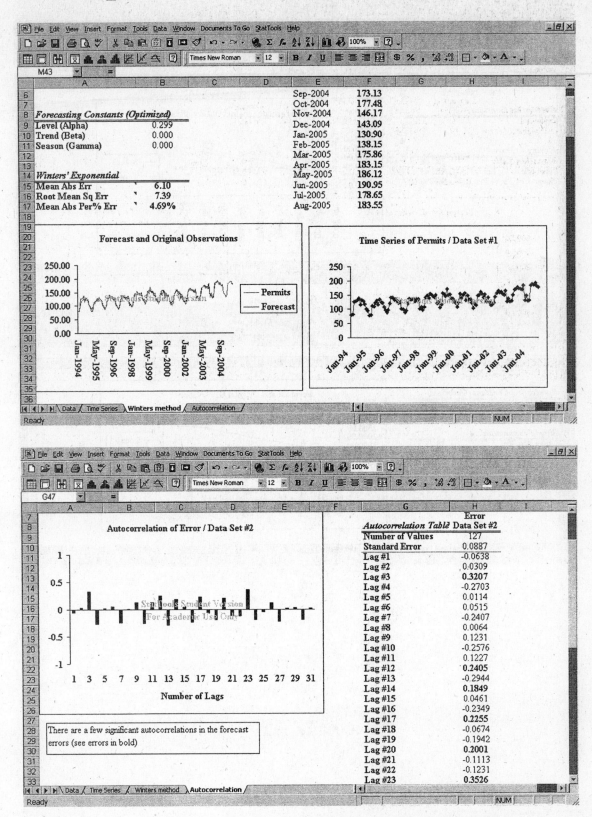

Problem 13_79

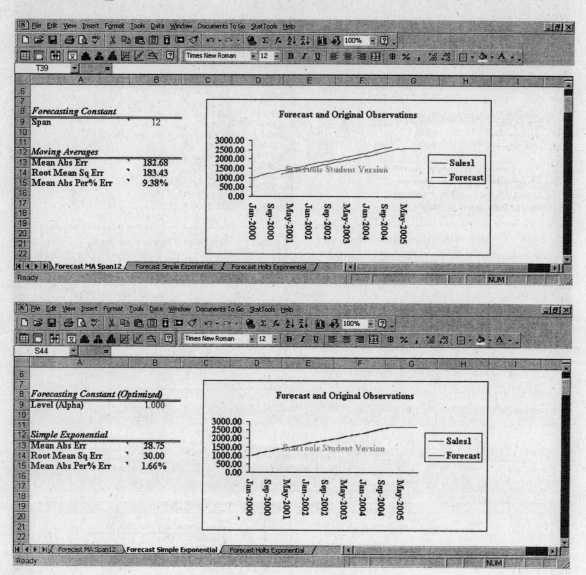

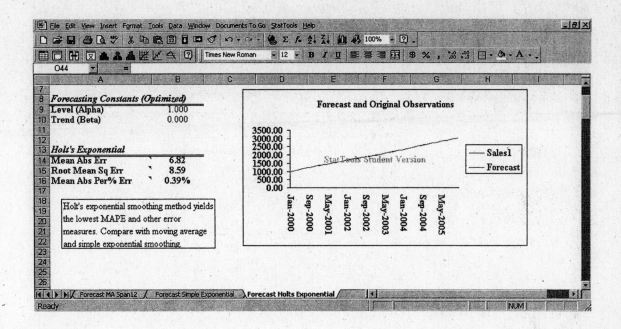

CHAPTER 14

All problems will be set up using the following system:

- **input cells**　　　**thick border**
- **changing cells**　　**gray shading and boldface**
- **target cell**　　　**double line border**

Problem 14_5

The grams constraint line is currently the thick one. As its right-hand side increases, it moves up and to the right. Once it gets beyond the dashed line, i.e., beyond the point where the other two constraint lines cross, there will be no feasible solutions. We know that the point where the other two constraint lines cross is (1.25, 1.875). (This is the optimal solution from the text.) Plugging these values into the left-hand side of the grams constraint gives 37(1.25)+65(1.875) = 168.125. This is the largest the right-hand side of the grams constraint can be before there will be no feasible solutions.

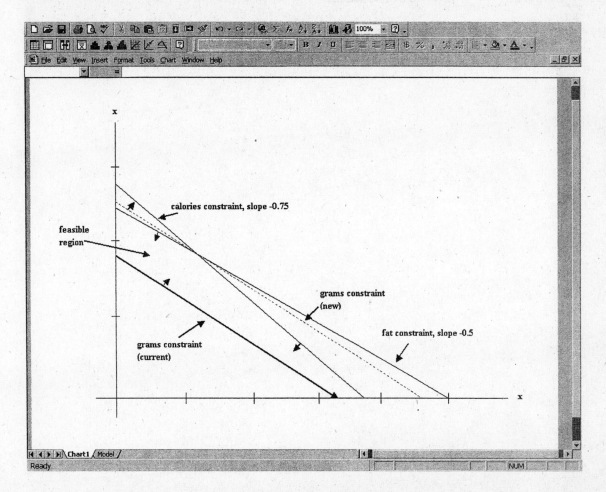

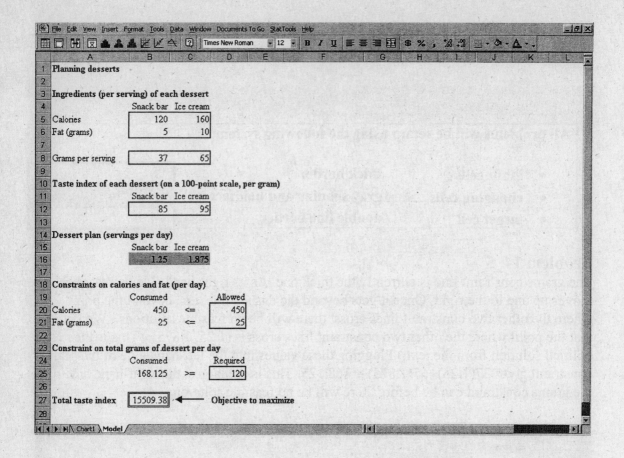

Problem 14_9

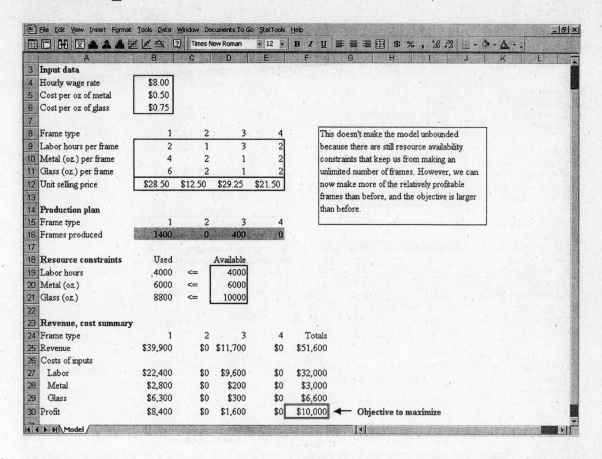

	File Edit View Insert Format Tools Data Window Documents To Go StatTools Help										

	A	B	C	D	E	F	G	H	I	J	K	L
3	**Input data**											
4	Hourly wage rate	$8.00										
5	Cost per oz of metal	$0.50										
6	Cost per oz of glass	$0.75										
7												
8	Frame type	1	2	3	4							
9	Labor hours per frame	2	1	3	2							
10	Metal (oz.) per frame	4	2	1	2							
11	Glass (oz.) per frame	6	2	1	2							
12	Unit selling price	$28.50	$12.50	$29.25	$21.50							
13												
14	**Production plan**											
15	Frame type	1	2	3	4							
16	Frames produced	1400	0	400	0							
17												
18	**Resource constraints**	Used		Available								
19	Labor hours	4000	<=	4000								
20	Metal (oz.)	6000	<=	6000								
21	Glass (oz.)	8800	<=	10000								
22												
23	**Revenue, cost summary**											
24	Frame type	1	2	3	4	Totals						
25	Revenue	$39,900	$0	$11,700	$0	$51,600						
26	Costs of inputs											
27	Labor	$22,400	$0	$9,600	$0	$32,000						
28	Metal	$2,800	$0	$200	$0	$3,000						
29	Glass	$6,300	$0	$300	$0	$6,600						
30	Profit	$8,400	$0	$1,600	$0	$10,000	← Objective to maximize					

This doesn't make the model unbounded because there are still resource availability constraints that keep us from making an unlimited number of frames. However, we can now make more of the relatively profitable frames than before, and the objective is larger than before.

Problem 14_11
Part a:

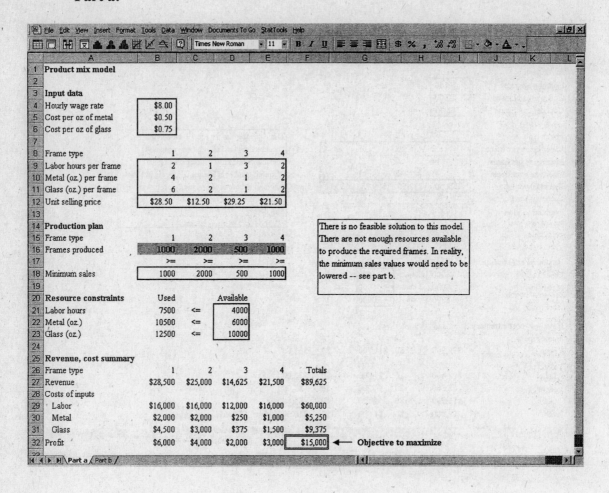

Part b:

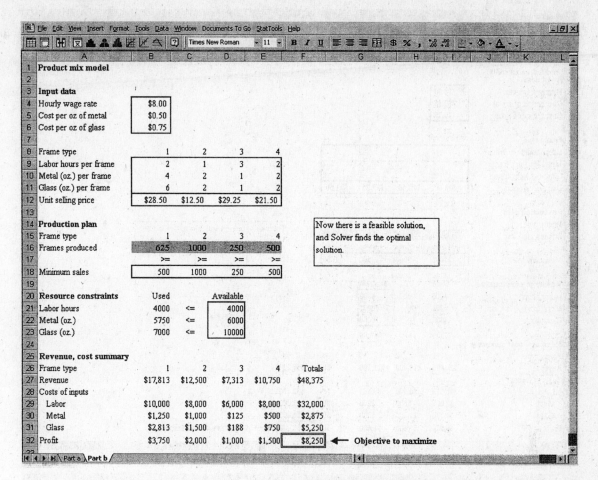

	A	B	C	D	E	F	G
1	**Product mix model**						
2							
3	**Input data**						
4	Hourly wage rate	$8.00					
5	Cost per oz of metal	$0.50					
6	Cost per oz of glass	$0.75					
7							
8	Frame type	1	2	3	4		
9	Labor hours per frame	2	1	3	2		
10	Metal (oz.) per frame	4	2	1	2		
11	Glass (oz.) per frame	6	2	1	2		
12	Unit selling price	$28.50	$12.50	$29.25	$21.50		
13							
14	**Production plan**						
15	Frame type	1	2	3	4		
16	Frames produced	625	1000	250	500		
17		>=	>=	>=	>=		
18	Minimum sales	500	1000	250	500		
19							
20	**Resource constraints**	Used		Available			
21	Labor hours	4000	<=	4000			
22	Metal (oz.)	5750	<=	6000			
23	Glass (oz.)	7000	<=	10000			
24							
25	**Revenue, cost summary**						
26	Frame type	1	2	3	4	Totals	
27	Revenue	$17,813	$12,500	$7,313	$10,750	$48,375	
28	Costs of inputs						
29	Labor	$10,000	$8,000	$6,000	$8,000	$32,000	
30	Metal	$1,250	$1,000	$125	$500	$2,875	
31	Glass	$2,813	$1,500	$188	$750	$5,250	
32	Profit	$3,750	$2,000	$1,000	$1,500	$8,250	← Objective to maximize

Now there is a feasible solution, and Solver finds the optimal solution.

Problem 14_13

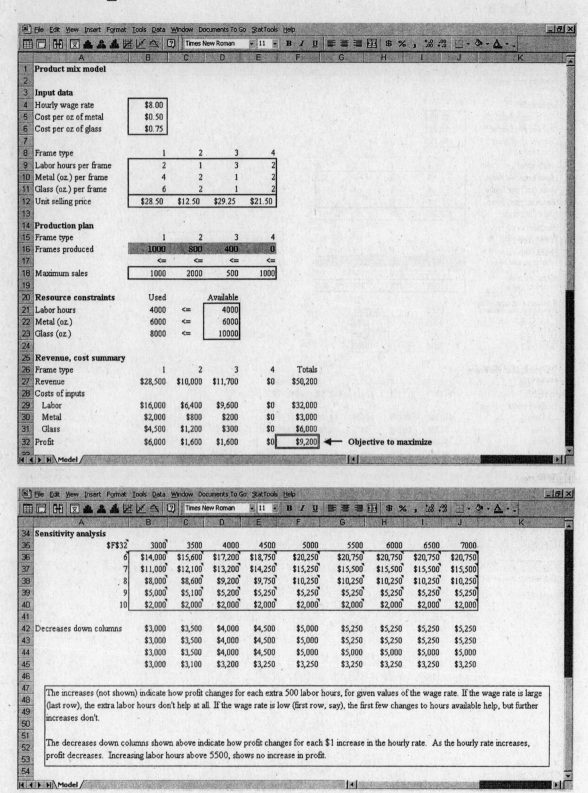

Top spreadsheet:

	A	B	C	D	E	F	G	H	I	J	K
1	Product mix model										
2											
3	Input data										
4	Hourly wage rate	$8.00									
5	Cost per oz of metal	$0.50									
6	Cost per oz of glass	$0.75									
7											
8	Frame type	1	2	3	4						
9	Labor hours per frame	2	1	3	2						
10	Metal (oz.) per frame	4	2	1	2						
11	Glass (oz.) per frame	6	2	1	2						
12	Unit selling price	$28.50	$12.50	$29.25	$21.50						
13											
14	Production plan										
15	Frame type	1	2	3	4						
16	Frames produced	1000	800	400	0						
17		<=	<=	<=	<=						
18	Maximum sales	1000	2000	500	1000						
19											
20	Resource constraints	Used		Available							
21	Labor hours	4000	<=	4000							
22	Metal (oz.)	6000	<=	6000							
23	Glass (oz.)	8000	<=	10000							
24											
25	Revenue, cost summary										
26	Frame type	1	2	3	4	Totals					
27	Revenue	$28,500	$10,000	$11,700	$0	$50,200					
28	Costs of inputs										
29	Labor	$16,000	$6,400	$9,600	$0	$32,000					
30	Metal	$2,000	$800	$200	$0	$3,000					
31	Glass	$4,500	$1,200	$300	$0	$6,000					
32	Profit	$6,000	$1,600	$1,600	$0	$9,200					

$9,200 ⟵ **Objective to maximize**

Bottom spreadsheet:

	A	B	C	D	E	F	G	H	I	J	K
34	Sensitivity analysis										
35	$F$32	3000	3500	4000	4500	5000	5500	6000	6500	7000	
36	6	$14,000	$15,600	$17,200	$18,750	$20,250	$20,750	$20,750	$20,750	$20,750	
37	7	$11,000	$12,100	$13,200	$14,250	$15,250	$15,500	$15,500	$15,500	$15,500	
38	8	$8,000	$8,600	$9,200	$9,750	$10,250	$10,250	$10,250	$10,250	$10,250	
39	9	$5,000	$5,100	$5,200	$5,250	$5,250	$5,250	$5,250	$5,250	$5,250	
40	10	$2,000	$2,000	$2,000	$2,000	$2,000	$2,000	$2,000	$2,000	$2,000	
41											
42	Decreases down columns	$3,000	$3,500	$4,000	$4,500	$5,000	$5,250	$5,250	$5,250	$5,250	
43		$3,000	$3,500	$4,000	$4,500	$5,000	$5,250	$5,250	$5,250	$5,250	
44		$3,000	$3,500	$4,000	$4,500	$5,000	$5,000	$5,000	$5,000	$5,000	
45		$3,000	$3,100	$3,200	$3,250	$3,250	$3,250	$3,250	$3,250	$3,250	

The increases (not shown) indicate how profit changes for each extra 500 labor hours, for given values of the wage rate. If the wage rate is large (last row), the extra labor hours don't help at all. If the wage rate is low (first row, say), the first few changes to hours available help, but further increases don't.

The decreases down columns shown above indicate how profit changes for each $1 increase in the hourly rate. As the hourly rate increases, profit decreases. Increasing labor hours above 5500, shows no increase in profit.

Problem 14_15

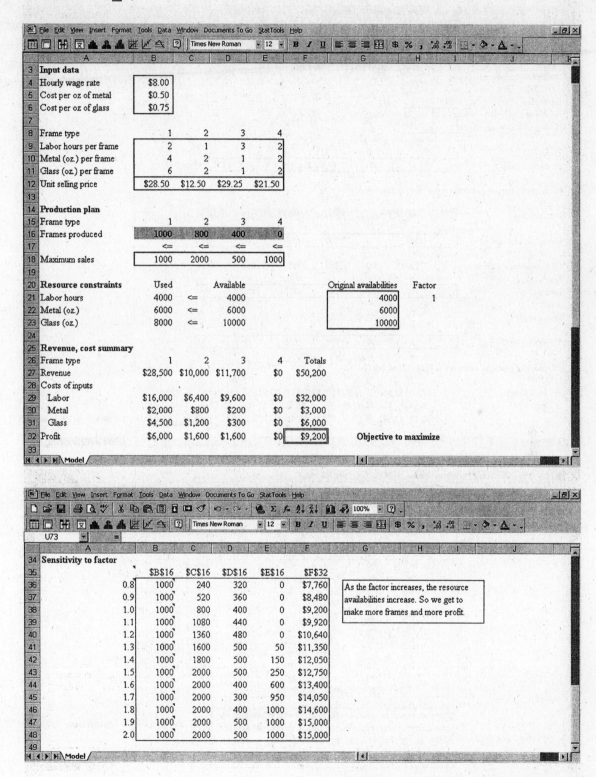

	A	B	C	D	E	F	G	H	I	J	K
3	**Input data**										
4	Hourly wage rate	$8.00									
5	Cost per oz of metal	$0.50									
6	Cost per oz of glass	$0.75									
7											
8	Frame type	1	2	3	4						
9	Labor hours per frame	2	1	3	2						
10	Metal (oz.) per frame	4	2	1	2						
11	Glass (oz.) per frame	6	2	1	2						
12	Unit selling price	$28.50	$12.50	$29.25	$21.50						
13											
14	**Production plan**										
15	Frame type	1	2	3	4						
16	Frames produced	1000	800	400	0						
17		<=	<=	<=	<=						
18	Maximum sales	1000	2000	500	1000						
19											
20	**Resource constraints**	Used		Available			Original availabilities		Factor		
21	Labor hours	4000	<=	4000			4000		1		
22	Metal (oz.)	6000	<=	6000			6000				
23	Glass (oz.)	8000	<=	10000			10000				
24											
25	**Revenue, cost summary**										
26	Frame type	1	2	3	4	Totals					
27	Revenue	$28,500	$10,000	$11,700	$0	$50,200					
28	Costs of inputs										
29	Labor	$16,000	$6,400	$9,600	$0	$32,000					
30	Metal	$2,000	$800	$200	$0	$3,000					
31	Glass	$4,500	$1,200	$300	$0	$6,000					
32	Profit	$6,000	$1,600	$1,600	$0	$9,200	Objective to maximize				

	A	B	C	D	E	F	G	H	I	J
34	**Sensitivity to factor**									
35			$B$16	$C$16	$D$16	$E$16	$F$32			
36		0.8	1000	240	320	0	$7,760	As the factor increases, the resource		
37		0.9	1000	520	360	0	$8,480	availabilities increase. So we get to		
38		1.0	1000	800	400	0	$9,200	make more frames and more profit.		
39		1.1	1000	1080	440	0	$9,920			
40		1.2	1000	1360	480	0	$10,640			
41		1.3	1000	1600	500	50	$11,350			
42		1.4	1000	1800	500	150	$12,050			
43		1.5	1000	2000	500	250	$12,750			
44		1.6	1000	2000	400	600	$13,400			
45		1.7	1000	2000	300	950	$14,050			
46		1.8	1000	2000	400	1000	$14,600			
47		1.9	1000	2000	500	1000	$15,000			
48		2.0	1000	2000	500	1000	$15,000			

Problem 14_17

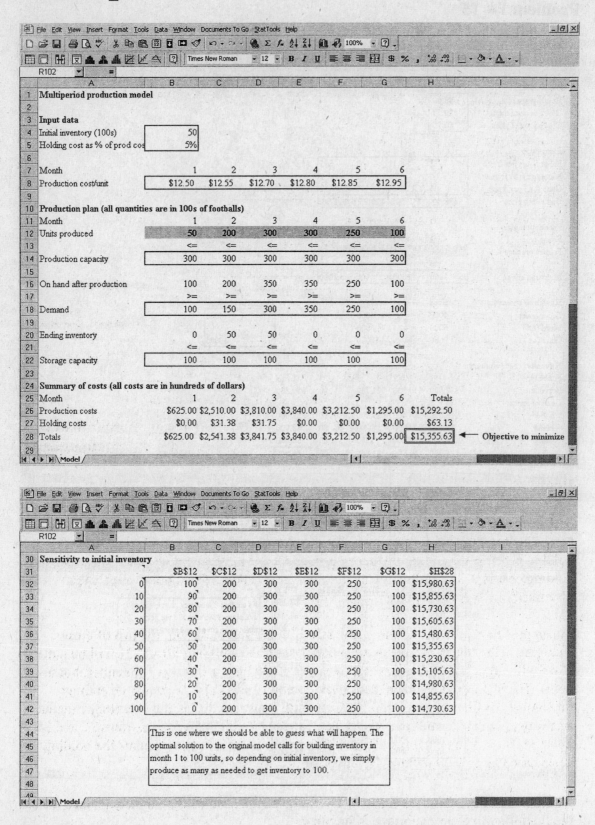

Problem 14_19

	A	B	C	D	E	F	G	H	I	J	K
1	Multiperiod production model										
2											
3	Input data										
4	Initial inventory (100s)	50									
5	Holding cost as % of prod cost	5%									
6											
7	Month	1	2	3	4	5	6				
8	Production cost/unit	$12.50	$12.55	$12.70	$12.80	$12.85	$12.95				
9											
10	Production plan (all quantities are in 100s of footballs)										
11	Month	1	2	3	4	5	6				
12	Units produced	50	200	300	300	250	100				
13		<=	<=	<=	<=	<=	<=				
14	Production capacity	300	300	300	300	300	300				
15											
16	Demand	100	150	300	350	250	100				
17											
18	Ending inventory	0	50	50	0	0	0	← Constrain these to be nonnegative			
19		<=	<=	<=	<=	<=	<=				
20	Storage capacity	100	100	100	100	100	100				
21											
22	Summary of costs (all costs are in hundreds of dollars)										
23	Month	1	2	3	4	5	6	Totals			
24	Production costs	$625.00	$2,510.00	$3,810.00	$3,840.00	$3,212.50	$1,295.00	$15,292.50			
25	Holding costs	$0.00	$31.38	$31.75	$0.00	$0.00	$0.00	$63.13			
26	Totals	$625.00	$2,541.38	$3,841.75	$3,840.00	$3,212.50	$1,295.00	$15,355.63	← Objective to minimize		

Problem 14_21

This is trickier than it looks. First, we constrain onhand after production to be >= demand only in month 6. This will allow negative ending inventories in months 1-5. The tricky part is getting the holding cost right. The obvious approach is to use IF functions for holding costs: if the ending inventory is positive, we have a holding cost; otherwise, the holding cost is 0. The problem is that Solver can't handle IF functions reliably (as discussed in the next chapter).

The approach here is to add three new rows, 20-22, and make the first two of these changing cells. In any month, at most one of the values in rows 20 and 21 will be nonzero -- we will either have inventory left over or we will have a shortage (or neither, but not both). The difference between them (row 20 minus row 21) is logically the ending inventory. To tie everything together, we must constrain the ending inventory calculated this way to equal the ending inventory calculated the original way, i.e., rows 22 and 24 must be equal. The nice thing about this approach is that we can calculate the holding costs based on row 20 without IF functions.

As for the optimal solution, it is slightly cheaper than for the original model, since we use the flexibility to have a shortage in month 4.

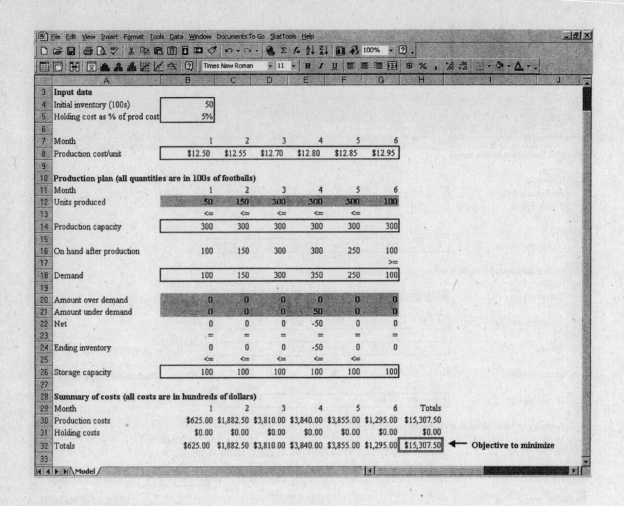

Problem 14_25

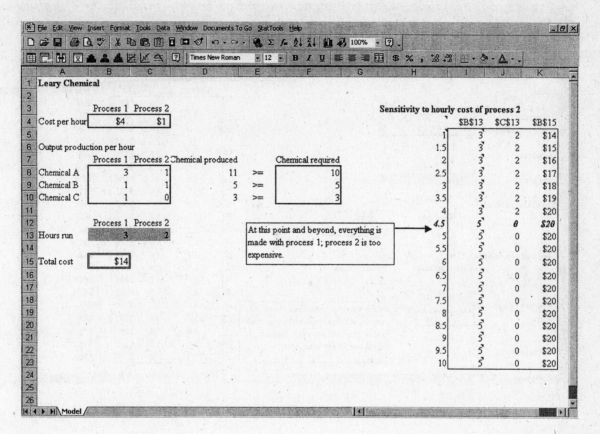

Problem 14_27

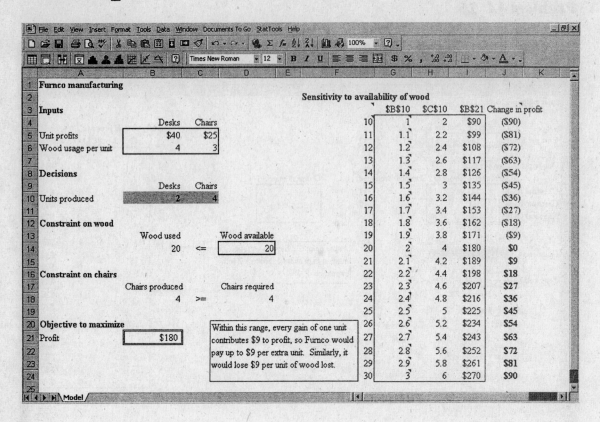

Problem 14_29

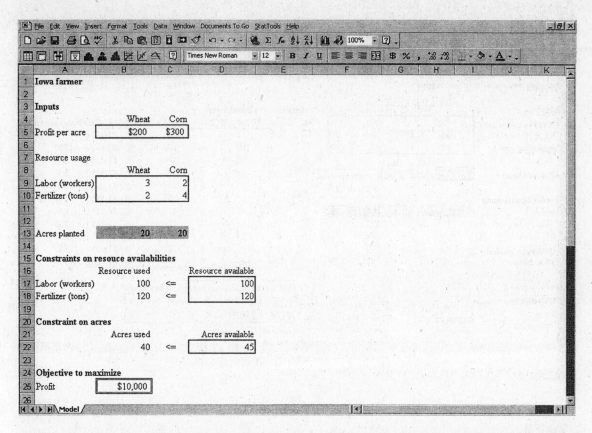

	A	B	C	D	E	F
1	**Iowa farmer**					
2						
3	**Inputs**					
4		Wheat	Corn			
5	Profit per acre	$200	$300			
6						
7	Resource usage					
8		Wheat	Corn			
9	Labor (workers)	3	2			
10	Fertilizer (tons)	2	4			
11						
12						
13	Acres planted	20	20			
14						
15	**Constraints on resouce availabilities**					
16		Resource used		Resource available		
17	Labor (workers)	100	<=	100		
18	Fertilizer (tons)	120	<=	120		
19						
20	**Constraint on acres**					
21		Acres used		Acres available		
22		40	<=	45		
23						
24	**Objective to maximize**					
25	Profit	$10,000				
26						

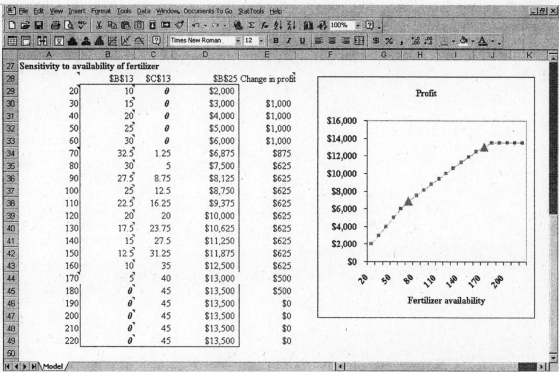

	A	B	C	D	E
27	**Sensitivity to availability of fertilizer**				
28		$B$13	$C$13	$B$25	Change in profit
29	20	10	0	$2,000	
30	30	15	0	$3,000	$1,000
31	40	20	0	$4,000	$1,000
32	50	25	0	$5,000	$1,000
33	60	30	0	$6,000	$1,000
34	70	32.5	1.25	$6,875	$875
35	80	30	5	$7,500	$625
36	90	27.5	8.75	$8,125	$625
37	100	25	12.5	$8,750	$625
38	110	22.5	16.25	$9,375	$625
39	120	20	20	$10,000	$625
40	130	17.5	23.75	$10,625	$625
41	140	15	27.5	$11,250	$625
42	150	12.5	31.25	$11,875	$625
43	160	10	35	$12,500	$625
44	170	5	40	$13,000	$500
45	180	0	45	$13,500	$500
46	190	0	45	$13,500	$0
47	200	0	45	$13,500	$0
48	210	0	45	$13,500	$0
49	220	0	45	$13,500	$0
50					

Problem 14_31

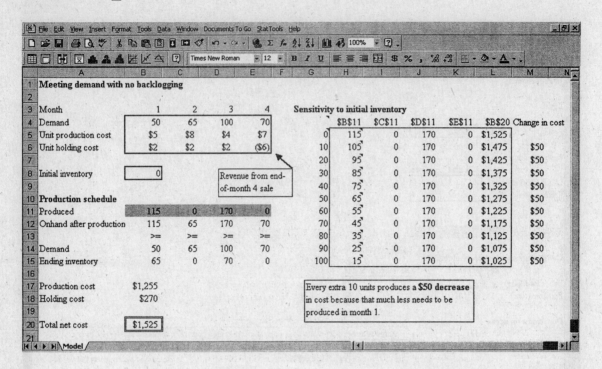

| File | Edit | View | Insert | Format | Tools | Data | Window | Documents To Go | StatTools | Help |

	A	B	C	D	E	F	G	H	I	J	K	L	M	N
1	**Meeting demand with no backlogging**													
2														
3	Month		1	2	3	4		**Sensitivity to initial inventory**						
4	Demand	50	65	100	70			$B$11	$C$11	$D$11	$E$11	$B$20	Change in cost	
5	Unit production cost	$5	$8	$4	$7		0	115	0	170	0	$1,525		
6	Unit holding cost	$2	$2	$2	($6)		10	105	0	170	0	$1,475	$50	
7							20	95	0	170	0	$1,425	$50	
8	Initial inventory	0					30	85	0	170	0	$1,375	$50	
9							40	75	0	170	0	$1,325	$50	
10	**Production schedule**						50	65	0	170	0	$1,275	$50	
11	Produced	115	0	170	0		60	55	0	170	0	$1,225	$50	
12	Onhand after production	115	65	170	70		70	45	0	170	0	$1,175	$50	
13		>=	>=	>=	>=		80	35	0	170	0	$1,125	$50	
14	Demand	50	65	100	70		90	25	0	170	0	$1,075	$50	
15	Ending inventory	65	0	70	0		100	15	0	170	0	$1,025	$50	
16														
17	Production cost	$1,255												
18	Holding cost	$270												
19														
20	Total net cost	$1,525												
21														

Revenue from end-of-month 4 sale

Every extra 10 units produces a **$50 decrease** in cost because that much less needs to be produced in month 1.

Problem 14_33

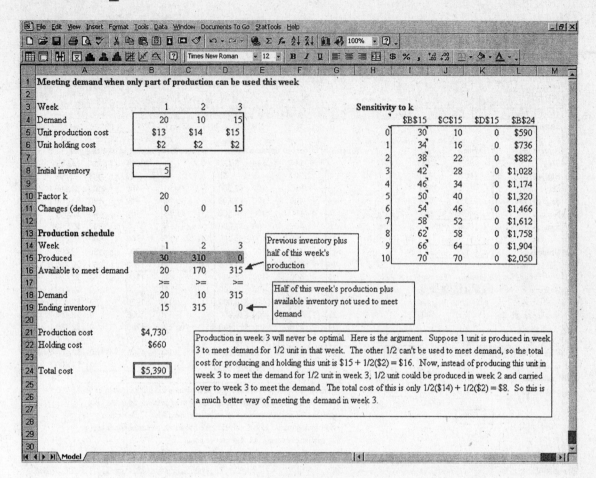

Problem 14_37

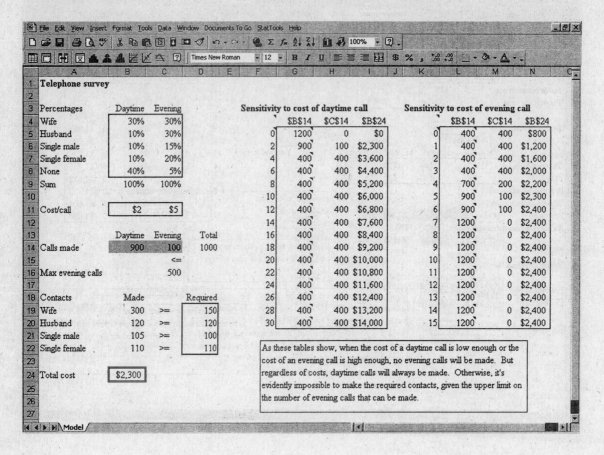

	A	B	C	D	E	F	G	H	I	J	K	L	M	N
1	Telephone survey													
2														
3	Percentages	Daytime	Evening			Sensitivity to cost of daytime call					Sensitivity to cost of evening call			
4	Wife	30%	30%				$B$14	$C$14	$B$24			$B$14	$C$14	$B$24
5	Husband	10%	30%			0	1200	0	$0		0	400	400	$800
6	Single male	10%	15%			2	900	100	$2,300		1	400	400	$1,200
7	Single female	10%	20%			4	400	400	$3,600		2	400	400	$1,600
8	None	40%	5%			6	400	400	$4,400		3	400	400	$2,000
9	Sum	100%	100%			8	400	400	$5,200		4	700	200	$2,200
10						10	400	400	$6,000		5	900	100	$2,300
11	Cost/call	$2	$5			12	400	400	$6,800		6	900	100	$2,400
12						14	400	400	$7,600		7	1200	0	$2,400
13		Daytime	Evening	Total		16	400	400	$8,400		8	1200	0	$2,400
14	Calls made	900	100	1000		18	400	400	$9,200		9	1200	0	$2,400
15			<=			20	400	400	$10,000		10	1200	0	$2,400
16	Max evening calls		500			22	400	400	$10,800		11	1200	0	$2,400
17						24	400	400	$11,600		12	1200	0	$2,400
18	Contacts	Made		Required		26	400	400	$12,400		13	1200	0	$2,400
19	Wife	300	>=	150		28	400	400	$13,200		14	1200	0	$2,400
20	Husband	120	>=	120		30	400	400	$14,000		15	1200	0	$2,400
21	Single male	105	>=	100										
22	Single female	110	>=	110										
23														
24	Total cost	$2,300												
25														
26														
27														

As these tables show, when the cost of a daytime call is low enough or the cost of an evening call is high enough, no evening calls will be made. But regardless of costs, daytime calls will always be made. Otherwise, it's evidently impossible to make the required contacts, given the upper limit on the number of evening calls that can be made.

Problem 14_41

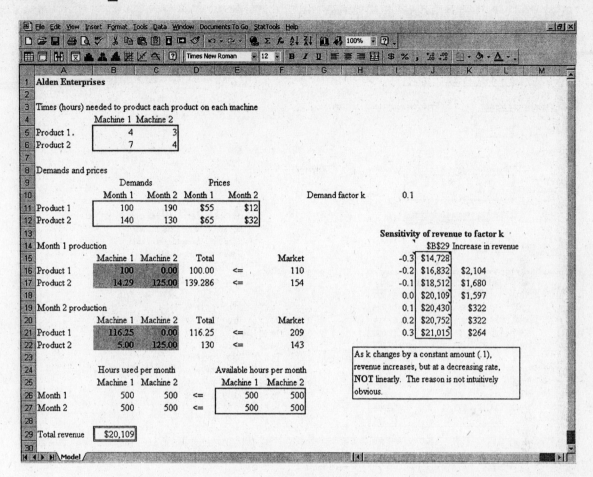

Problem 14_43

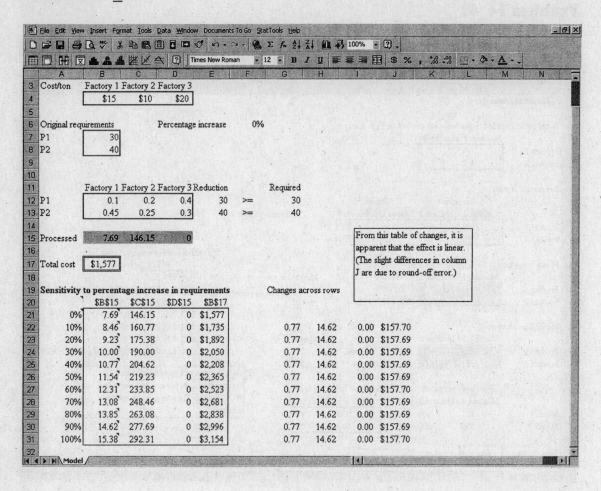

Problem 14_45

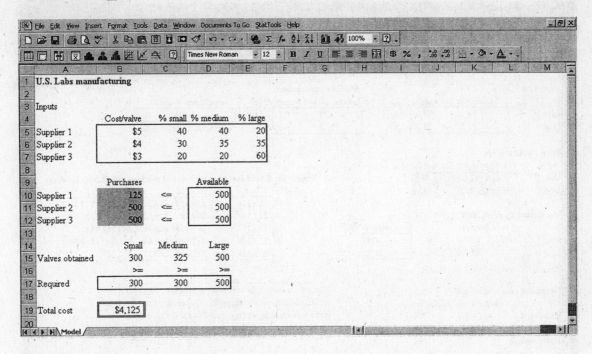

Problem 14_53

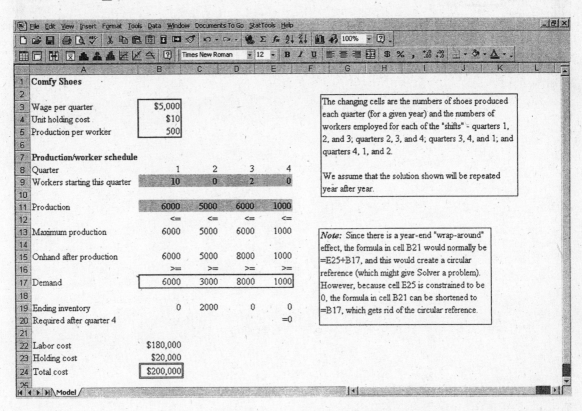

Problem 14_57

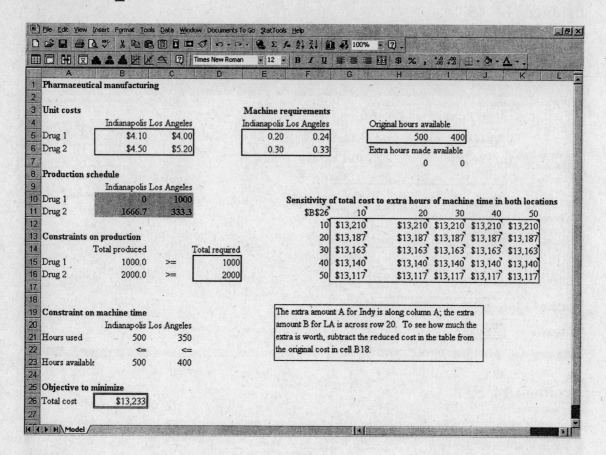

CHAPTER 15

All problems will be set up using the following system:

- **input cells**   **thick border**
- **changing cells**   **gray shading and boldface**
- **target cell**   **double line border**

Problem 15_3

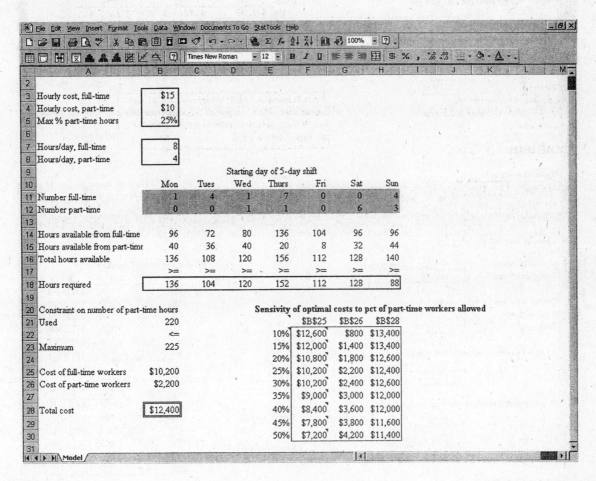

Problem 15_5

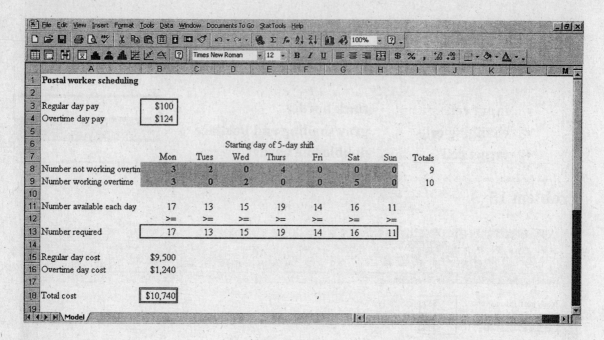

Problem 15_7

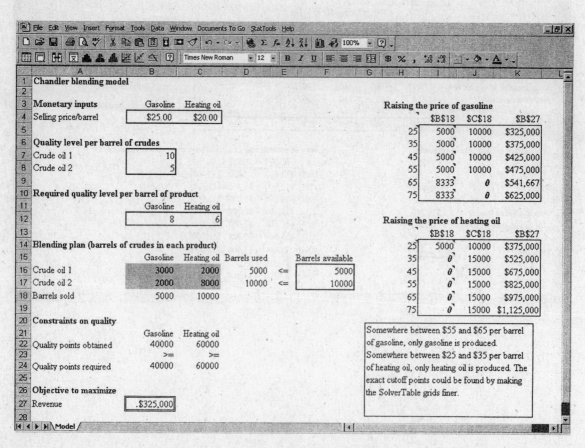

Problem 15_11

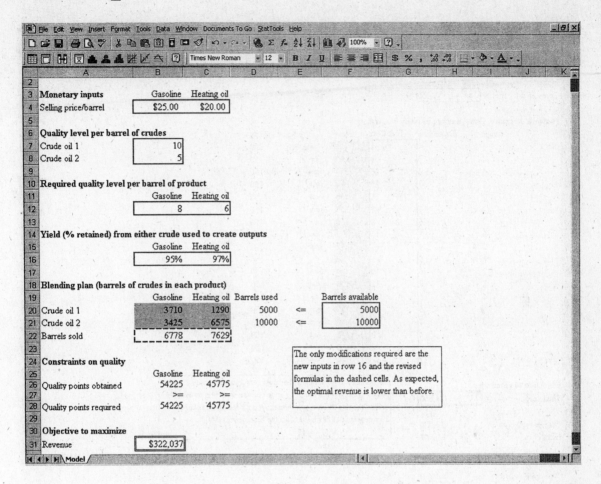

Problem 15_13

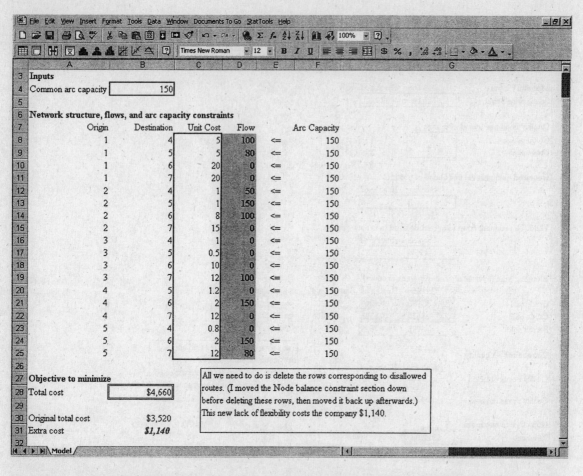

	A	B	C	D	E	F	G
3	**Inputs**						
4	Common arc capacity	150					
5							
6	**Network structure, flows, and arc capacity constraints**						
7	Origin	Destination	Unit Cost	Flow		Arc Capacity	
8	1	4	5	100	<=	150	
9	1	5	5	80	<=	150	
10	1	6	20	0	<=	150	
11	1	7	20	0	<=	150	
12	2	4	1	50	<=	150	
13	2	5	1	150	<=	150	
14	2	6	8	100	<=	150	
15	2	7	15	0	<=	150	
16	3	4	1	0	<=	150	
17	3	5	0.5	0	<=	150	
18	3	6	10	0	<=	150	
19	3	7	12	100	<=	150	
20	4	5	1.2	0	<=	150	
21	4	6	2	150	<=	150	
22	4	7	12	0	<=	150	
23	5	4	0.8	0	<=	150	
24	5	6	2	150	<=	150	
25	5	7	12	80	<=	150	
26							
27	**Objective to minimize**						
28	Total cost	$4,660					
29							
30	Original total cost	$3,520					
31	Extra cost	*$1,140*					

All we need to do is delete the rows corresponding to disallowed routes. (I moved the Node balance constraint section down before deleting these rows, then moved it back up afterwards.) This new lack of flexibility costs the company $1,140.

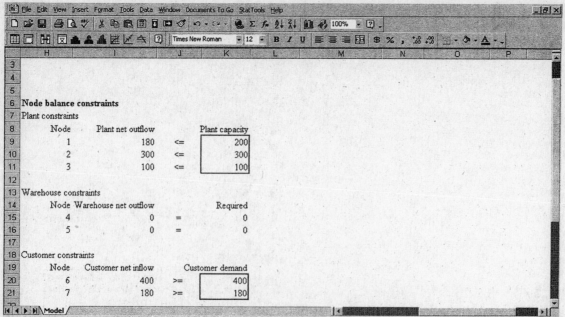

	H	I	J	K	L	M	N	O	P
6	**Node balance constraints**								
7	Plant constraints								
8	Node	Plant net outflow		Plant capacity					
9	1	180	<=	200					
10	2	300	<=	300					
11	3	100	<=	100					
12									
13	Warehouse constraints								
14	Node	Warehouse net outflow		Required					
15	4	0	=	0					
16	5	0	=	0					
17									
18	Customer constraints								
19	Node	Customer net inflow		Customer demand					
20	6	400	>=	400					
21	7	180	>=	180					

Problem 15_25

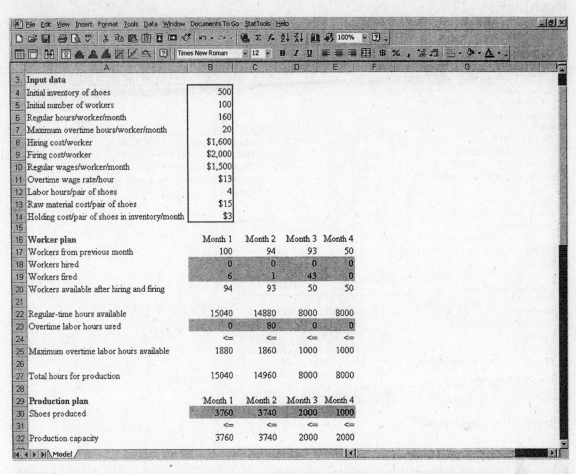

		A	B	C	D	E	F	G
3		Input data						
4		Initial inventory of shoes	500					
5		Initial number of workers	100					
6		Regular hours/worker/month	160					
7		Maximum overtime hours/worker/month	20					
8		Hiring cost/worker	$1,600					
9		Firing cost/worker	$2,000					
10		Regular wages/worker/month	$1,500					
11		Overtime wage rate/hour	$13					
12		Labor hours/pair of shoes	4					
13		Raw material cost/pair of shoes	$15					
14		Holding cost/pair of shoes in inventory/month	$3					
15								
16		Worker plan	Month 1	Month 2	Month 3	Month 4		
17		Workers from previous month	100	94	93	50		
18		Workers hired	0	0	0	0		
19		Workers fired	6	1	43	0		
20		Workers available after hiring and firing	94	93	50	50		
21								
22		Regular-time hours available	15040	14880	8000	8000		
23		Overtime labor hours used	0	80	0	0		
24			<=	<=	<=	<=		
25		Maximum overtime labor hours available	1880	1860	1000	1000		
26								
27		Total hours for production	15040	14960	8000	8000		
28								
29		Production plan	Month 1	Month 2	Month 3	Month 4		
30		Shoes produced	3760	3740	2000	1000		
31			<=	<=	<=	<=		
32		Production capacity	3760	3740	2000	2000		

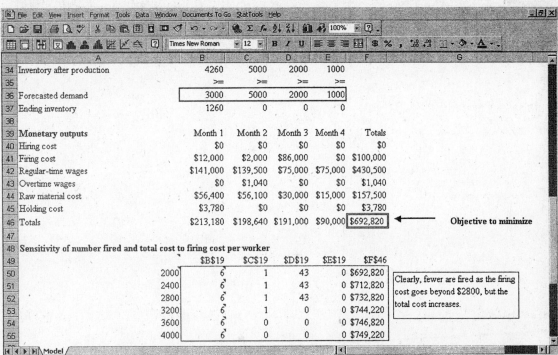

	A	B	C	D	E	F	G
34	Inventory after production	4260	5000	2000	1000		
35		>=	>=	>=	>=		
36	Forecasted demand	3000	5000	2000	1000		
37	Ending inventory	1260	0	0	0		
38							
39	Monetary outputs	Month 1	Month 2	Month 3	Month 4	Totals	
40	Hiring cost	$0	$0	$0	$0	$0	
41	Firing cost	$12,000	$2,000	$86,000	$0	$100,000	
42	Regular-time wages	$141,000	$139,500	$75,000	$75,000	$430,500	
43	Overtime wages	$0	$1,040	$0	$0	$1,040	
44	Raw material cost	$56,400	$56,100	$30,000	$15,000	$157,500	
45	Holding cost	$3,780	$0	$0	$0	$3,780	
46	Totals	$213,180	$198,640	$191,000	$90,000	$692,820	← Objective to minimize

48 Sensitivity of number fired and total cost to firing cost per worker

49			$B$19	$C$19	$D$19	$E$19	$F$46
50		2000	6	1	43	0	$692,820
51		2400	6	1	43	0	$712,820
52		2800	6	1	43	0	$732,820
53		3200	6	1	0	0	$744,220
54		3600	6	0	0	0	$746,820
55		4000	6	0	0	0	$749,220

Clearly, fewer are fired as the firing cost goes beyond $2800, but the total cost increases.

Problem 15_27

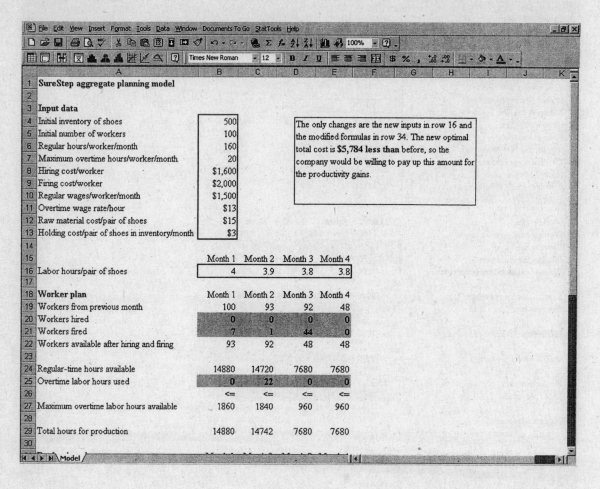

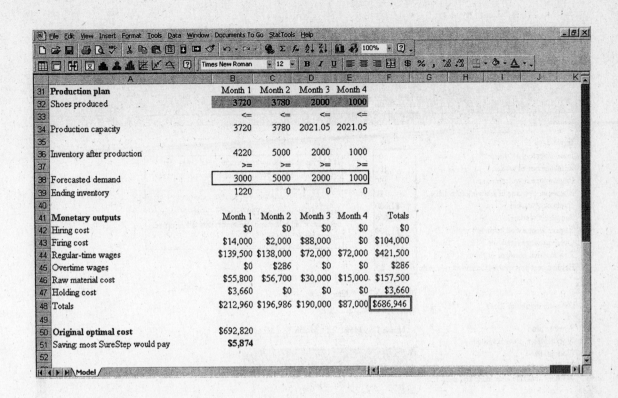

	A	B	C	D	E	F
31	**Production plan**	Month 1	Month 2	Month 3	Month 4	
32	Shoes produced	3720	3780	2000	1000	
33		<=	<=	<=	<=	
34	Production capacity	3720	3780	2021.05	2021.05	
35						
36	Inventory after production	4220	5000	2000	1000	
37		>=	>=	>=	>=	
38	Forecasted demand	3000	5000	2000	1000	
39	Ending inventory	1220	0	0	0	
40						
41	**Monetary outputs**	Month 1	Month 2	Month 3	Month 4	Totals
42	Hiring cost	$0	$0	$0	$0	$0
43	Firing cost	$14,000	$2,000	$88,000	$0	$104,000
44	Regular-time wages	$139,500	$138,000	$72,000	$72,000	$421,500
45	Overtime wages	$0	$286	$0	$0	$286
46	Raw material cost	$55,800	$56,700	$30,000	$15,000	$157,500
47	Holding cost	$3,660	$0	$0	$0	$3,660
48	Totals	$212,960	$196,986	$190,000	$87,000	$686,946
49						
50	**Original optimal cost**	$692,820				
51	Saving most SureStep would pay	**$5,874**				
52						

Problem 15_29

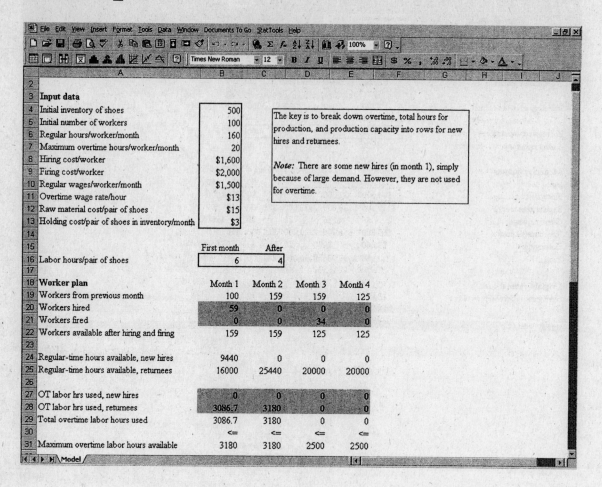

	A	B	C	D	E
2					
3	**Input data**				
4	Initial inventory of shoes	500			
5	Initial number of workers	100			
6	Regular hours/worker/month	160			
7	Maximum overtime hours/worker/month	20			
8	Hiring cost/worker	$1,600			
9	Firing cost/worker	$2,000			
10	Regular wages/worker/month	$1,500			
11	Overtime wage rate/hour	$13			
12	Raw material cost/pair of shoes	$15			
13	Holding cost/pair of shoes in inventory/month	$3			
14					
15		First month	After		
16	Labor hours/pair of shoes	6	4		
17					
18	**Worker plan**	Month 1	Month 2	Month 3	Month 4
19	Workers from previous month	100	159	159	125
20	Workers hired	59	0	0	0
21	Workers fired	0	0	34	0
22	Workers available after hiring and firing	159	159	125	125
23					
24	Regular-time hours available, new hires	9440	0	0	0
25	Regular-time hours available, returnees	16000	25440	20000	20000
26					
27	OT labor hrs used, new hires	0	0	0	0
28	OT labor hrs used, returnees	3086.7	3180	0	0
29	Total overtime labor hours used	3086.7	3180	0	0
30		<=	<=	<=	<=
31	Maximum overtime labor hours available	3180	3180	2500	2500

The key is to break down overtime, total hours for production, and production capacity into rows for new hires and returnees.

Note: There are some new hires (in month 1), simply because of large demand. However, they are not used for overtime.

	A	B	C	D	E	F	G	H	I	J
33	Total hours for production, new hires	9440	0	0	0					
34	Total hours for production, returnees	19086.7	28620	20000	20000					
35										
36	**Production plan**	Month 1	Month 2	Month 3	Month 4					
37	Shoes produced	6345	7155	5000	3000					
38		<=	<=	<=	<=					
39	Total production capacity	6345	7155	5000	5000					
40	Production capacity, new hires	1573.3	0	0	0					
41	Production capacity, returnees	4771.7	7155	5000	5000					
42										
43	Inventory after production	6845	8000	5000	3000					
44		>=	>=	>=	>=					
45	Forecasted demand	6000	8000	5000	3000					
46	Ending inventory	845	0	0	0					
47										
48	**Monetary outputs**	Month 1	Month 2	Month 3	Month 4	Totals				
49	Hiring cost	$94,400	$0	$0	$0	$94,400				
50	Firing cost	$0	$0	$68,000	$0	$68,000				
51	Regular-time wages	$238,500	$238,500	$187,500	$187,500	$852,000				
52	Overtime wages	$40,127	$41,340	$0	$0	$81,467				
53	Raw material cost	$95,175	$107,325	$75,000	$45,000	$322,500				
54	Holding cost	$2,535	$0	$0	$0	$2,535				
55	Totals	$470,737	$387,165	$330,500	$232,500	$1,420,902				
56										

Model

Chapter 15 Optimization Modeling: Applications   271

Problem 15_31

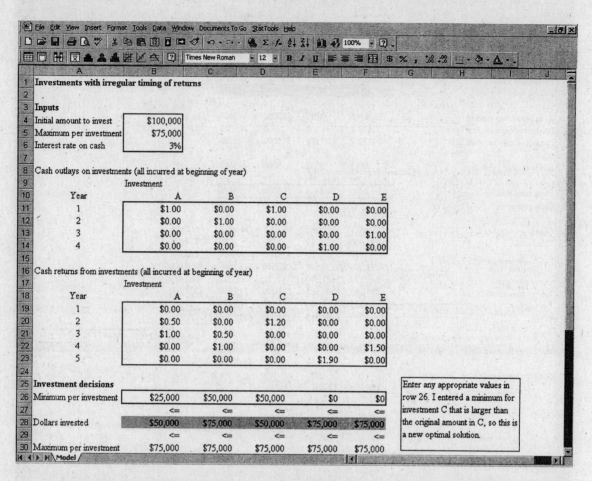

		Investment				
1	**Investments with irregular timing of returns**					
2						
3	**Inputs**					
4	Initial amount to invest	$100,000				
5	Maximum per investment	$75,000				
6	Interest rate on cash	3%				
7						
8	Cash outlays on investments (all incurred at beginning of year)					
9		Investment				
10	Year	A	B	C	D	E
11	1	$1.00	$0.00	$1.00	$0.00	$0.00
12	2	$0.00	$1.00	$0.00	$0.00	$0.00
13	3	$0.00	$0.00	$0.00	$0.00	$1.00
14	4	$0.00	$0.00	$0.00	$1.00	$0.00

Cash returns from investments (all incurred at beginning of year)

	Investment				
Year	A	B	C	D	E
1	$0.00	$0.00	$0.00	$0.00	$0.00
2	$0.50	$0.00	$1.20	$0.00	$0.00
3	$1.00	$0.50	$0.00	$0.00	$0.00
4	$0.00	$1.00	$0.00	$0.00	$1.50
5	$0.00	$0.00	$0.00	$1.90	$0.00

Investment decisions

	A	B	C	D	E
Minimum per investment	$25,000	$50,000	$50,000	$0	$0
	<=	<=	<=	<=	<=
Dollars invested	$50,000	$75,000	$50,000	$75,000	$75,000
	<=	<=	<=	<=	<=
Maximum per investment	$75,000	$75,000	$75,000	$75,000	$75,000

Enter any appropriate values in row 26. I entered a minimum for investment C that is larger than the original amount in C, so this is a new optimal solution.

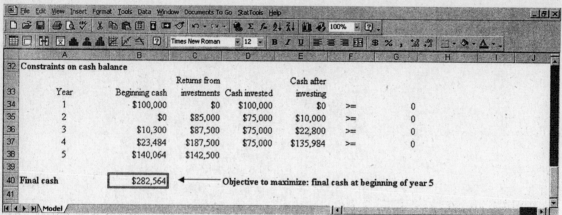

Constraints on cash balance

Year	Beginning cash	Returns from investments	Cash invested	Cash after investing		
1	$100,000	$0	$100,000	$0	>=	0
2	$0	$85,000	$75,000	$10,000	>=	0
3	$10,300	$87,500	$75,000	$22,800	>=	0
4	$23,484	$187,500	$75,000	$135,984	>=	0
5	$140,064	$142,500				

Final cash | $282,564 | ← Objective to maximize: final cash at beginning of year 5

Problem 15_37

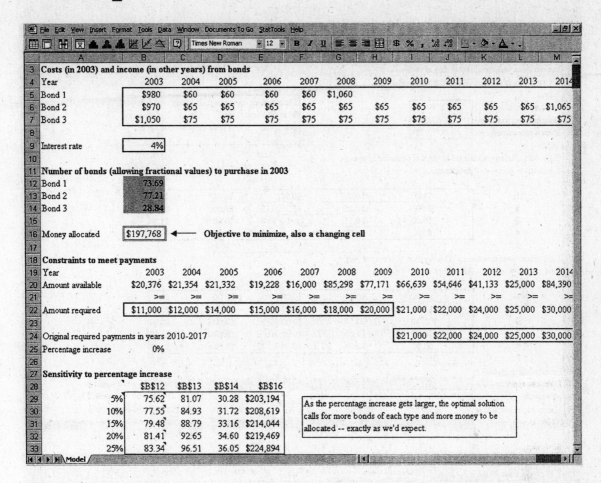

Problem 15_39

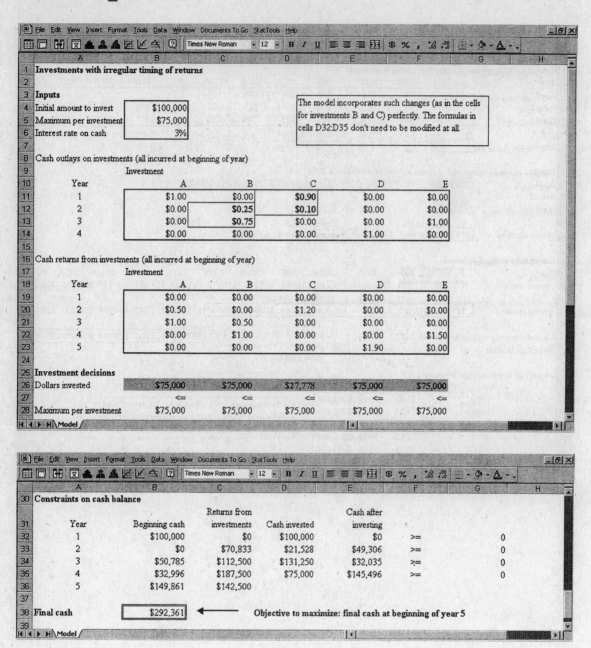

Problem 15_47

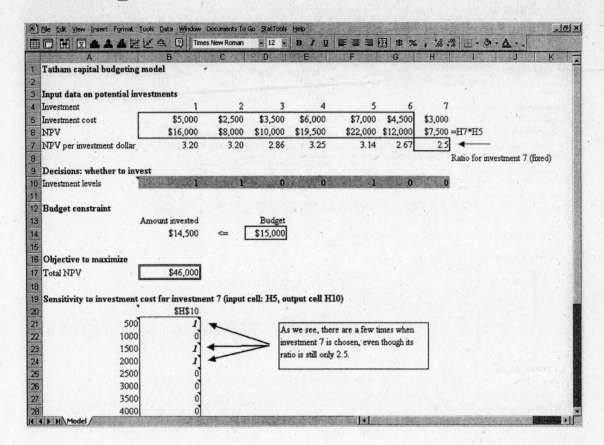

Problem 15_49
Part a:

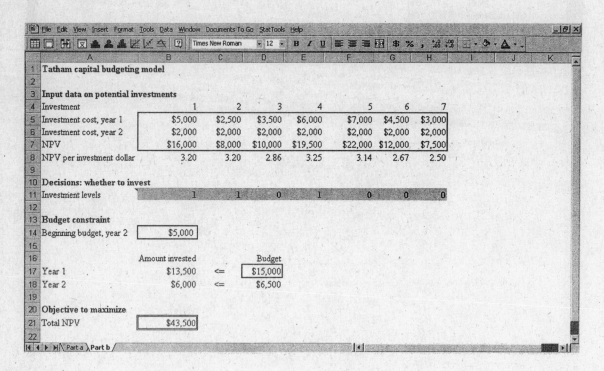

Part b:

Problem 15_51

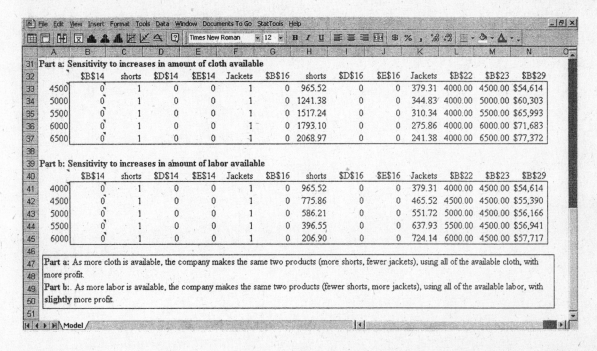

		Shirts	Shorts	Pants	Skirts	Sweatshirts	Jackets
3	**Input data on products**						
5	Labor hours/unit	2	1	6	4	1	8
6	Cloth (sq. yd.)/unit	3	2.5	4	4.5	3.5	5.5
8	Selling price/unit	$35	$40	$65	$70	$45	$110
9	Variable cost/unit	$20	$10	$25	$30	$15	$35
10	Fixed cost for equipment	$1,500	$1,200	$1,600	$1,500	$1,100	$1,600

Sensitivity to lowered fixed cost of machinery for sweatshirts.

	$F$14	$F$16
0	0	0
100	0	0
200	0	0
300	0	0
400	0	0
500	0	0
600	0	0
700	0	0
800	0	0
900	0	0
1000	0	0
1100	0	0

Production plan, constraints on capacity

		Shirts	Shorts	Pants	Skirts	Sweatshirts	Jackets
14	Produce any?	0	1	0	0	0	1
16	Units produced	0	965.52	0	0	0	379.31
17		<=	<=	<=	<=	<=	<=
18	Logical upper limit	0.00	1800.00	0.00	0.00	0.00	500.00

Constraints on resources

		Resource used		Available
22	Labor hours	4000.00	<=	4000
23	Cloth	4500.00	<=	4500

Evidently, the fixed cost for the sweatshirt machinery is irrelevant. Even when it is lowered to $0, the company still produces **no** sweatshirts.

Monetary outputs

26	Revenue	$80,345
27	Variable cost	$22,931
28	Fixed cost for equipment	$2,800
29	Profit	$54,614

← Objective to maximize

Problem 15_53

For basic problem set up see Problem 15_51.

Part a: Sensitivity to increases in amount of cloth available

	$B$14	shorts	$D$14	$E$14	Jackets	$B$16	shorts	$D$16	$E$16	Jackets	$B$22	$B$23	$B$29
4500	0	1	0	0	1	0	965.52	0	0	379.31	4000.00	4500.00	$54,614
5000	0	1	0	0	1	0	1241.38	0	0	344.83	4000.00	5000.00	$60,303
5500	0	1	0	0	1	0	1517.24	0	0	310.34	4000.00	5500.00	$65,993
6000	0	1	0	0	1	0	1793.10	0	0	275.86	4000.00	6000.00	$71,683
6500	0	1	0	0	1	0	2068.97	0	0	241.38	4000.00	6500.00	$77,372

Part b: Sensitivity to increases in amount of labor available

	$B$14	shorts	$D$14	$E$14	Jackets	$B$16	shorts	$D$16	$E$16	Jackets	$B$22	$B$23	$B$29
4000	0	1	0	0	1	0	965.52	0	0	379.31	4000.00	4500.00	$54,614
4500	0	1	0	0	1	0	775.86	0	0	465.52	4500.00	4500.00	$55,390
5000	0	1	0	0	1	0	586.21	0	0	551.72	5000.00	4500.00	$56,166
5500	0	1	0	0	1	0	396.55	0	0	637.93	5500.00	4500.00	$56,941
6000	0	1	0	0	1	0	206.90	0	0	724.14	6000.00	4500.00	$57,717

Part a: As more cloth is available, the company makes the same two products (more shorts, fewer jackets), using all of the available cloth, with more profit.

Part b: As more labor is available, the company makes the same two products (fewer shorts, more jackets), using all of the available labor, with **slightly** more profit.

Problem 15_55

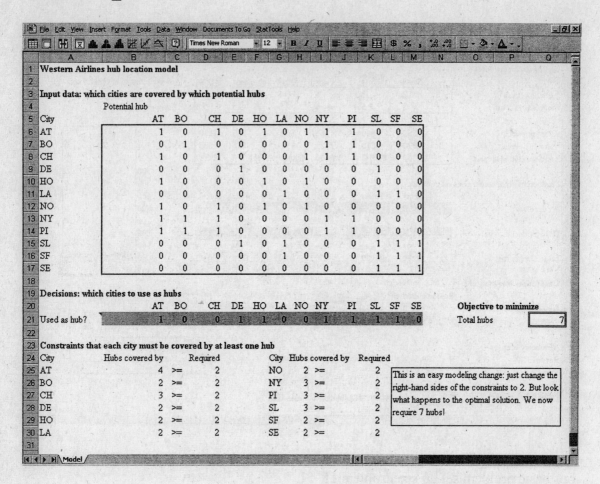

Western Airlines hub location model

Input data: which cities are covered by which potential hubs

City	Potential hub											
	AT	BO	CH	DE	HO	LA	NO	NY	PI	SL	SF	SE
AT	1	0	1	0	1	0	1	1	1	0	0	0
BO	0	1	0	0	0	0	0	1	1	0	0	0
CH	1	0	1	0	0	0	1	1	1	0	0	0
DE	0	0	0	1	0	0	0	0	0	1	0	0
HO	1	0	0	0	1	0	1	0	0	0	0	0
LA	0	0	0	0	0	1	0	0	0	1	1	0
NO	1	0	1	0	1	0	1	0	0	0	0	0
NY	1	1	1	0	0	0	0	1	1	0	0	0
PI	1	1	1	0	0	0	0	1	1	0	0	0
SL	0	0	0	1	0	1	0	0	0	1	1	1
SF	0	0	0	0	0	1	0	0	0	1	1	1
SE	0	0	0	0	0	0	0	0	0	1	1	1

Decisions: which cities to use as hubs

	AT	BO	CH	DE	HO	LA	NO	NY	PI	SL	SF	SE		Objective to minimize	
Used as hub?	1	0	0	1	1	0	0	1	1	1	0		Total hubs	7

Constraints that each city must be covered by at least one hub

City	Hubs covered by		Required	City	Hubs covered by		Required
AT	4	>=	2	NO	2	>=	2
BO	2	>=	2	NY	3	>=	2
CH	3	>=	2	PI	3	>=	2
DE	2	>=	2	SL	3	>=	2
HO	2	>=	2	SF	2	>=	2
LA	2	>=	2	SE	2	>=	2

This is an easy modeling change: just change the right-hand sides of the constraints to 2. But look what happens to the optimal solution. We now require 7 hubs!

Problem 15_57

Input data: which cities are covered by which potential hubs

Potential hub

City	AT	BO	CH	DE	HO	LA	NO	NY	PI	SL	SF	SE
AT	1	0	1	0	1	0	1	1	1	0	0	0
BO	0	1	0	0	0	0	0	1	1	0	0	0
CH	1	0	1	0	0	0	1	1	1	0	0	0
DE	0	0	0	1	0	0	0	0	0	1	0	0
HO	1	0	0	0	1	0	1	0	0	0	0	0
LA	0	0	0	0	0	1	0	0	0	1	1	0
NO	1	0	1	0	1	0	1	0	0	0	0	0
NY	1	1	1	0	0	0	0	1	1	0	0	0
PI	1	1	1	0	0	0	0	1	1	0	0	0
SL	0	0	0	1	0	0	0	0	0	1	1	1
SF	0	0	0	0	0	1	0	0	0	1	1	1
SE	0	0	0	0	0	0	0	0	0	1	1	1

Decisions: which cities to use as hubs

	AT	BO	CH	DE	HO	LA	NO	NY	PI	SL	SF	SE		Objective to minimize	
Used as hub?	0	1	0	0	0	0	1	0	0	1	0	0		Total hubs	3

Constraints that each city must be covered by at least one hub

City	Hubs covered by		Required	City	Hubs covered by		Required
AT	1	>=	1	NO	1	>=	1
BO	1	>=	1	NY	1	>=	1
CH	1	>=	1	PI	1	>=	1
DE	1	>=	1	SL	1	>=	1
HO	1	>=	1	SF	1	>=	1
LA	1	>=	1	SE	1	>=	1

There may be other solutions, but here are four.

Solutions found (all with 3 hubs)

0	0	0	0	1	0	0	1	0	1	0	0
0	0	0	0	1	0	0	0	1	1	0	0
0	1	0	0	0	0	1	0	0	1	0	0
1	1	0	0	0	0	0	0	0	1	0	0

Model

Problem 15_63

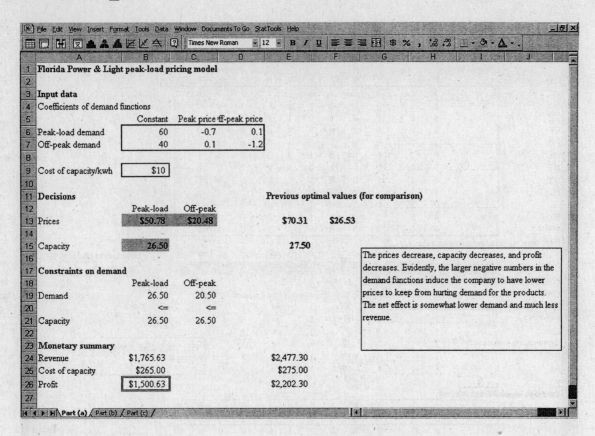

Problem 15_75

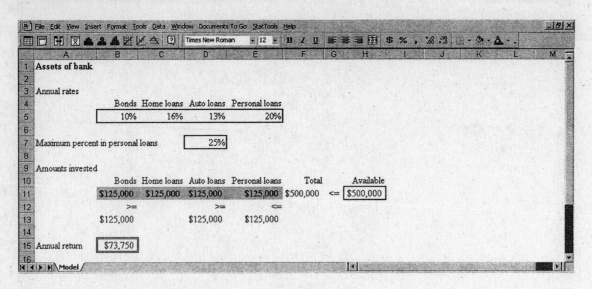

Problem 15_87

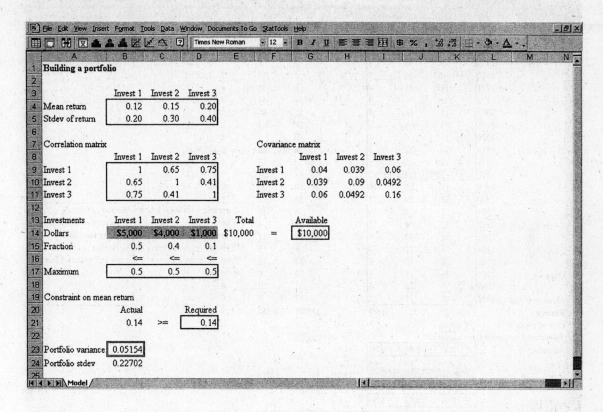

Problem 15_89

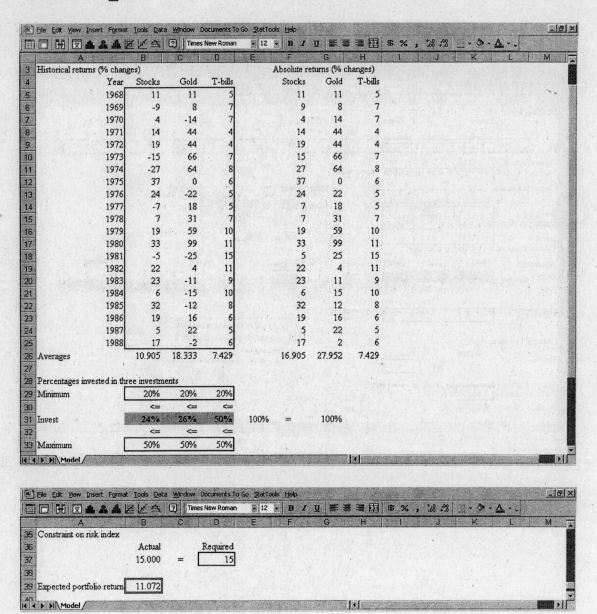

	Year	Stocks	Gold	T-bills		Stocks	Gold	T-bills
3	Historical returns (% changes)				Absolute returns (% changes)			
4	Year	Stocks	Gold	T-bills		Stocks	Gold	T-bills
5	1968	11	11	5		11	11	5
6	1969	-9	8	7		9	8	7
7	1970	4	-14	7		4	14	7
8	1971	14	44	4		14	44	4
9	1972	19	44	4		19	44	4
10	1973	-15	66	7		15	66	7
11	1974	-27	64	8		27	64	8
12	1975	37	0	6		37	0	6
13	1976	24	-22	5		24	22	5
14	1977	-7	18	5		7	18	5
15	1978	7	31	7		7	31	7
16	1979	19	59	10		19	59	10
17	1980	33	99	11		33	99	11
18	1981	-5	-25	15		5	25	15
19	1982	22	4	11		22	4	11
20	1983	23	-11	9		23	11	9
21	1984	6	-15	10		6	15	10
22	1985	32	-12	8		32	12	8
23	1986	19	16	6		19	16	6
24	1987	5	22	5		5	22	5
25	1988	17	-2	6		17	2	6
26	Averages	10.905	18.333	7.429		16.905	27.952	7.429
27								
28	Percentages invested in three investments							
29	Minimum	20%	20%	20%				
30		<=	<=	<=				
31	Invest	24%	26%	50%	100%	=	100%	
32		<=	<=	<=				
33	Maximum	50%	50%	50%				

35	Constraint on risk index				
36		Actual		Required	
37		15.000	=	15	
38					
39	Expected portfolio return	11.072			

Problem 15_97

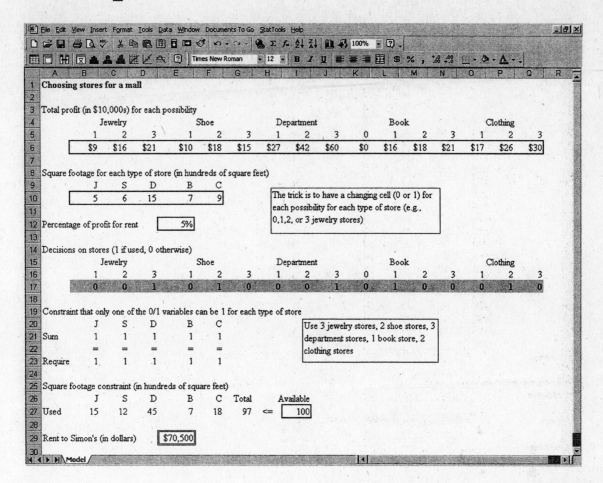

CHAPTER 16

@RISK problems will be set up using the following system:

- input cells   **thick border**
- changing cells   **gray shading and boldface**
- target cell   **double line border**

Problem 16_1

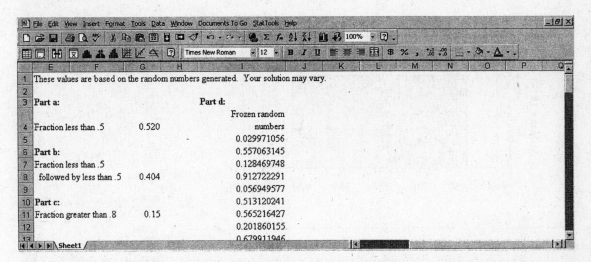

Problem 16_5
This comes from RISKview's Graph/Graph in Excel menu item. It's not interactive, but here are the answers to the questions.

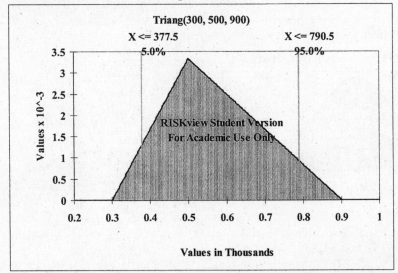

Part a: Mean = 566.67, Stdev = 124.72
Part b: 5th percentile = 377.5, 95th percentile = 790.5
Part c: P(X<450) = 0.188
Part d: P(X>650) = 0.260
Part e: P(500<X<700) = 0.5

Problem 16_9

Part a: The "no idea" suggests the uniform distribution. The statements about 450K and 650K means there is 90% of the probability between these two values, so 5% is in each tail. A little arithmetic implies that the left and right endpoint should be approximately 439K and 661K.

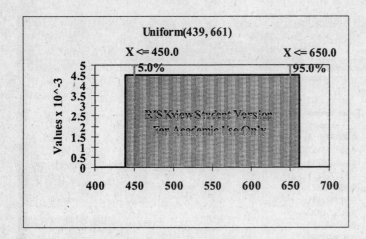

Part b: Symmetric and bell-shaped suggests the normal distribution, with mean 550K. From statistics, we know that the mean plus or minus 1.645 stdevs captures 90% of the area, so 1.645 times sigma equals 100K. Therefore, the stdev sigma is approximately 100K/1.645 = 60.8.

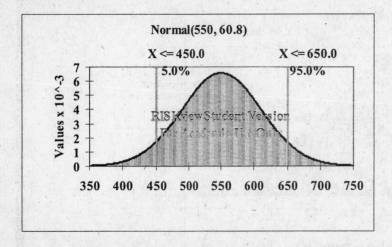

Part c: Since we're told it's not symmetric and skewed to the right, and we're given a mostly likely value, we might try the triangular. Then it's a matter of trial and error to get the min and max so that the statements about 450K and 650K are approximately correct. RISKview actually makes it pretty easy to do the experimenting with its spinner controls. We find the approximate min and max to be 415 and 705.

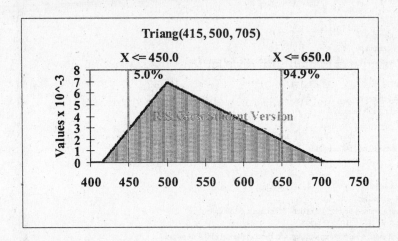

Problem 16_13

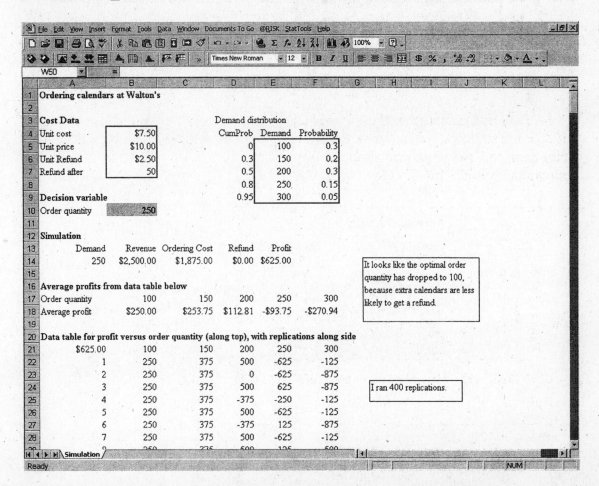

Problem 16_15

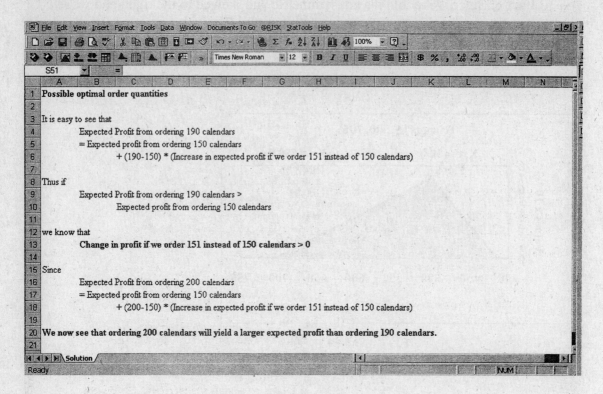

Problem 16_17

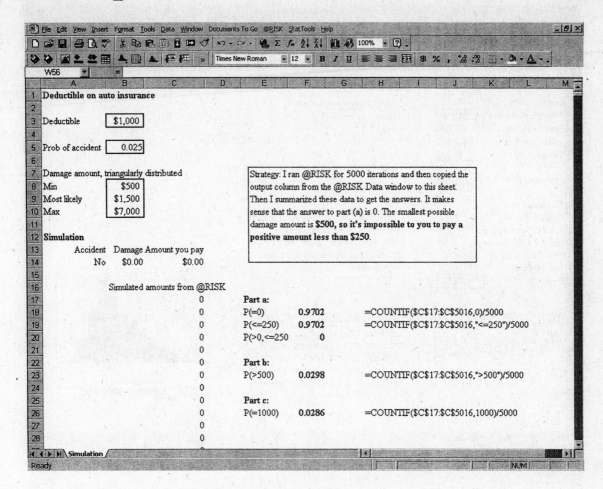

Problem 16_19

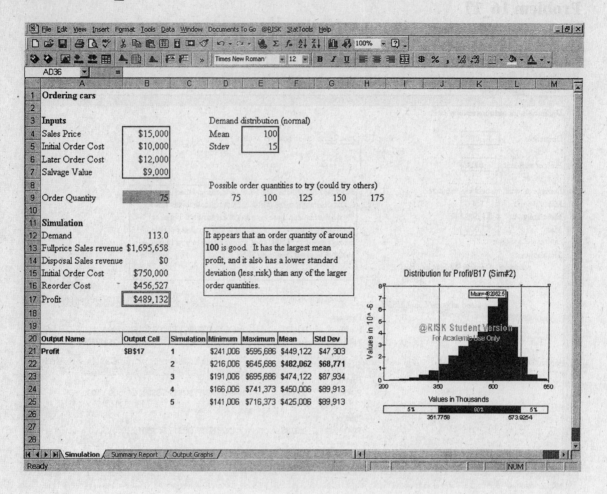

Problem 16_21

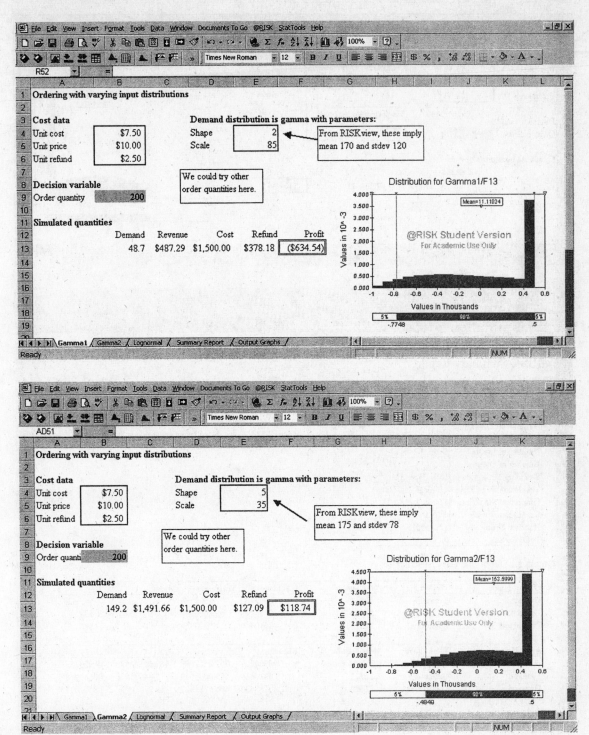

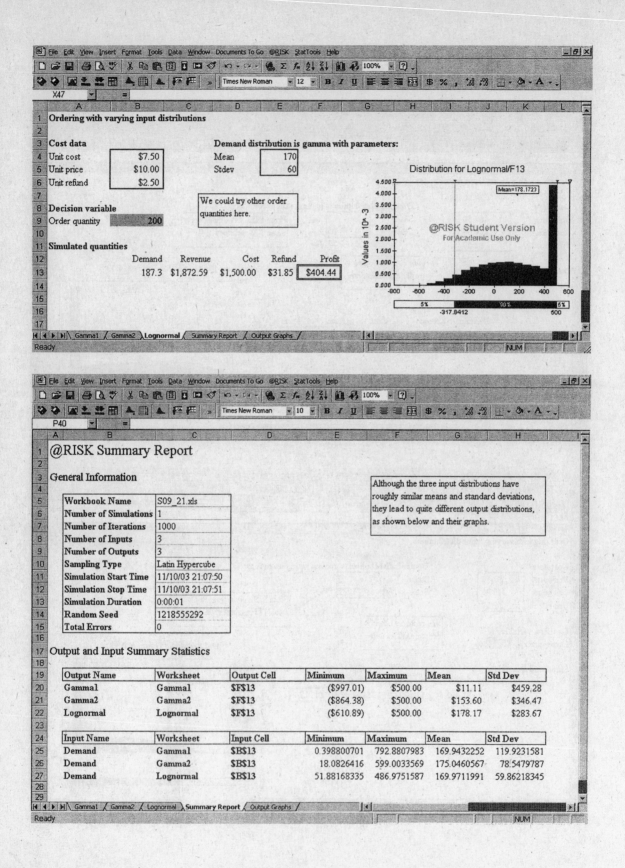

Problem 16_23

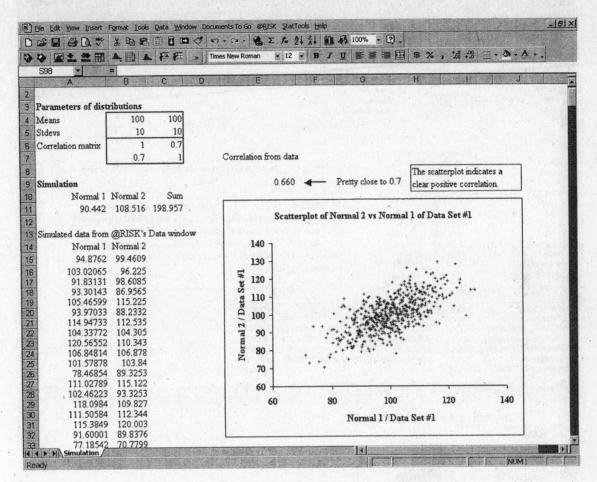

Problem 16_27

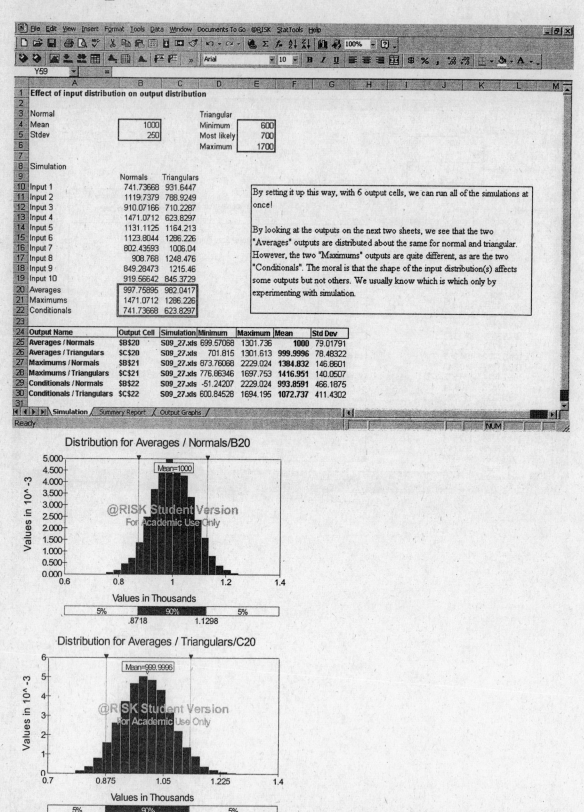

By setting it up this way, with 6 output cells, we can run all of the simulations at once!

By looking at the outputs on the next two sheets, we see that the two "Averages" outputs are distributed about the same for normal and triangular. However, the two "Maximums" outputs are quite different, as are the two "Conditionals". The moral is that the shape of the input distribution(s) affects some outputs but not others. We usually know which is which only by experimenting with simulation.

Distribution for Averages / Normals/B20

Distribution for Averages / Triangulars/C20

Problem 16_29

Part a:

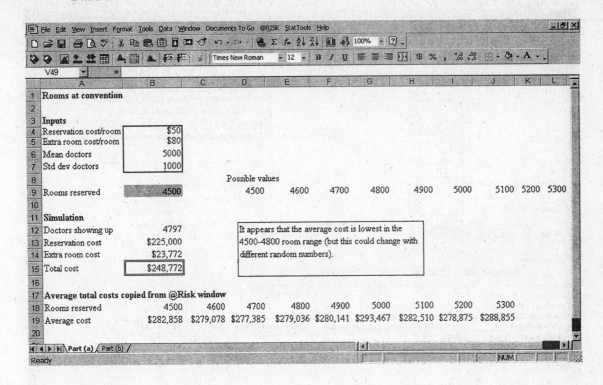

Part b:

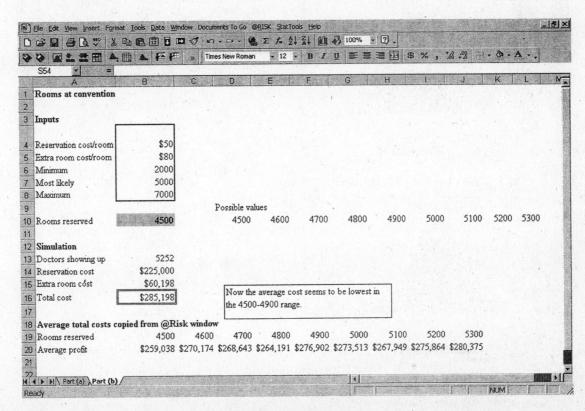

Problem 16_33

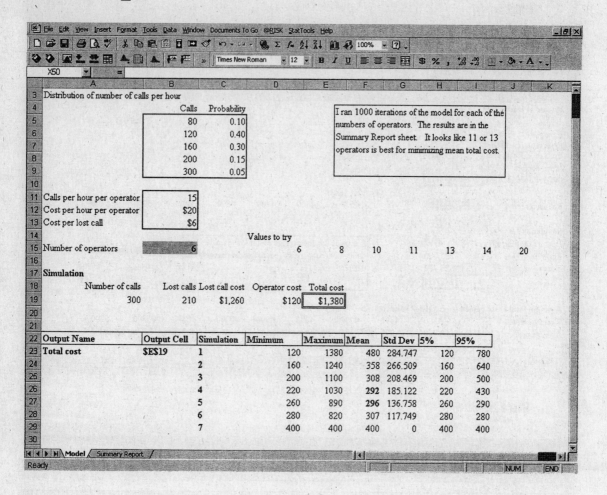

	A	B	C	D	E	F	G	H	I	J	K
3	Distribution of number of calls per hour										
4			Calls	Probability			I ran 1000 iterations of the model for each of the				
5			80	0.10			numbers of operators. The results are in the				
6			120	0.40			Summary Report sheet. It looks like 11 or 13				
7			160	0.30			operators is best for minimizing mean total cost.				
8			200	0.15							
9			300	0.05							
10											
11	Calls per hour per operator		15								
12	Cost per hour per operator		$20								
13	Cost per lost call		$6								
14					Values to try						
15	Number of operators		6		6	8	10	11	13	14	20
16											
17	Simulation										
18		Number of calls	Lost calls	Lost call cost	Operator cost	Total cost					
19		300	210	$1,260	$120	$1,380					
20											
21											
22	Output Name		Output Cell	Simulation	Minimum		Maximum	Mean	Std Dev	5%	95%
23	Total cost		$E$19	1	120		1380	480	284.747	120	780
24				2	160		1240	358	266.509	160	640
25				3	200		1100	308	208.469	200	500
26				4	220		1030	292	185.122	220	430
27				5	260		890	296	136.758	260	290
28				6	280		820	307	117.749	280	280
29				7	400		400	400	0	400	400
30											

Problem 16_35

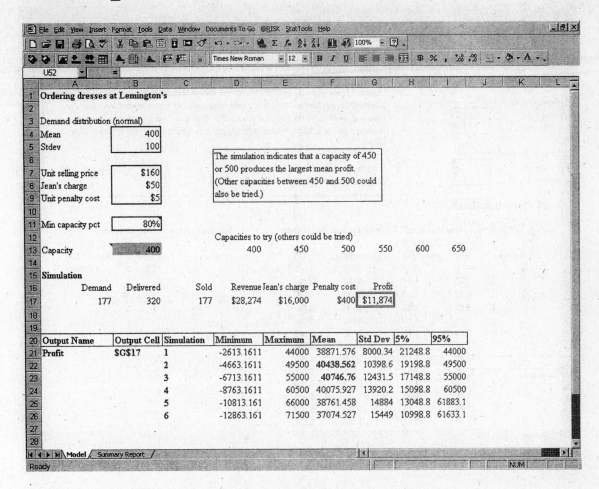

Problem 16_39

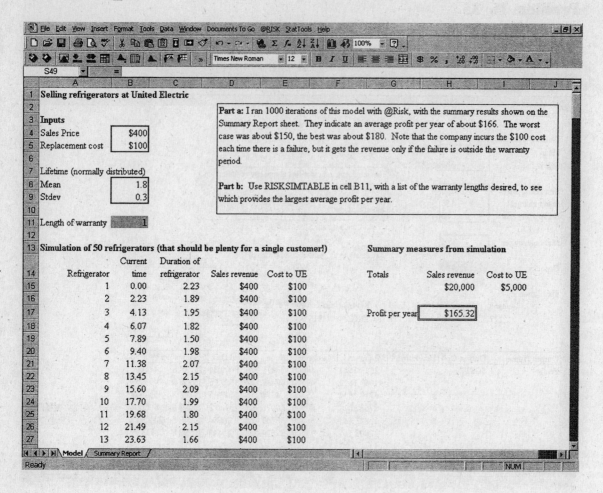

Problem 16_43

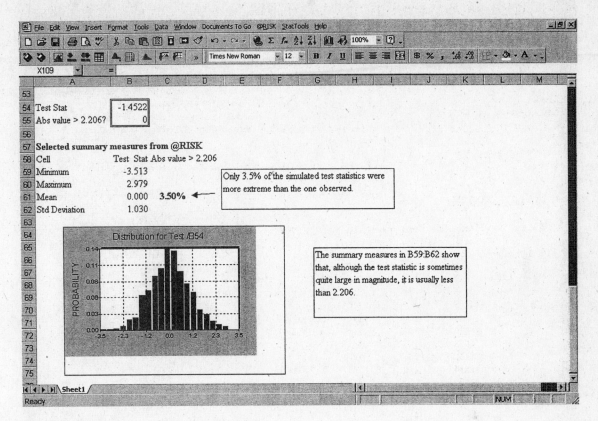

Problem 16_45

We need to fit some distribution for the size of claims. Probably lognormal (a distribution with positive values that's skewed to the right) will work here. Policies such as file if claim >$500, file if claim>$1000, etc. should be evaluated against goal of minimizing average cost per year. We must also model the frequency of accidents (time between accidents is probably exponentially distributed).

CHAPTER 17

@RISK problems will be set up using the following system:

- **input cells**   thick border
- **changing cells**   gray shading and boldface
- **target cell**   double line border

Problem 17_1

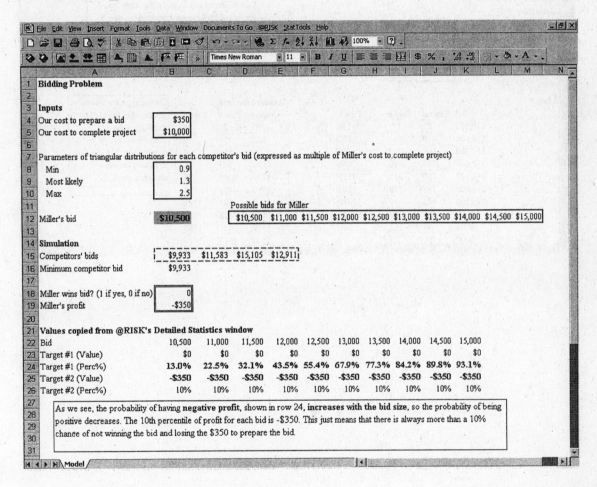

Problem 17_3

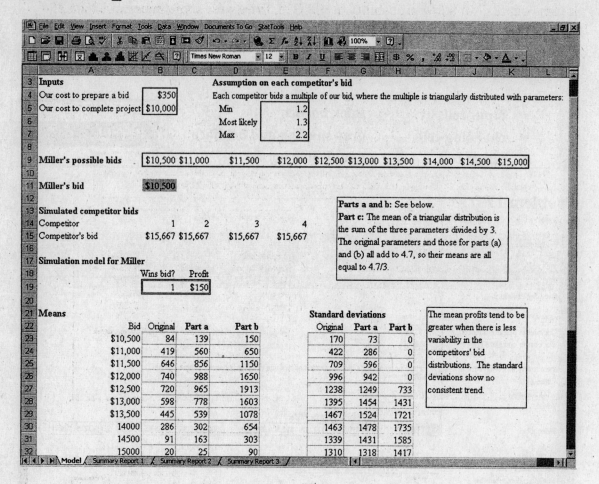

Problem 17_7

It turns out that for a low probability in cell B25, there were sometimes more than 25 batches, so increase the potential number of batches to 40 (copied the logic down) just to be safe. In particular, the 95th percentile of the number of days required to complete the order decreases dramatically as the probability of inspection increases.

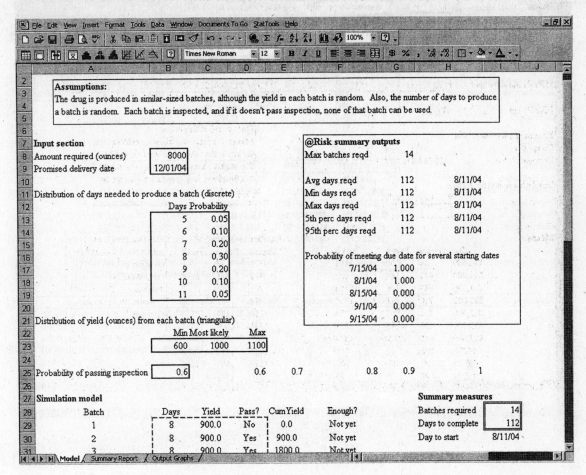

Problem 17_9

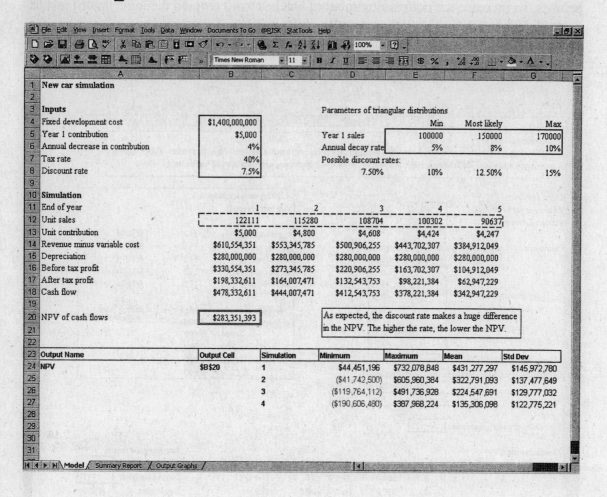

New car simulation

Inputs				Parameters of triangular distributions			
Fixed development cost	$1,400,000,000				Min	Most likely	Max
Year 1 contribution	$5,000			Year 1 sales	100000	150000	170000
Annual decrease in contribution	4%			Annual decay rate	5%	8%	10%
Tax rate	40%			Possible discount rates:			
Discount rate	7.5%			7.50%	10%	12.50%	15%

Simulation

End of year	1	2	3	4	5
Unit sales	122111	115280	108704	100302	90637
Unit contribution	$5,000	$4,800	$4,608	$4,424	$4,247
Revenue minus variable cost	$610,554,351	$553,345,785	$500,906,255	$443,702,307	$384,912,049
Depreciation	$280,000,000	$280,000,000	$280,000,000	$280,000,000	$280,000,000
Before tax profit	$330,554,351	$273,345,785	$220,906,255	$163,702,307	$104,912,049
After tax profit	$198,332,611	$164,007,471	$132,543,753	$98,221,384	$62,947,229
Cash flow	$478,332,611	$444,007,471	$412,543,753	$378,221,384	$342,947,229

NPV of cash flows $283,351,393

As expected, the discount rate makes a huge difference in the NPV. The higher the rate, the lower the NPV.

Output Name	Output Cell	Simulation	Minimum	Maximum	Mean	Std Dev
NPV	$B$20	1	$44,451,196	$732,078,848	$431,277,297	$145,972,780
		2	($41,742,500)	$605,960,384	$322,791,093	$137,477,649
		3	($119,764,112)	$491,736,928	$224,547,691	$129,777,032
		4	($190,606,480)	$387,968,224	$135,306,098	$122,775,221

Problem 17_17

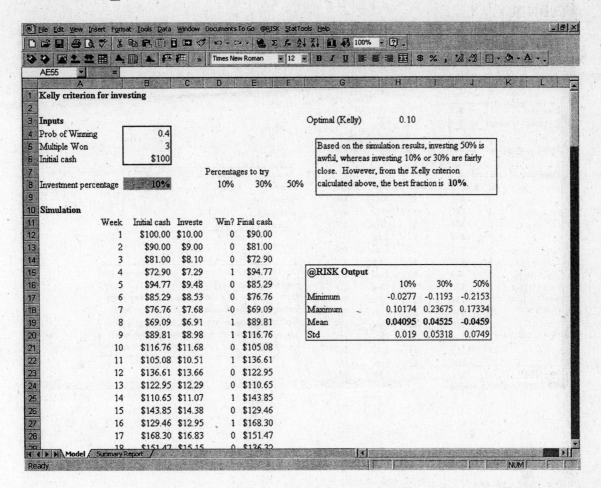

Problem 17_25

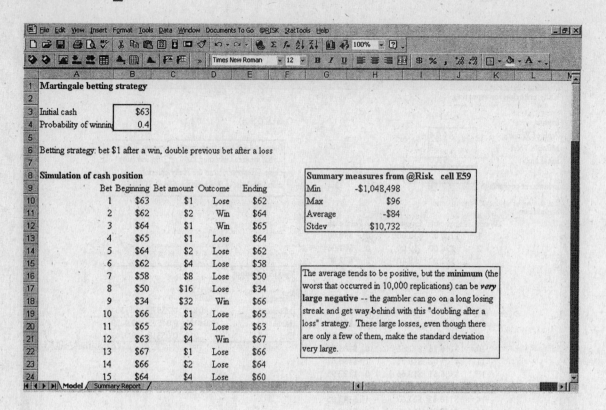

Problem 17_29

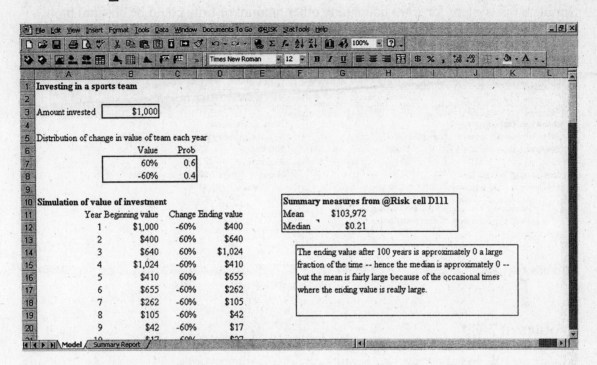

Problem 17_35

Simulate this system for 2000 hours (any other amount of time could be chosen) by generating enough failures to be sure that 2000 hours elapse.

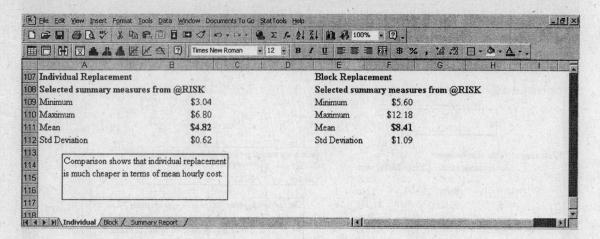

	A	B		E	F
107	**Individual Replacement**			**Block Replacement**	
108	**Selected summary measures from @RISK**			**Selected summary measures from @RISK**	
109	Minimum	$3.04		Minimum	$5.60
110	Maximum	$6.80		Maximum	$12.18
111	Mean	**$4.82**		Mean	**$8.41**
112	Std Deviation	$0.62		Std Deviation	$1.09

Comparison shows that individual replacement is much cheaper in terms of mean hourly cost.

Sheet tabs: Individual / Block / Summary Report

Problem 17_39

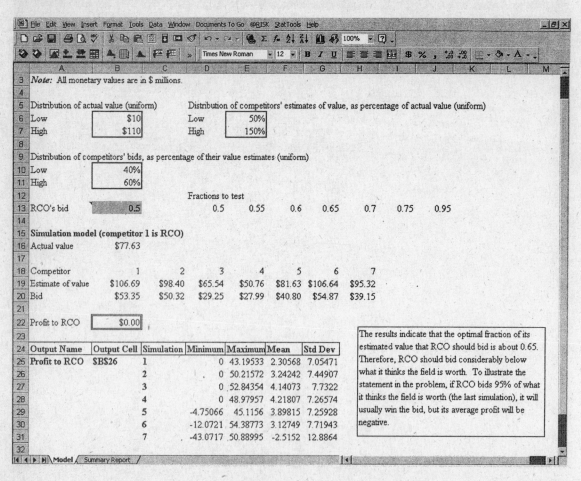

3 *Note:* All monetary values are in $ millions.

Distribution of actual value (uniform)

Low	$10
High	$110

Distribution of competitors' estimates of value, as percentage of actual value (uniform)

Low	50%
High	150%

Distribution of competitors' bids, as percentage of their value estimates (uniform)

Low	40%
High	60%

Fractions to test

RCO's bid 0.5

| 0.5 | 0.55 | 0.6 | 0.65 | 0.7 | 0.75 | 0.95 |

Simulation model (competitor 1 is RCO)

Actual value $77.63

Competitor	1	2	3	4	5	6	7
Estimate of value	$106.69	$98.40	$65.54	$50.76	$81.63	$106.64	$95.32
Bid	$53.35	$50.32	$29.25	$27.99	$40.80	$54.87	$39.15

Profit to RCO $0.00

Output Name	Output Cell	Simulation	Minimum	Maximum	Mean	Std Dev
Profit to RCO	$B$26	1	0	43.19533	2.30568	7.05471
		2	0	50.21572	3.24242	7.44907
		3	0	52.84354	4.14073	7.7322
		4	0	48.97957	4.21807	7.26574
		5	-4.75066	45.1156	3.89815	7.25928
		6	-12.0721	54.38773	3.12749	7.71943
		7	-43.0717	50.88995	-2.5152	12.8864

The results indicate that the optimal fraction of its estimated value that RCO should bid is about 0.65. Therefore, RCO should bid considerably below what it thinks the field is worth. To illustrate the statement in the problem, if RCO bids 95% of what it thinks the field is worth (the last simulation), it will usually win the bid, but its average profit will be negative.

Sheet tabs: Model / Summary Report

Problem 17_43

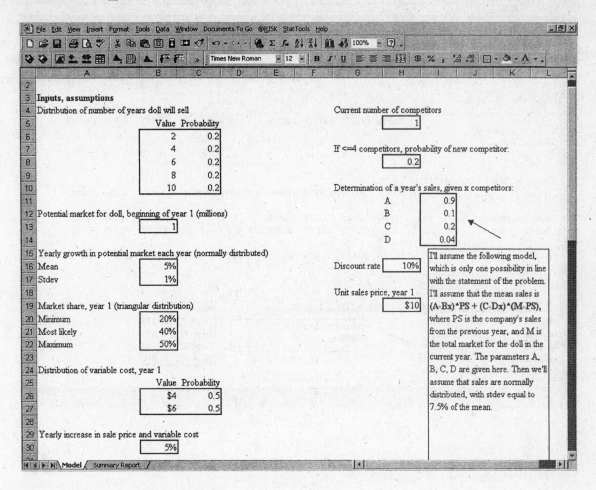

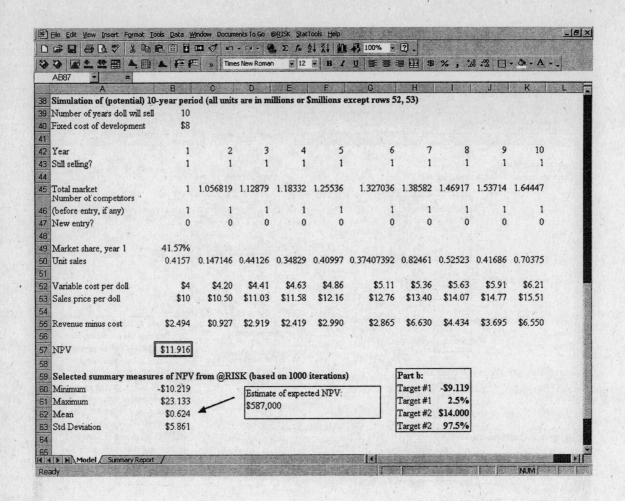

	A	B	C	D	E	F	G	H	I	J	K
38	**Simulation of (potential) 10-year period (all units are in millions or $millions except rows 52, 53)**										
39	Number of years doll will sell	10									
40	Fixed cost of development	$8									
41											
42	Year	1	2	3	4	5	6	7	8	9	10
43	Still selling?	1	1	1	1	1	1	1	1	1	1
44											
45	Total market	1	1.056819	1.12879	1.18332	1.25536	1.327036	1.38582	1.46917	1.53714	1.64447
46	Number of competitors (before entry, if any)	1	1	1	1	1	1	1	1	1	1
47	New entry?	0	0	0	0	0	0	0	0	0	0
48											
49	Market share, year 1	41.57%									
50	Unit sales	0.4157	0.147146	0.44126	0.34829	0.40997	0.37407392	0.82461	0.52523	0.41686	0.70375
51											
52	Variable cost per doll	$4	$4.20	$4.41	$4.63	$4.86	$5.11	$5.36	$5.63	$5.91	$6.21
53	Sales price per doll	$10	$10.50	$11.03	$11.58	$12.16	$12.76	$13.40	$14.07	$14.77	$15.51
54											
55	Revenue minus cost	$2.494	$0.927	$2.919	$2.419	$2.990	$2.865	$6.630	$4.434	$3.695	$6.550
56											
57	NPV	$11.916									
58											
59	**Selected summary measures of NPV from @RISK (based on 1000 iterations)**										
60	Minimum	-$10.219									
61	Maximum	$23.133									
62	Mean	$0.624									
63	Std Deviation	$5.861									

Estimate of expected NPV: $587,000

Part b:
Target #1 -$9.119
Target #1 2.5%
Target #2 $14.000
Target #2 97.5%

Problem 17_45

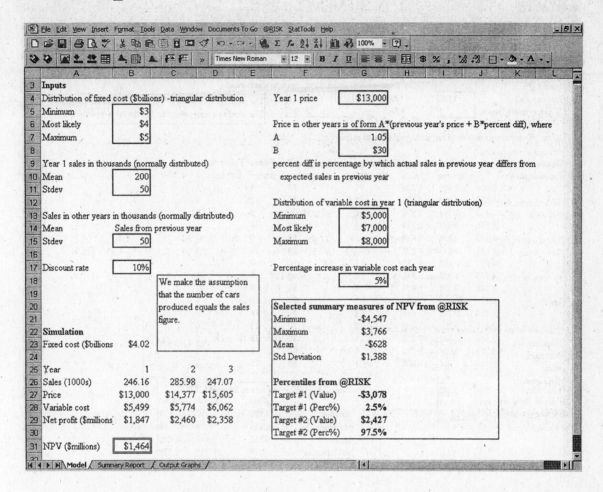

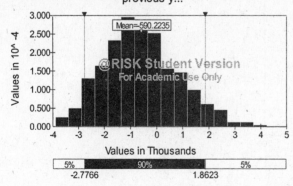

Distribution for NPV ($millions) / Sales from previous y...

Problem 17_47

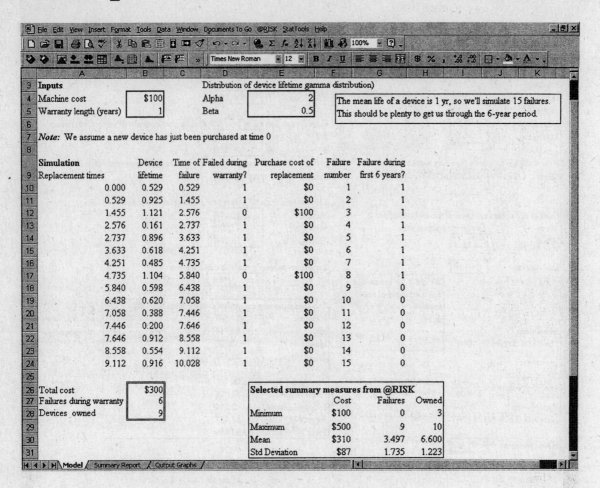

	A	B	C	D	E	F	G	H
3	**Inputs**			Distribution of device lifetime gamma distribution)				
4	Machine cost	$100		Alpha	2		The mean life of a device is 1 yr, so we'll simulate 15 failures.	
5	Warranty length (years)	1		Beta	0.5		This should be plenty to get us through the 6-year period.	
6								
7	*Note:* We assume a new device has just been purchased at time 0							
8								
9	**Simulation** Replacement times	Device lifetime	Time of failure	Failed during warranty?	Purchase cost of replacement	Failure number	Failure during first 6 years?	
10	0.000	0.529	0.529	1	$0	1	1	
11	0.529	0.925	1.455	1	$0	2	1	
12	1.455	1.121	2.576	0	$100	3	1	
13	2.576	0.161	2.737	1	$0	4	1	
14	2.737	0.896	3.633	1	$0	5	1	
15	3.633	0.618	4.251	1	$0	6	1	
16	4.251	0.485	4.735	1	$0	7	1	
17	4.735	1.104	5.840	0	$100	8	1	
18	5.840	0.598	6.438	1	$0	9	0	
19	6.438	0.620	7.058	1	$0	10	0	
20	7.058	0.388	7.446	1	$0	11	0	
21	7.446	0.200	7.646	1	$0	12	0	
22	7.646	0.912	8.558	1	$0	13	0	
23	8.558	0.554	9.112	1	$0	14	0	
24	9.112	0.916	10.028	1	$0	15	0	
25								
26	Total cost	$300						
27	Failures during warranty	6						
28	Devices owned	9						

Selected summary measures from @RISK	Cost	Failures	Owned
Minimum	$100	0	3
Maximum	$500	9	10
Mean	$310	3.497	6.600
Std Deviation	$87	1.735	1.223

Model / Summary Report / Output Graphs /

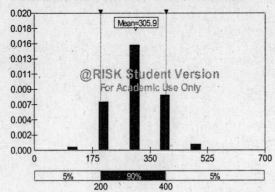

Distribution for Total cost / Device lifetime/B31

Mean=305.9

@RISK Student Version
For Academic Use Only

5%   90%   5%

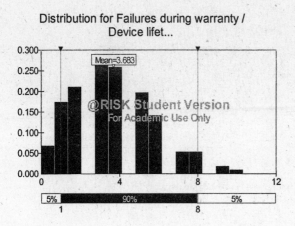

Distribution for Failures during warranty /
Device lifet...

Problem 17_49

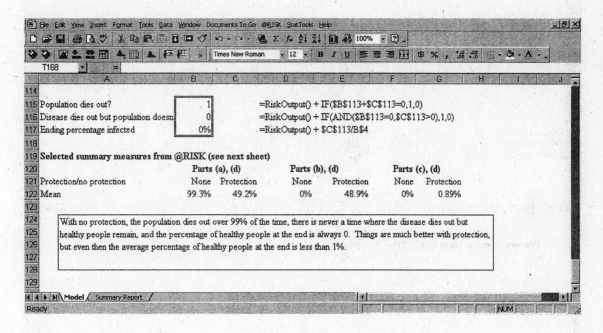